Fire-Breathing Liberal

Fire-Breathing
LIBERAL

How I Learned
to Survive
(and Thrive)
in the
Contact Sport
of Congress

★

Rep. ROBERT WEXLER

with David Fisher

THOMAS DUNNE BOOKS 〽 NEW YORK

ST. MARTIN'S PRESS

THOMAS DUNNE BOOKS.
An imprint of St. Martin's Press.

www.thomasdunnebooks.com
www.stmartins.com

Library of Congress Cataloging-in-Publication Data

Wexler, Robert, 1961–
    Fire-breathing liberal : how I learned to survive (and thrive) in the contact sport of
Congress / Rep. Robert Wexler; with David Fisher. — 1st ed.
        p.   cm.
    Includes index.
    ISBN-13: 978-0-312-36644-5 (alk. paper)
    ISBN-10: 0-312-36644-2 (alk. paper)
    1. Wexler, Robert, 1961– 2. Legislators—United States—Biography. 3. United
States. Congress. House—Biography. 4. United States—Politics and government—
21st century. 5. United States—Politics and government—21st century.
6. Liberalism—United States—History—20th century. 7. Liberalism—United
States—History—20th century. I. Fisher, David, 1946– II. Title.
    E901.1.W49A33 2008
    328.73092—dc22
    [B]   2008012473

First Edition: July 2008

10 9 8 7 6 5 4 3 2 1

For all the wonderful people who invited me
to sit on their couches;
who taught me the lessons of rebuilding this nation
after the Depression;
who shared with me their stories of fighting in WWII and Korea;
and who, in their retirement years, entrusted me
to be their voice in Washington.

What do our opponents mean when they apply to us the label
"liberal"? If by a "liberal" they mean someone who looks ahead
and not behind, someone who welcomes new ideas without rigid
reactions, someone who cares about the welfare of the people—
their health, their housing, their schools, their jobs, their civil rights,
and their civil liberties—someone who believes we can break through
the stalemate and suspicions that grip us in our policies abroad,
if that is what they mean by a "liberal," then I'm proud to say
I'm a "liberal."

—John F. Kennedy,
September 14, 1960

CONTENTS

INTRODUCTION

It's Time to Be Mad as Hell

———————

Dissent is the highest form of patriotism.

—Thomas Jefferson

On November 17, 2005, Congressman Jack Murtha (D-PA) stood before the House of Representatives and startled the nation by saying out loud what many of us had been thinking: It was time to bring our troops home from Iraq. "The U.S. cannot accomplish anything further in Iraq militarily," he said. "It is time to bring them home . . . It's a flawed policy wrapped in illusion. It's time for a change of direction. My plan calls for immediate redeployment of U.S. troops consistent with the safety of U.S. forces. The American public is way ahead of the members of Congress."

Today this statement wouldn't be news at all. Almost all Democrats and many Republicans consider the war a catastrophe. But when Murtha stood up and made this statement, that was not the case. It was not at all politically correct for a politician to proclaim that our troops should come home from Iraq, and it was all the more astonishing and courageous coming from Jack Murtha. Murtha had served in the Marines for thirty-seven years and in 2005 was the ranking Democrat on the House Appropriations subcommittee that oversees military spending. Jack was the most consistent and staunch supporter of the military in Congress—and now he had decided that President Bush's Iraq policy had failed and it was time to start withdrawing our troops.

The Republicans were irate. Almost universally they had supported the Bush war policy. Several Republican members immediately issued statements denouncing Murtha, calling him a coward. Freshman Ohio conservative Jean Schmidt, then just two months into her first term, said smugly on the floor, "Cowards cut and run. Marines never do." Democrats responded with boos, and later she was forced to apologize.

In my office, Murtha's statement generated quite a stir. I'm Robert Wexler and I'm a proud liberal Democratic member of the United States House of Representatives. I've represented Florida's 19th Congressional District on the southeast coast for six terms. Like Murtha and most of my colleagues, I'd voted to give President Bush the power he needed to launch an attack on Iraq. It was the worst vote of my career. Within months I'd realized that Congress and the nation had been manipulated by Bush and Cheney's faulty intelligence and misleading briefings, and it was a vote I had come to regret tremendously. But I'd voted that way. Since that time I'd been strongly critical of how the war was being waged. And now Jack Murtha, a highly respected and hawkish member serving his sixteenth term, had challenged the rest of us to end it.

Murtha's statement initiated an intense debate in my office. Initially, my chief of staff, Eric Johnson, felt that having voted for the war, we had a special obligation to see it through and said flatly, "We're not supporting the withdrawal in six months."

My office is loosely run, so much so that when we recently hired a new employee and he asked about the office rules, the others all looked at one another, waiting for someone else to tell him there were none. And no member of my staff is shy about disagreeing with me—or with anyone else. I'm extremely fortunate: I have a very intelligent, dedicated, and committed staff. In fact, the documentarian Ivy Meeropol produced and directed a six-part series titled *The Hill* for the Sundance Channel focusing on my staff and the way Congress works. One reviewer commented that in dealing with my staff I resembled "a beleaguered camp counselor."

Among the members of my staff was Halie Soifer, my legislative assistant. Halie is idealistic and passionate, and especially knowledgeable about foreign policy. And like all members of my staff, she wasn't afraid to speak up. She was quick to disagree with Eric's assessment. "Maybe we should," she said. "It's sound policy."

I appreciated the views of my staff, but I hadn't reached a conclusion. And in the end it *is* my decision. While I desperately wanted to end the war and get our troops out of Iraq, I wasn't certain that an immediate withdrawal was practical, possible, or desirable. Going into Iraq had turned out to be a colossal mistake, but I didn't want to compound this error with anything but the most thoughtful withdrawal plan. Obviously it takes considerable time to safely and responsibly redeploy or withdraw 150,000 troops. I wondered aloud, "I guess my reaction to it is, Do you dislike George Bush so much that you jeopardize the stability of the entire region?"

Halie responded, "The question is, Is our being there doing anything to ensure the stability of the region? Murtha is actually saying our leaving will empower the Iraqi soldiers to step up to the plate."

Eric Johnson has been at my side for eleven years. We'd met almost two decades earlier, when I was twenty-eight years old and running for the Florida Senate while nineteen-year-old Eric was running for the school board. Eric still looks like he's nineteen years old—even though he and his partner, James, now own a house and have an adorable adopted son. Eventually Eric became my chief of staff, which means he is essentially my alter ego. He is in charge of every task from running the office to helping shape policy. And as is often the case, Eric was disgusted. "The administration didn't have a good plan going into the war; they don't have a plan to get out of the war. To impose one means we have a half-assed exit, too."

"People are dying," Halie said.

"People can die on the way out, too, if it's sloppy or screwed up," Eric responded.

I wanted the troops out as rapidly as possible, but I also wanted to consider all the consequences. "Okay," I said, "let's say you withdraw. Let's say you avoid massive American casualties on the way out, but let's say you destabilize Egypt, you break up Iraq into three parts, you almost guarantee the instability of the region by withdrawing. What about the credibility of America?"

Halie scored the final point—and stopped us all in our tracks. "Where is our credibility now?" she asked.

Where indeed? Every month we were losing more than a hundred soldiers, in addition to the many hundreds more suffering life-altering injuries, and we were spending almost $5.5 billion. There was no long-range plan, and no end in sight. Worse, our reputation and credibility in the world were in tatters. It was obvious to me that a dramatic change was needed. But was Murtha's approach the right change?

We spent most of the afternoon discussing how to respond to Murtha's statement. We considered issuing a press release in which I would announce my support for Murtha's call for withdrawal, but also my belief that it should be completed in phases. And then I would denounce the disgusting Republican attacks on Murtha.

This did not appear to be an issue on which I would have to vote. With Republicans in control of the House, it didn't seem possible that Murtha's proposal would ever be brought to the floor. At least that's the way it appeared until the Republicans decided to use the war for political gain.

Republicans saw this as an opportunity to brand Democrats as traitors. California conservative Duncan Hunter, chairman of the Armed Services Committee, introduced a resolution urging "that the deployment of the United States forces in Iraq be terminated immediately." The Republican leadership intended to bring that resolution to the floor and force Democrats to vote on it.

Hunter told reporters, "I hope the message that goes back to our troops in Iraq is that we do not support a precipitous pullout."

Normally, legislation is introduced and first heard and debated in a committee. Only after a laborious process of testimony, amendments, and voting does legislation come to the full House for consideration. But this resolution was being treated very differently. It was going directly to the floor. Eva Dominguez, my senior legislative assistant, was furious. "How could they bring it to the floor without even going to a committee?"

Halie had the answer. "They can do whatever they want. They're writing the rules as we speak. It's a dictatorship."

Hunter's resolution wasn't precisely what Murtha was advocating, but as the Republicans intended, it was close enough to confuse Americans and the media into believing we were voting on the Murtha proposal. Murtha was terribly upset by this. "I didn't introduce this as a partisan resolution," he said. "I go by Arlington Cemetery every day, and the vice president, he criticizes Democrats? Let me tell you, those gravestones don't say Democrat or Republican. They say American."

For the Republicans this was smart politics; for Democrats it was a true dilemma. This resolution was a deadly serious version of the unanswerable question, Have you stopped beating your wife? If we Democrats voted for the Hunter resolution, the Republicans would smear us as cowards who wanted to "cut and run," but a vote against the resolution would appear to be sanctioning the president's "stay the course" position.

The Republicans were all going to vote against it. Even Duncan Hunter was going to oppose his own resolution. Democrats who supported it, blustered Republican Speaker of the House Denny Hastert, wanted to "wave the white flag of surrender to the terrorists of the world."

"You all on the left opened up this debate," postured Tennessee Republican Marsha Blackburn. "Now they would like to sneak out of the room and avoid this topic . . . They're going to take the heat . . ." The Republicans had set it up to become a big political victory.

Before the vote, the Democratic caucus—all the Democratic members—met to discuss our strategy. We were split. For several hours we debated the pros and cons of the vote. Caucus meetings sometimes get very . . . democratic. There is no single, unified Democratic position, and we hear it in these caucus meetings. At this meeting, Democratic leader Nancy Pelosi spoke, our whip, Steny Hoyer, spoke, and Jim Clyburn, the chairman of the caucus, chimed in. We had experts on Iraq and foreign policy come before us to answer questions. There were divided opinions about what would actually happen if we withdrew our troops. People asked pointed questions. This was a tumultuous meeting; there was a great deal of shouting and ranting. There were angry people on both sides of this debate. Some Democrats against the war wanted to vote for the resolution, while others insisted it was a political trap and the party must not fall into it: Rather than debating the issue, this was simply another example of the Republicans using the war for political gain. The caucus ended with no final decision.

In my office, my staff and I continued to debate how I should vote. Eric and I were coming to realize that this was a rare opportunity for Democrats to put up or shut up on the war. He said, "I think Democrats should call their bluff . . . Let's make them sorry for the day they did it. Let America talk about how the Democrats stood for something."

I rarely have difficulty deciding how to vote on an issue. But this was a unique situation. "It's not Murtha's resolution," I said. "They think it's a bad vote for Democrats to withdraw immediately. But this vote is still a referendum on how the president went to war and how he conducted it. I have no confidence in the president." As I spoke, my voice grew louder and louder. No one on my staff even seemed to notice. Most of us have worked together for a long time. "He's running us into the ground," I continued. "People are dying, and I'm not voting with it anymore. It's time to be mad as hell, and this is my mad as hell vote. If I vote no, I'm saying carte blanche, Mr. President, you've done the right thing. I'm not saying that. I wouldn't have the vote this way, but we don't get to pick and choose our votes."

Finally we got a call from Fred Turner, chief of staff for Congressman Alcee Hastings (D-FL), informing us that a memo from our leadership had gone out. Nancy Pelosi had laid down the law: "The Democratic leadership recommends all Members vote no," it read. Nancy believed it was extremely important that this internal debate within the party be kept within the party. That's what a leader does. Publicly, we had to show a unified face. So the Democratic leadership had decided the best thing to do was vote as a bloc against the resolution, deriding it as a Republican grandstand ploy.

I turned on the TV to watch the debate taking place on the floor of the House. "Like the intelligence that led to war," Californian Henry Waxman said, "the resolution before this body is a fake."

Steny Hoyer labeled it "the rankest of politics and the absence of any sense of shame."

Massachusetts representative Jim McGovern protested that this resolution was a distortion of Murtha's proposal. "Give us a real debate," he said. "Don't bring this piece of garbage to the floor."

Even Jack Murtha was going to vote against it. But something just didn't sit right with me, and I still wasn't certain that voting no was the right thing for Democrats to do. I'd been terribly wrong when I voted to give Bush the power to commit troops in Iraq, and suddenly I was being given a second chance, which under Republican control was not likely to happen again.

Fred was still on the speakerphone with my staff. "There's no good result for Democrats from this vote, agreed?" Fred asked Eric, stating the party position.

I jumped in and said, "Well, I actually think there is—if two hundred Democrats voted yes and said this was a referendum on the president's war in Iraq and we think it's a lousy war that he's running."

Time had run out. My beeper announced that the vote had been called, and the television in my office showed the vote clock on the floor steadily clicking down. I still had to walk from my office across the street to the Capitol and get to the floor in time to cast my vote. In the minutes before I left, my staff and I huddled to discuss the issue for the last time. Lale Mamaux, my press secretary, said, "If you don't want the immediate withdrawal of troops, you should vote no."

"That's not what this vote is," I said. "This vote is about the president. This vote is about what Jack Murtha did yesterday."

Eric and my legislative director, Jonathan Katz, were deeply concerned about the repercussions if I were the only yes vote. "I'm saying no," Eric said. "N.O. But my heart says yes."

When I walked out of the office, I still wasn't certain how I would vote. After I'd left, my staff took its own poll on how I'd finally cast my vote. It was evenly split.

On the floor of the House, Duncan Hunter had boasted that this would be "a clear and convincing no vote on the question of whether we should leave Iraq immediately."

Democratic Leader Nancy Pelosi countered that "Mr. Hunter's resolution . . . is a political stunt and it should be rejected by this House."

"This is not what I envisioned," Jack Murtha said. "Not what I introduced."

Finally it was time to vote. For me, this vote was ultimately a referendum on the Bush administration's Iraq policy. I decided that making a strong, clear statement in opposition to the president's failed war strategy was the only vote I could live with.

The final vote was 403 against, with three Democrats voting for the resolution. I was one of those three. Several Democrats criticized me for my vote, reminding me that other members who had been leaders in the anti–Iraq War movement had compromised their political position for the "good of the party" on this vote. I understood that, and I respected them. But this was my vote.

The Republicans had won an important political victory. The Democrats had suffered another humiliation—manipulated into giving the president a nearly unanimous vote to stay the course in Iraq. But the fact was that we had all lost. It is cynical votes like this one that have contributed greatly to the almost universal disdain in which the American public holds Congress. The Republicans had their strategy, we Democrats countered with our strategy, and what the American people saw was nothing changing, nothing getting accomplished. It had become obvious to a majority of the public that the administration had no coherent plan, that our troops were bogged down, and that the Republican Congress was doing nothing about it.

Today Democrats have a small majority in the House and Senate, but unfortunately Congress is still held in extremely low regard. That's not surprising; as an institution, Congress has rarely been a popular branch of the government. Actually, that's slightly misleading: Most people like their own representative but don't think much of Congress as a whole. There are several reasons for this dismal state of affairs. I don't think most people are fully aware of the breadth of the activities carried out by members of Congress. I know that as Democrats, our party is diverse and diffuse. And President Bush has blocked much of what we have tried to accomplish.

But mostly I believe people hold Congress in such low esteem because they don't see substantial results. They're mad as hell, too. In 2006 the country voted for a Democratic majority with the expectation that Washington would change, but we have not delivered. Things haven't changed enough, and people have justifiably gotten upset.

If people saw congressional action positively affecting their everyday lives, they would have a different perspective on Congress. But we haven't fought those difficult battles, so instead people focus on a system that too often appears to be hopelessly deadlocked.

What I've tried to do in this book is take you inside the House of Representatives. I hope to give you a broad picture of what it is members of Congress do when we go to work every day. The job of a congressman actually does extend from the shelves of your grocery store to remote capitals throughout the world. Some of what we do will surprise you, and I suspect that some of it will disappoint you. I hope to show you how the system actually works, how a bill really becomes a law, and a bit of the human side of being a member of Congress.

In addition, I want to give you a candid sense of a political life, from my first election to my present position. I am proud and privileged to be a member of the United States Congress. It's a job I love. Often it's a terribly frustrating job—but those frustrations are balanced by remarkable moments when my work has affected lives in a positive way.

And finally, I want to proclaim on every page of this book that I am a liberal Democrat and proud of it. I am tired of watching conservatives distort the meaning of liberalism in their quest to divide the country for their partisan purposes. I've watched as the conservative leadership collaborated with an out-of-control executive branch to diminish the powers constitutionally granted to Congress. By our inaction we have allowed the Bush-Cheney administration to expand its reach—in secrecy—far beyond what was intended by the Founding Fathers and create an imperial presidency.

I want to bring you inside the system in the hope that we can begin to change it together.

Fire-Breathing Liberal

1

Capitol Warfare:
When Do Liberals Have Their Surge?

Big old Wexler, that lousy phony. Another liberal fraud from Brooklyn. Wexler. See him ripping into [Attorney General Alberto] Gonzales. A fake case if I ever saw one. Screaming at him. The last time I saw a politician scream at someone like that was in Nazi Germany in the kangaroo court trial against people who conspired to kill Hitler. Wexler really went crazy. Oh, the tough guy. He has more hatred for Gonzales than he does for Osama bin Laden and the Islamists.

—Right-wing talk-show host Michael Savage

I was elected to the House of Representatives in 1996. For a decade I served not so quietly in the minority, watching with dismay as the Republican majority raged out of control. During my first term the right-wing Congress attempted to destroy the presidency of Bill Clinton by raising a personal failing to the level of a high crime or misdemeanor against the nation. And then, with the Supreme Court's appointment to the presidency of George W. Bush following the stolen 2000 election, the Republican Congress wholeheartedly abrogated its responsibility to serve as an equal branch of the government, instead acting in concert with a woefully incompetent administration to all but drain our country of meaningful political debate, dangerously minimize our standing in the world, and mortgage the economic future of our children. These so-called conservatives who have taken control of the Republican Party stood by willingly as the Bush administration invaded our privacy and violated our personal liberties while making all of us less safe. They have done this repeatedly, but certainly their most significant action was lying and manipulating America into the calamitous war in Iraq—and then using that war as a political weapon to question the patriotism of anyone who dared utter a peep of dissension.

These same right-wing Republicans have done everything possible to destroy the progressive movement in America—the people actively trying to stop them—by creating and utilizing an effective propaganda machine intended to turn the word *liberal,* or even simply *Democrat,* into a synonym for traitor. Unable or unwilling to debate issues on the facts, they have resorted to name-calling—which is why my simple act of asking legitimate questions to inept and disingenuous public officials such as Attorney General Alberto Gonzales can so casually be equated to the horrors of Nazi Germany.

To these people, opposing the policies of the Bush administration is not a philosophical or intellectual disagreement. Rather it is an affront to the core values of so-called true Americans. Rush Limbaugh actually told his listeners, "Liberalism is a kind of perversion." In the vernacular of the right there is no such thing as the loyal opposition; instead, anyone who disagrees with them is vilified, attacked, and if possible destroyed. Rarely will they have the courage to debate the issues. It's not "This is what Robert Wexler said, and this is why he's wrong." It's "Robert Wexler is a pacifist, unpatriotic, turncoat wacko who is committing treason." Their strategy of character assassination isn't limited to liberals and Democrats, either; even mainstream Republicans who do not embrace their agenda are subjected to vitriolic political and verbal attacks. They've even created a word, *Rino,* meaning "Republican in name only," to describe Republicans who dare to deviate from the party line.

I would be happy to debate these people about the issues facing this country—or about the damage they inflict upon this nation by spewing political hatred for their own profit—in front of a neutral audience. But I have little expectation that any of them—Limbaugh, Coulter, Savage—would have the courage to accept that offer. They refuse to engage in discussions they don't control completely. They have to own the microphone. George W. Bush set the standard for them during his election campaigns when the carefully vetted audiences at his appearances consisted solely of people who supported him.

Well, I am a proud liberal Democrat. I believe without reservation in the greatness of America and our Constitution. I'm a patriot. I love and respect our flag and what it stands for at least as much as the Rush Limbaughs and Tom DeLays of this world—I dare say even more, because I'm also brave enough to hold sacrosanct the rights conferred on every American by that Constitution—even those with whom I disagree. And that commitment to true justice is owed equally to the most and least deserving among us. I take freedom seriously. In my view, a liberal is someone who cherishes our liberties so much that at times he or she is compelled to take unpopular positions to protect and preserve our rights.

The most popular conservatives consider liberals to be their enemy. Rush Limbaugh told his listeners, "Every day we come in here and have to defend this country against Democrats and liberals." He has referred to me as "the disgusting Robert Wexler" and my constituents in Florida's 19th Congressional District as "deranged," "lunatics," "wacko," and "devoid of rationality or reason." In 2000 Sean Hannity complained that Al Gore had "unleashed the most partisan people in the country, like Robert Wexler, to go out there and purposely distort issues." Neil Boortz ridiculously claimed that Senator Barack Obama chose not to wear an American flag pin on his lapel because "the U.S. flag—regardless of what he thinks—the flag of this country irritates a lot of Democrat voters."

Perhaps the most troubling aspect of these people—the conservative politicians and their media support group—is that they religiously appeal to the basest instincts of certain segments of the American people.

They foment fear, they foment hatred, they employ stereotypes, and the net result is anger. There may well be times when anger is an appropriate emotion, but the conservative movement in America seems to me to be an ongoing effort to encourage people to be bothered and inflamed. These conservatives actively attempt to stoke profound division between Americans for right-wing political gain by using the most personal issues, issues like race and religion and sexual preference, to arouse that anger. This harsh tactic dates back to conservative icon Ronald Reagan, who launched his campaign for the presidency in 1980 with an appearance in Philadelphia, Mississippi, where only sixteen years earlier three young civil rights workers had been murdered and buried in a dam, a crime for which no one had then been convicted. In his speech that day Reagan proudly supported "states' rights," a code term at that time for racism and segregation. These wink-and-nod tactics continued through 2000 when George W. Bush spoke at Bob Jones University—which at that time officially prohibited interracial dating—as a means of appealing to white, fundamentalist voters. Right-wing conservatives like Bill O'Reilly fight the fictional "War on Christmas" allegedly being waged against Christians; they roil their political base by scapegoating homosexuals who seek only the same legal rights of partnership offered to heterosexuals, by claiming that their desire to marry would somehow threaten traditional marriages.

As a proud liberal I have been fighting these people throughout my political career. When the right wing disregarded the good of the nation and attempted to impeach President Clinton, I found myself, mostly by an accident of timing, acting as one of his most public defenders. When my congressional district and our butterfly ballots became the epicenter of the battle for the presidency in 2000—during which conservatives ignored their own long-established support for states' rights to hijack the election—I became one of the most vocal advocates for election reform. Who could have imagined that concepts as basic to our democracy as one person, one vote, and that the right to vote includes the right to have your vote counted, would still be considered controversial in America? In fact, at every opportunity available to me I have spoken out against these right-wing attempts to subvert our political process, and along the way earned the enmity of their defenders.

Certainly a telling example of their way of doing political business was the appearance in September 2007 of General David Petraeus, the senior American commander in Iraq and the architect of the so-called "surge strategy," before a joint panel composed of members of both the House Foreign Affairs Committee, of which I am a member, and the House Armed Services Committee. This hearing was held supposedly to report the results of President Bush's decision to send thirty thousand additional troops to Iraq to provide the time and security necessary for the Iraqi government to move forward toward stability and political reconciliation. Rather than appearing himself to answer these vitally important questions, or sending a ranking member of his administration to defend his policy, the president sent General Petraeus. The general appeared before us in his impressive full-dress uniform—and the message was clear: To scrutinize the administration policy we would have to cross-examine a courageous soldier, and by inference we would be slighting our brave military men and women. It was a typically cynical Bush administration strategy.

And it reminded me of two historical appearances before Congress by soldiers in uniform: conservative hero and talk-show host Colonel Oliver North, who came before Congress wearing all his medals and smugly lied under oath by denying he had been selling weapons to the Iranian government; and the commanding general of our troops in Vietnam, General William Westmoreland, who gave Congress a glowing and misleading report about the military's progress in that country. I have tremendous respect for the men and women of our military, and have become convinced that they, too, have been victimized by the Bush administration, and so I was determined not to be cowed into silence. I had no intention of blindly supporting General Petraeus because of his impressive uniform and distinguished résumé.

Several times throughout this war, military commanders had appeared before Congress to echo the political desires of the administration—and then, seemingly moments after they retired, they publicly offered scathing criticisms of the conduct of the war. Apparently they were just following orders. The truth is the truth whether you are an active general or a retired general. How was it responsible to the men and women they were commanding, to support a strategy that apparently they didn't believe in when they were in command? This country has paid a staggering price for their silence, but the men and women in uniform have paid the dearest price. More than twenty retired generals have defied military tradition by publicly criticizing the Bush Iraq war policy after they retired. Major General Paul Eaton, for example, who helped revive the Iraqi army, called Secretary of Defense Donald Rumsfeld "incompetent strategically, operationally, and tactically." Retired four-star Marine General Anthony Zinni, the former head of Central Command, described the behavior of the Bush administration as ranging from "true dereliction, negligence, and irresponsibility" to "lying, incompetence, and corruption." Imagine what might have changed had these generals spoken up years earlier. Knowing this, being angry about this, I was ready to confront General Petraeus when he appeared before Congress to testify.

I wish I could claim that I was one of those few brave politicians who spoke out against this war from the very beginning and voted against giving President Bush the authority he needed to wage military action against Iraq, but I was not. I came too late to that position. I remember the week Congress voted on the Iraq resolution. There is a homeless gentleman who can be found most days sitting on a bench outside the Rayburn building, a House office building. Sometimes he sings, sometimes he rants. Truthfully, I assumed he was mentally ill. As I walked to the Capitol one afternoon that week that we voted to give Bush the power he had requested, this man was screaming loudly, "There's no weapons of mass destruction! There's no weapons of mass destruction!"

I walked past him thinking, He's just another "crazy nut." The crazy nut turned out to be absolutely right. Admittedly it took me some time to understand how wrong I had been to trust the Bush administration. One afternoon I was being interviewed by Randi Rhodes on her Air America radio program. Randi Rhodes is the liberal answer to the Limbaugh-Coulter-Boortz axis of misinformation—the difference being that Randi deals with facts and reality, exudes integrity, and passionately appeals to our highest ideals of intellectual honesty and public service. Randi had been against the war from the very beginning. On this occasion, she listed simply and concisely all the administration's lies, all its fabrications, all its misdeeds and manipulations, and at the end asked me, "How could you buy this? How could you be fooled?"

As I sat there listening I thought, Randi makes a strong case. I hope I'm not wrong. How could I have bought it? I had voted to give President Bush the authority he requested based on a series of confidential briefings given to members of the House by high-ranking government and military officials. There had been a great deal of descriptive discussion about weapons of mass destruction (WMDs). We'd been warned about the horrors that America would encounter if we didn't support the administration's policy. These briefings certainly reinforced my belief that Saddam Hussein was a repugnant and dangerous man and that the world would be safer if he was deposed. I'd believed the testimony detailing the possibility of nuclear weapons in a suitcase. I'd believed Secretary of State Colin Powell when he came before the Foreign Affairs Committee, and later stood in the United Nations, and presented evidence that Hussein possessed these horrific weapons. That was my mistake. Having seen up close the way the Bush team operated following the 2000 election, perhaps I should have been more suspicious. As jaded as I was about George W. Bush and his administration, I could not fathom that even Bush and Cheney would be so dishonest as to lead us to war on cherry-picked intelligence, manipulated data, and a series of blatant misstatements.

I was not going to repeat my initial mistake. Since that first vote I'd been a consistent critic of the manner in which the Iraq War was being prosecuted. About six months after the war began, in September 2003, Ambassador L. Paul Bremer, then in charge of the provisional government, appeared before the Foreign Affairs Committee. At that time the full extent of the administration's postwar incompetence was yet to be known. The American people were still in the midst of the postcombat euphoria. Saddam Hussein had been deposed. The search for the non-existent weapons of mass destruction was still in progress, but the assumption was that they would be found.

During my career in the Florida Senate and then the United States Congress I had questioned countless witnesses at innumerable hearings about an extraordinary variety of subjects, and rarely had I heard an answer that surprised me, much less shocked me. But that day I did. I asked Bremer, "I was wondering if you could share with us in terms of civilians and soldiers how many Iraqis have been killed during the military operation and how many have died since President Bush declared the military operation over."

Bremer replied, "I don't have those numbers, sir."

That seemed to me to be a pertinent piece of information. How many enemy soldiers had died in the war? How many civilian casualties had there been? Bremer seemed somewhat incredulous that anyone even cared. When he admitted he didn't know I was stunned. "You have never asked how many Iraqis have been killed?"

"No."

"Why not?"

"Well, it is not at the moment relevant to what I am trying to do, which is rebuild the country."

I was astonished by both the substance of Bremer's response and his arrogance. I am respectful of witnesses, but at times that gets difficult. Bremer's complete disinterest in the human cost of the war on the Iraqi side was telling. Supposedly our most important mission was to win the hearts and minds, the loyalty of the Iraqi people. It seemed to me that the number of dead innocents would profoundly affect this goal. "So whether there were ten Iraqis killed or four hundred thousand would not be relevant to your program?"

"Congressman, let's be realistic here," he said, practically swatting me away. "We are not talking about four hundred thousand under any circumstances."

"Good. I'm glad to hear that . . ."

Eventually it became clear that the president and vice president and senior members of the administration had indeed manipulated evidence, presenting half-truths and distorted intelligence to create a climate for war. Reports concluding that there were no WMDs had been disregarded. In 2007 the Defense Department's inspector general concluded that the Pentagon had taken "inappropriate" action when it "did draw conclusions that were not fully supported by the available intelligence."

Even worse, it became clear that in the administration's rush into war, there had been almost no planning or preparation for the postwar period. Troops had been sent to Iraq with a confused mission and without the protective equipment they needed. The rebuilding of the country and the form of government to be established were essentially made up as they went along. As a direct result of the administration's malfeasance, Iraq was embroiled in a civil war, and hundreds, then thousands, of Americans were dying there. As Secretary of Defense Donald Rumsfeld's top aide, Doug Feith, admitted in 2007, in one of the great understatements of all time, "Mistakes were made."

Mistakes were made! Mistakes were made! It was an incomprehensible disgrace, a fiasco—yet anyone who dared question or criticize the administration's policy was attacked and smeared. The objective was to kill the messenger to ensure that little attention would be paid to the message. In 2005, for example, after I'd voted for the so-called Murtha resolution—which was actually Duncan Hunter's cynical resolution—I explained, "Every now and then you're allowed to vote your conscience in Congress. Nobody is calling for a cut and run. Our troops have every reason to be proud. We got rid of an awful dictator and we've given the Iraqi people the opportunity to form a government, write a constitution, and have elections. The mission has been accomplished . . . and now it's time for us to get out of there and let the Iraqis take over."

In response the Republicans attacked my patriotism. The chairman of the Palm Beach County Republican Party told the media, "He called for a surrender to the terrorists. What else do you want to call it? Surrender is surrender." He added that my vote was anti-Israel, a serious charge in my heavily Jewish district. Fortunately, my constituents know that I am one of the strongest supporters of Israel in Congress and ignored him completely.

The Democrats won control of the House in 2006 at least partially because of our commitment to end the war and bring our troops home. So, like the growing majority of Americans, I was frustrated by our inability to successfully counter the president's stubborn policy in Iraq. In January 2007 the president announced his new strategy: Rather than finally beginning a staged withdrawal, he was going to send an additional thirty thousand troops to Iraq. The newly elected Democratic majority almost immediately introduced a nonbinding resolution supporting the troops but disapproving the surge strategy. On the floor of the House I said loudly (I always speak loudly), "I stand in opposition to a president who failed the American people by initiating an ill-conceived war, an administration that misled the nation . . . into believing that Saddam Hussein had weapons of mass destruction, an administration that invented links between Baghdad and al-Qaeda . . . I only wish we were voting on a binding resolution that mandates a redeployment of troops and cuts off funding for this tragic escalation." Instead, we passed a nonbinding resolution. This is simply a "sense of the House." It has no claws, no mandates, no real meaning except to influence public opinion. It wouldn't save a single life. We failed to force the president to begin withdrawing soldiers from Iraq—and our troops continued to be killed and wounded.

And it was clear we were running out of troops. In order to meet military recruitment levels, the standards had to be lowered. In April, Secretary of Defense Robert Gates extended the tour of duty in Iraq and Afghanistan from a year to sixteen months. Those few allies we had, most of whom contributed very few soldiers, began withdrawing. Even worse, we began to discover that American soldiers who had been wounded in battle were not receiving the care they deserved after coming home. What was already a disastrous situation was continually getting worse.

Our next opportunity to end this insanity came in May 2007 when the president requested an additional $120 billion to pay for the war. The cost of this war was rapidly approaching half a trillion dollars, more than three thousand Americans had been killed and an estimated thirty thousand seriously wounded—and the Iraqi government had decided to adjourn for the summer.

This was another opportunity to force the administration to commit to a timetable for withdrawal, a plan that would put pressure on the Iraqis to finally take control of their country. Instead, Congress worked out a deal that set out certain benchmarks for the Iraqi government to meet—but refused to demand a timetable. It was agreed that the administration would report to Congress the following September on the success of the Iraqi government in reaching those benchmarks. I voted against that agreement, pointing out, "Each day American troops fight and die in an increasingly violent civil war . . . This war must end, and Congress must end it. I will not support any legislation that funds this war without mandating that our troops are swiftly redeployed from Iraq. This legislation is yet another blank check for President Bush."

So it was in September 2007 that General Petraeus came before Congress to report on the progress of the Bush administration's surge strategy. This was to be a major milestone and was the first real opportunity Democrats had to affect the conduct of the war. The feeling was that this hearing would help determine the next steps and perhaps even lead to a withdrawal plan. In preparation for this hearing, I had read General Westmoreland's testimony to Congress forty years earlier detailing the "progress" in Vietnam. Reading it, you would have thought the Vietnam War was going as planned, and if the United States had just stuck it out a little more, just a little bit more, everything would have turned out just fine. Reading that turned out to be an instructive choice.

Westmoreland had made an argument that President Lyndon Johnson could never have made because no one would have believed him. And here we were in the same situation again.

The Republicans were going to have the difficult task of defending the failed Bush strategy. As *The Washington Post* reported, the Iraqi government had failed to meet most political, economic, and security benchmarks. In fact, that government was essentially dysfunctional, doing nothing as their country fell into the hands of the local armed militias that had taken control of regions and neighborhoods. So rather than trying to defend it, the Republicans went on the attack.

Against a newspaper ad. A day or so before the hearing, the liberal political group MoveOn.org bought a full-page ad in *The New York Times* headlined "General Petraeus or General Betrayus: Cooking the Books for the White House." That gave the Republicans the excuse they so desperately needed to change the focus; it enabled them to question the patriotism of everyone who spoke out against the administration or the general's report. How dare MoveOn—and by extension all Democrats—question the integrity of a general wearing his uniform? Not one of them mentioned the prewar appearance at the United Nations of retired general Colin Powell, who compromised his own reputation by presenting the administration's phony case for war. As then senator Fred Thompson (R-TN) claimed, completely erroneously, "This is the group that funds the Democratic Party. I call upon the Democratic Party . . . to repudiate the libel of this patriotic American."

President Bush, who ordered underequipped troops into combat without a coherent strategy, called the newspaper ad "disgusting." Rudy Giuliani, who had avoided service in Vietnam by receiving a deferment, referred to it as "character assassination on an American general who is putting his life at risk." Republican congresswoman Ileana Ros-Lehtinen, who like me represents a district in South Florida, said, "I offer my colleagues the opportunity to use this hearing to distance themselves from the despicable ad that was published today calling into question the patriotism of General Petraeus."

The right-wing attack machine mobilized, employing all its resources to criticize the Democrats for an ad run by a private group. Actually, MoveOn.org—in addition to several other Internet groups—has been an important contributor to the recent electoral success of the Democratic Party. By mobilizing voters and running issue ads, as well as serving as a forum of ideas, MoveOn has become an influential player in American politics. MoveOn.org was started during the Clinton impeachment proceedings. The name actually means "Let's move on to the important business of the country." I worked with them at that time, when the "org" consisted of a few guys and a Web site. I may not always agree with MoveOn, and in fact it's been critical of me several times, but I respect its willingness to be provocative and its courage to tackle issues few other groups do. It has done exemplary work, and I was quite surprised that more Democrats didn't come to its defense.

Conservatives understand that MoveOn is a real threat to them, so they have maligned it—as well as financier George Soros, who has been one of the primary contributors to MoveOn. The names they've called Soros are despicable—"Communist" is probably the kindest—while at the same time they've celebrated Richard Mellon Scaife, the far-right-wing multimillionaire who provided almost two million dollars to fund the Arkansas Project, an attempt "to unearth damaging information about President Clinton." Scaife's money funded the private investigations into Whitewater as well as the absurd allegations that the Clintons were somehow involved in the suicide of White House aide and family friend Vince Foster.

The Republican onslaught successfully twisted the impact of Petraeus's appearance. Rather than addressing the reality that American troops were being wounded and dying every day in Iraq, they feigned outrage at this ad. Even worse, they introduced a resolution to censure MoveOn in both the House and Senate. "Congress should not be in the business of policing ads," I pointed out. "The priorities of Congress are ridiculously misplaced when we condemn an organization for a pun that some people found offensive, while previously failing to condemn vicious campaign ads against decorated veterans like Senators John Kerry and Max Cleland . . . Further, it is blatantly hypocritical of certain Republican senators who repeatedly block efforts to vote on legitimate Iraq war policy, to then vote on ridiculous resolutions [about] independent interest groups." Many Democrats voted for the resolution to distance themselves from MoveOn and the substance of the newspaper advertisement. Just imagine the furor that would have resulted had we proposed a resolution to censure the right-wing Christian Coalition or Pat Robertson for one of their more outrageous proclamations, such as blaming 9/11 on homosexuals. I voted against the resolution, but unfortunately many of my colleagues did not, and it passed. It was not our proudest day.

My focus remained on General Petraeus. In the six terms I'd served in the United States Congress there had never been a hearing quite like this one. I was surprised that the Democratic caucus hadn't met to discuss how we were going to proceed, perhaps to outline those areas we wanted to pursue to make sure we used our time effectively. Instead, each representative was completely on his or her own. After reading Westmoreland's testimony, I'd written the statement I intended to deliver. Generally when I'm going to be questioning an important witness I prepare a statement and a few questions.

Every seat in the large Cannon Caucus Room was taken, and people were standing in the back and along the walls. Only rarely do two committees hold a joint hearing, and for the first time in my eleven years in Congress, at least twenty-five members of the House and Senate who were not on either committee attended the hearing and sat in the audience. I listened quietly as one after another of the most senior members of Congress questioned Petraeus. And I was astonished that my Democratic colleagues were downright deferential and nonconfrontational. A tragic war was raging in Iraq and we were playing patty-cake with the general. I began thinking, Oh no, we're not going to be duped again. We're not going to be lackeys for this administration and for generals who don't speak the truth until they leave the service. But apparently we were.

Ironically, the people who were treated the most harshly in that room were members of the feminist antiwar group named Code Pink. Twice while General Petraeus was speaking these women interrupted loudly and were forcibly removed from the room—the guards pulled them out. The Democratic leadership, rather than respecting their civil disobedience to protest this war, instead threatened to prosecute them. Please. I understand that we cannot allow congressional hearings to be disrupted by antics from the audience, but it would be nice if we could muster as much anger toward those responsible for perpetrating the failed strategy in Iraq as we do toward the Code Pink ladies!

While listening to both Democrats and Republicans make statements and question the general, I started writing down some thoughts.

In the middle of the hearing, my office passed me a message from a high-ranking Democratic leader. My first thought was, Okay, finally someone wants me to ask Petraeus a hard-hitting question. This hearing was being televised. I happened to be sitting in the middle of the panel, directly below the most senior people on the committees, so each time they were on camera I was visible. In the middle of this vitally important hearing the message was clear: "Tell Robert to stop chewing gum. He's on camera. It doesn't look respectful."

At first I thought perhaps that was a joke. As I'd told several people, during the Clinton impeachment hearings my mother had complained about the fact that I was chewing gum on camera. Maybe this was a reaction to that. It wasn't. Our leadership wanted me to stop chewing gum. I took the gum out of my mouth.

By the time I was called upon, not a single one of my colleagues had mentioned the Westmoreland testimony. The Democrats had been polite, courteous, and respectful. During the few hours the hearings had been in progress, it had been announced that six more American soldiers had been killed in Iraq. I had my written statement, which I referred to as I started speaking, but then I ignored most of what I'd written. After reminding General Petraeus and Ambassador Ryan Crocker, who was also testifying, that I had opposed the surge from its inception, I told the general:

Cherry-picking statistics or selectively massaging information will not change the basic truth . . . I do not question your credibility. You are a true patriot. I admire your service to our nation. But I do question your facts. And it is my patriotic duty to represent my constituents and question you about your arguments that the surge in troops be extended . . . especially when your testimony stating that the dramatic reduction in sectarian deaths is opposite from the National Intelligence Estimate, the Government Accounting Office, and several other nonbiased, nonpartisan reports. I am skeptical, General, but more important, the American people are skeptical because four years ago very credible people both in uniform and not in uniform came before this Congress and sold us a bill of goods that turned out to be false. And that's why we went to war based on false pretenses to begin with.

There was no holding back. I continued my argument:

> This testimony today is eerily similar to the testimony the American people heard on April 28, 1967, from General William Westmoreland when he told the American people America was making progress in Vietnam. General, you say we're making progress in Iraq, but the Iraqi parliament simply left Baghdad and shut down operations last month. You say we're making progress, but the nonpartisan GAO concluded that the Iraqi government has failed to meet fifteen of the eighteen political, economic, and security benchmarks that Congress mandated. You say we're making progress, but war-related deaths have doubled . . . and 70 percent of Iraqis say that the surge has worsened their lives.

I asked him, "General, there are fifty-eight thousand one hundred and fifty-nine names etched into the Vietnam War Memorial. Twenty years from now, when we build the Iraq War Memorial on the National Mall, how many more men and women will have been sacrificed to protect our so-called credibility? How many more names will be added to the wall before we admit we need to leave? How many more names, General?"

The right-wing propaganda machine roared into action. "You have to understand Wexler's constituency to understand this," Limbaugh said. "They are deranged . . . You Democrats down there are absolutely delusional, devoid of any rationality or reason." And then he went on to add, "I'll bet it was everything Petraeus could do not to reach across the table and start strangling this little guy. I'll just bet you. He's sitting there, Wexler, making it sound like nobody cares these three thousand seven hundred deaths matter. He's telling that to a four-star general in a dress uniform! . . . Folks, this is not far off from the rest of the kook, liberal population throughout this country."

Imagine that, a congressman having the audacity to challenge "a four-star general in a dress uniform!"

Eventually the administration got almost exactly what it wanted: more time and more money to continue fighting a senseless war in Iraq that cannot be won by any conventional standards while continuing a too-feeble effort to defeat the Taliban in Afghanistan. It's vital to remember that the objective of the surge was to make political progress. There is little doubt that the huge increase in the number of U.S. soldiers on the ground in Iraq will increase security—that was the reason so many military experts argued at the beginning of the war that thousands more troops were needed to occupy the country. But adding more troops at this point is a temporary solution, a Band-Aid that we are paying for in American lives and billions of dollars. Yet the Republicans insist the surge has been a success because the level of violence has been reduced. Success might be better measured by examining how close the surge has come to achieving its original objectives—and on that scale it has been a dismal failure.

It was so frustrating. After a decade in the minority, voters had delivered a Democratic majority to Congress—and we simply weren't using it.

2

Will Work for Votes:
A Campaign Education

It's a sin in politics to land a soft punch.

—Alf Landon

I was asked once what surprised me most about being in Congress. The answer was easy: everything. My colleague Ron Klein (D-FL) said that being a congressman was like trying to drink out of a fire hose—everything comes at you so fast and then it just keeps coming. The reality is that your congressional representative is your direct connection to the federal government. The House of Representatives was established by the Founding Fathers to be directly responsive to the beliefs and needs of citizens. While originally senators were appointed by state legislators for six-year terms—that didn't change until the Seventeenth Amendment was passed in 1913—members of the House of Representatives were given only two-year terms and were elected directly by the people. That meant they had to answer to the voters every two years. And if they didn't adequately represent the beliefs of their constituents, they were easily replaced. It's amazing to me how many people either don't know or forget that the entire House is up for election every two years. I'm constantly asked by informed Americans, "When's your next election? Is it this time or three or four years from now?"

I tell them the truth: "I'm always up for reelection." The elections come so quickly that most members of the House are in perpetual campaign mode. Unfortunately, the system has created a permanent campaign.

To me, being a congressman is the greatest possible job in the world. On a daily basis I'll deal with local, national, and international issues—either directly or through a member of my staff. The range of issues a representative will confront is limitless, from trying to find a kidney for a constituent to global climate change. I have enabled World War II veterans to finally get the honors they earned, voted on appropriating funds for each aspect of the Iraq War, and carried messages from Syrian President Bashar Assad to Israeli Prime Minister Ariel Sharon. I've worked to make sure my constituents get their mail delivered directly to their homes rather than having to go to a central mailbox, defended President Clinton during his impeachment proceedings, and, as cofounder of the Turkey caucus, worked hard to improve relations between the United States and that democratic, secular Muslim nation, a critical ally in the fight against terrorism. I have spoken at high schools, helped my son deliver one thousand soccer balls to young survivors of the tsunami in Aceh, Indonesia, and nominated many of my young constituents to the service academies. I've answered hundreds of questions about Medicare and changes in Social Security at town meetings, protested vocally on national TV against the fraudulent presidential election of 2000, and been a leader in the fight for a verifiable paper trail for voting machines. I've grilled Attorney General Alberto Gonzales in congressional hearings about the firing of eight U.S. attorneys for purely political reasons. I've met with everyone from presidents and prime ministers to hardworking people who are desperately trying to survive on a limited fixed income.

That just begins to describe the possibilities made available by the job. Most people, I've learned, don't know what their congressman or congresswoman really does, or how they do it, and how it influences their lives on a daily basis. Their knowledge of Congress is limited to what they read in the newspapers or on the Internet or hear on television and radio. And most of that generally isn't very positive. The ordinary things we do rarely make the news.

I REPRESENT FLORIDA'S 19th Congressional District in the House of Representatives. My district is made up of over seven hundred thousand people in Palm Beach and Broward Counties, so I represent a mix of young suburbanites and retirees, most of whom have moved down from the Northeast. It's a strong Democratic district: In the 2004 election George W. Bush got only 36 percent of the vote. Slightly more than a third of my district is Jewish, and we have a large number of Italian-Americans and a growing Latino community. A substantial number of my constituents are senior citizens; in fact, we rank second in the nation in terms of the number of people in the district who collect Social Security. When Al Gore made a campaign visit in 2000, I introduced him by explaining, "Maybe you don't know why prescription drug coverage is so important to South Florida, Mr. Vice President. Well, I'm proud to represent the district with the highest per capita use of Viagra anywhere in the world!"

Generally, it's a relatively affluent, reasonably liberal district. Liberal— yet traditional people. A place where traditional values matter. Many of my constituents are immigrants or first-generation Americans. These are hardworking, patriotic people, a lot of them veterans who fought in World War II or Korea. They owned small businesses, they were union leaders, they worked for the government. I represent many retired teachers, particularly women who believe teaching is the most honorable profession a person could go into. These are not fancy people. These are people who value hard work and education and take their citizenship extremely seriously. Many times people have told me they haven't missed voting in a presidential election since 1938 or 1942. I have some constituents who remember voting for Al Smith in 1928. These are people who worked their whole lives so their children could have a better life, and they are very proud of their children's and grandchildren's and in some cases great-grandchildren's accomplishments.

In most congressional districts it's difficult to attract even fifty people to a political meeting. In Florida 19, a town hall meeting can easily attract three or four hundred people, more if you serve bagels or corned beef sandwiches! And when they disagree with me, they are not shy about telling me. My constituents have both the time and the interest. In my district it's not good enough to say you're from New York City; you're really from a neighborhood, you're from the Bronx or Brooklyn or Queens. And not just Queens, either, which neighborhood in Queens? A lot of residents of the district moved down to Florida with a group of close friends. Where they came from matters. One day, for example, New York senator Charles Schumer was speaking in a crowded condominium in my district. "Before moving down here, a lot of you were my constituents," he said. "Would everybody originally from Brooklyn please stand?" Nobody stood. "Okay, how about those people from Queens or the Bronx?" Again, nobody stood. He was a little surprised. "All right, anybody at all from the metropolitan area?" Not one person stood up.

I decided to step in. "Senator Schumer," I explained, "there's one thing you probably don't understand. When these people were your constituents, they *could* stand up." Everybody started laughing. "Now they stand up in the morning and they sit down at the end of the day. There's not a lot of unnecessary standing. So why don't you just try asking them to raise their hands."

Like so many of my constituents, I'm originally from New York. From Long Island. My father was a union man, a shop steward at *The New York Times*. As long as I can remember, politics was a passion of mine. My best friend and next-door neighbor was Norman Lent III, whose father, Norman Lent, Jr., was a state senator who eventually became a U.S. congressman. In 1970 he ran against the Democratic incumbent, Allard Lowenstein, who was a hero in my home. Norman's father is a wonderful man, but he was a Republican. I remember walking into the Lent home defiantly carrying a LOWENSTEIN FOR CONGRESS bag. To me, it was an easy decision. Lowenstein was the

Democrat. I had to support him. Years later I asked my parents how they ever let me do that. It was an awful thing to do, incredibly disrespectful, and I'm certainly not proud of it. Norman's father turned out to be a fine congressman.

Norman and I would play a game titled Mr. President. Other kids were playing All-Star Baseball or Electric Football. We played *Mr. President* for hours at a time, five days a week. I grew up believing this was the most phenomenal game ever devised, which in many ways describes me. The object of the game was to win the presidential election. How many nine-year-olds knew that New York State had 43 electoral votes? Norman and I did. That fact might well sum up my childhood. Florida, incidentally, had only 14 electoral votes. In those days, electorally it barely mattered.

The first time I ran for office Norman was my campaign manager. We were in fifth grade and I ran for class treasurer. Norman worked extremely hard making posters and helping me write my speech. I won. But as we walked home from school the day of the election, he admitted that he hadn't voted for me. Obviously I was surprised; my own campaign manager voted for my opponent! When I asked him why, he explained that he was worried that if I won it would affect our friendship.

When I was ten years old, my father bought a delicatessen in a Hollywood, Florida, mall. Pic-A-Deli, it was called, and my family became part of the great wave of New Yorkers moving south.

I don't really know why, but perhaps because of Norman's father, as long ago as I can remember I had dreamed of being a United States congressman. Truthfully, though, I didn't believe I had even a remote chance of actually accomplishing that dream. An ordinary person from a middle-class family, like me, a Jewish kid whose father owned a delicatessen, didn't become a successful politician. To me, at least, politicians seemed to come from a different world.

Certainly part of the reason I wanted to go into politics was my love for this country. I understand the magnificence of America. I know how corny this sounds, but I really love listening to "The Star-Spangled Banner." At ball games, at events, I absolutely love it. When my children were only a few weeks old and wouldn't go to sleep, I would walk around holding them and singing it to them. Admittedly, part of the reason for that was that I didn't know all the words to any other song, but "The Star-Spangled Banner" goes right to the essence of what I believe: There is nothing better than being a patriotic American.

Few things infuriate me more than someone questioning another person's patriotism because they have a different point of view. What the Republicans did to John Kerry, a true Vietnam War hero, in the 2004 election, by making up lies to disparage his reputation, was bad enough, but when they tried to paint Jack Murtha as dishonest and even discussed opening up an investigation into how he won his medals, that was too much. That was disgraceful.

But by the time that happened, I had been in Congress almost a decade, long enough not to be surprised by these tactics, just angry and disappointed. During my first week in the House, I was on the floor, probably looking around in awe, when David Bonior, then the minority whip—the person who makes sure members of their party show up and vote the party line—took me aside to give me a little advice. "Don't ever forget," he told me simply, "Congress is a contact sport."

I ran for public office for the first time in 1987. Entering politics had remained a dream of mine; I just didn't think I'd actually do it. It always seemed like something other people did. I had been working as a lawyer for almost three years. While it was a convenient way to make a living, there was just no passion in it for me. I liked the firm I was working for, I liked the people with whom I worked, but I couldn't imagine doing it for the next thirty-five years and being happy.

An opportunity presented itself when Florida senator Lawton Chiles announced he was retiring. That set off a chain reaction in which officials on just about every level of elective office wanted to move up. The incumbent congressman for my South Florida district decided to run for the open Senate seat. The county commissioner was running for Congress, which left open a seat on the Palm Beach County Commission. My wife, Laurie, and I discussed it, and with her support, I decided that I was going to run for that office.

I announced it, but unfortunately few people heard it. There was neither a bang nor a wimper. There was nothing. It was true grassroots politics. I had no campaign staff, no financial backing, no actual resources. What I had was my dream and my desire. This is how political careers begin. The hallmark of a first campaign is that you get to make every possible mistake for the first time. And I did. The first newspaper to interview me was the *Boca Raton News*. Their reporter asked me why I was running for this office and I explained seriously, "I'm twenty-six years old and I'm a product of the public school system in South Florida." I went into a reasoned analysis of the public school system, pointing out its successes and its deficiencies. The reporter listened carefully, took some notes, and then pointed out to me, "You're running for the county commission. The school board handles all those issues."

All right, I'd made a slight mistake. My campaign platform did not relate to the office for which I was running. I was completely wrong. Passionate, but wrong. There was absolutely no proper response to that reporter. As I left that interview I promised myself I would never again be unprepared.

In response to that disaster I began a three-month-long educational effort. I visited every county office to learn how each of them worked. I visited the water department, the utility department, the library department, the airport department. I asked to meet with the head of each of those departments to learn as much as possible about what they did, what problems they encountered, what support they needed. I spent several hours in every office. I'm told by people still in county government that I am the only county candidate who ever did that. But I had to. I was starting from less than scratch. Let me explain it this way: If my campaign was a game of Mr. President, I was starting from Candyland.

What I did have was determination. My next mistake was talking about all the things I learned. I would talk about specifics. I would compare the number of books in the library system to those in other similarly sized counties to show that Palm Beach County was deficient, and then I would explain in detail how I intended to devote specific resources to increase the number of books in the library. I spoke about the needs of senior citizens in the library system and how to best service rapidly growing areas of the county that were underserved by the library system.

I was passionate about it—and when I looked out at the audience, those few people who were willing to listen to me were glassy-eyed. I'd put them to sleep. Truthfully, I was even boring myself. Nobody wanted to hear about the library system in this campaign. They wanted to hear about "sexier" issues. No matter how important the water department might be, nobody wakes up in the morning and immediately starts worrying about it.

I learned. I learned from every mistake. I learned how to make a campaign speech focusing on those topics that directly affected my constituents' lives. But the most important lesson I learned was how to listen.

I visited every community leader who would speak with me. I probably sat on couches in three hundred living rooms. Mostly, these were older Jewish and Italian men and women. Some of them were Holocaust survivors. The first couch I ever sat on was in the condo of a gentleman named Harry Bilowsky, who lived with his wife, Helen, in Cypress Lakes. Harry was considered the King of the Condos in the northern part of the county. He was extremely well respected. I sat down on his couch, and to the extent that he let me speak, I told him why I was running for office. Then I sat with Sid Levine in Cresthaven and Sid Krutick in King's Point. These men were fifty years my senior. I had very little to offer them in terms of experience or wisdom; all I had was my enthusiasm and idealism. I ended up listening to these wise people, people whose life experiences had been so extraordinarily rich. They would offer me tea or coffee and some cookies, and then they would tell me everything there was to know about Florida politics and that they were not going to support me and why I had no business doing what I was doing. I began my political education on those couches.

It was the most valuable education a young politican could dream of getting. They taught me how the decisions made by politicians affected their lives. They told me about the lives they'd once lived, the pain their parents had experienced in Russia or Eastern Europe, the despair of the

Great Depression, or the difficulties their immigrant families had faced when they arrived in America. And they told me why they loved this country so much and what they expected of their government officials.

There was no reason why they should have supported me. My opponent in the first primary was a lovely woman named Shirley Stevens, who was an aide to the serving county commissioner. She was a responsible person, and her goal for a long time had been to become a county commissioner. That was all she wanted, to continue working in the community. That office would have been the culmination of her political career. I was in the race to be a good county commissioner, but for me that office was really a stepping-stone, a place to start. I had delusions of grandeur.

This was the first time I had to raise money to finance my campaign. Initially it was very difficult for me to ask people for money, but it quickly got easier. I got a lot of practice. I was a lawyer, and law firms were very active in local politics, so I spent a lot of time going to law firms raising money. Law firms that did land-use work were particularly helpful at the beginning. I suspect many of those firms donated to several candidates, betting on every horse in the race.

This was a very long campaign, lasting almost sixteen months and consisting of three different elections: two Democratic primaries and the general election. Initially there were four Democrats in the race, and admittedly the other three candidates were more mature than I was, more knowledgeable, and at that time more capable. Each of them was already deeply involved in local government. But while they had a lot to offer, none of them had a great deal of charisma. Rightfully I should have come in fourth, but I probably worked harder than my opponents. My campaign staff consisted of my father and myself. My father spent months building hundreds of two-by-three-foot blue-and-white wooden campaign signs that we nailed to telephone poles. He had a small station wagon, and every weekend the two of us would drive around nailing up these signs. This is how a political career starts.

The experience I gained during that campaign was invaluable. And truthfully, on occasion I did despair. Take a guess, what do you think is the worst thing that can happen to a candidate? Well, one afternoon my father was driving me out to Belle Glade, a rural area in the western part of the county, to a picnic at which I had been invited to give a speech. Neither one of us had ever been there. The sugar industry was a major economic force in the county and we had to drive right through those agricultural areas. It was only an hour from Boca Raton, but it was a different world.

My father's station wagon was my campaign office. There were signs affixed to its sides and a large taxicab-style sign on the roof reading ROBERT WEXLER, DEMOCRAT FOR COUNTY COMMISSION. I was wearing a suit, and my father had on a WEXLER FOR COUNTY COMMISSION T-shirt. We were late, so my dad was probably driving a little faster than he should have been. We were driving through a poor area, and out of nowhere a big dog darted out into the road. My father swerved, he slammed on the brakes, but there was really nothing he could do: The car slammed into the dog.

Within seconds, what felt like a thousand kids and their parents had gathered around this dead dog, all of them standing directly in front of the station wagon, which was covered with Wexler signs. It was just awful. If there is anything worse for a political campaign than a photograph of a crying little boy hunched over the body of his dead dog, and the car that killed the dog emblazoned with the candidate's name, I have yet to find it.

We were late and getting later, but beyond trying to console the children there was nothing we could do of any value but wait there. The only thing that came out of this incident was that a lot of people who had never heard my name before would never forget it.

But that was the exception. So much of elective politics is luck, and in general what I lacked in experience or sophistication I gained in luck. And timing; I was in the right place at the perfect time. The political structure in Palm Beach County was very loose, very flexible. I could never have run for office in any area with an established political structure. You can't just show up in Queens, New York, for example, and decide to run for office. It takes years to work your way up the ladder; there are a lot of dues to be paid. But Palm Beach County was growing so fast that the opportunity was there for me.

Perhaps most important for me, Palm Beach County had a large and rapidly growing Jewish community. I was one of the first young, aspiring Jewish politicians to come along, and in me people saw something similar to what they saw in their sons and grandsons. Many of these people had long believed that in America there was a limit to how far Jewish politicians could go. They were very realistic about that. Get an education, make a nice living for your family, but remember, this is still a Christian country. And then I came knocking on their door.

My candidacy tugged at the emotions of the older Jewish residents. One Sunday night, I spoke at Century Village, a large retirement community in West Palm Beach. I showed up wearing a dress shirt with an open collar and a sports jacket. No tie. After my speech, three of the condo leaders bawled me out for not wearing a tie. I was younger than anyone else in that meeting, and to show respect I should dress like a banker. This was their vision of what a young Jewish politician should look like. They wanted me to be successful in the broader spectrum of things, not just the Jewish community. They wanted me to look like what they thought a Protestant or Catholic politician looked like, the people they had long been supporting. I've never forgotten that night— and since then I've always worn a tie.

This was an intelligent electorate. Many of them had lived through some of the most horrific events in human history, so they were realists. During one campaign several years later, my opponent complained that I had the audacity to vote for an increase in my salary, causing someone in the audience to stand up and ask, "Well, what kind of schmuck wouldn't?"

With solid support from this population I won both Democratic primaries. My first real campaign and I'd won two primaries! My Republican opponent for the general election was named Ron Howard. As the newspapers pointed out, this gave him immediate name recognition, since a child actor of the same name had played Opie Taylor on *The Andy Griffith Show,* an advantage that became known as the "Opie factor." My inexperience became obvious during the campaign. There were two important local issues in the general election: the location of a proposed landfill in Boca Raton and the fact that a flight path from the brand-new Palm Beach County airport took planes directly over the most affluent neighborhoods of Palm Beach. But it was the airport issue that taught me a fundamental rule of politics: Negative campaigning works. Like it or not, that's simply a fact of political life. At the beginning of the race I made a commitment to run a positive campaign. I kept that commitment. That was mistake number one. If you make a commitment to run a completely positive campaign, you will lose every time. I'm not defending that reality, just acknowledging it. And it was very important that I learned it early in my career.

There are only a few instances I know of when negative campaigning backfired. Congressman Neil Abercrombie began his political career in Hawaii as a member of the state legislature. One of his goals was to turn a beautiful unused building on a sugar plantation into a public library. Even then Neil was considered a maverick, but the local Democratic Party told him that if he did his job and proved to be a loyal Democratic member, he could have his library. After proving his party loyalty for several months, he went to the chairman of the State Board of Education and asked for his library. "It's not going to happen," he was told.

He was furious. "This is what I was promised, and I've come through on my end," he protested.

The chairman agreed, but explained, "Well, nobody really expected you to do that, so the powers that be have decided it's not going to be a library."

Neil returned to his office, took out a sheet of letterhead stationery, and wrote carefully to the chairman, "Dear Nobu, F—k you." And signed his name. It was an instinctive act that he later regretted. During the next election cycle a union leader opposing him got hold of that letter and gleefully sent a copy of it to every constituent in the district, every one of them, accompanied by a note asking, "Is this the kind of person you want representing you in the state senate?" It was a perfect example of negative campaigning.

Ironically, when people opened this letter with this union leader's name at the bottom and read the note reading "F—k you," they got confused—and assumed it came from him! He successfully alienated a large block of voters, and Neil Abercrombie won the election.

In my first election, my opponent seized the opportunity to go negative—although looking back, it was Donald Trump's support that contributed more to my loss. Gorgeous Palm Beach airport, which was vital to opening up development and tourism in the area, had just opened. The primary flight path apparently went right over Mar-a-Lago, the sprawling mansion Trump had purchased and intended to turn into an exclusive golf club, as well as the homes of many of the wealthiest residents of Palm Beach. These estate owners created a political group to oppose the airport. They advocated building a new airport much farther away. One afternoon I received a phone call from a well-respected attorney named John McCracken, who was a partner at a prominent law firm in West Palm Beach. McCracken told me that not only would this group like to endorse me for the county commission, they wanted to hold a fund-raiser for me at Mar-a-Lago. Would I participate?

Fund-raiser? I certainly wasn't going to win by turning down too many of those. My wife, Laurie, strongly advised me to stay away from Donald Trump and Mar-a-Lago. I should have stopped right at that moment, but instead I called Harry Johnston, who worked for the same law firm as McCracken and had served as the president of the Florida senate. Harry was extremely knowledgeable about local politics. During this same election cycle, he was running for the United States Congress. McCracken was a great guy, he told me, which has proved to be completely accurate, and this was a legitimate group.

And the issue was legitimate. In fact, the noise from planes taking off and landing actually affected the poorer areas of West Palm Beach much more than the mansions. Just to find out for myself how bad it was, one morning I stayed in a modest home much closer to the airport than the estates. The noise was unbearable. You couldn't live with that booming sound every few minutes. It was obvious something had to be done.

That was the first major fund-raising event of my political career. Trump was not there, and I don't know if I ever got a contribution from him. But the event turned out to be substantially more valuable for my opponent. He used it perfectly. I was trying to run a positive campaign, and he sent out a caricature of me with strings attached to my body, being played like a puppet by Donald Trump. It was a devastating hit. I learned something extremely important from that: Follow my wife's advice!

Ron Howard knew how to run a campaign. The next most important lesson I learned was never allow your opponent to define you in the minds of the voters. Howard portrayed me as a young, inexperienced kid. He sent out a mail piece comparing the two of us. The one thing I thought was unfair, although it was true, was his emphasis on the fact that he was a married man with several children, a family man, while Laurie and I had no children. No children? Of course we had no children. We'd been married only three months.

Howard and I had two debates, I believe. He emphasized my age and lack of experience. I didn't do very well in those debates because I didn't go negative.

My real problem was that Ron Howard's claim was accurate. I was young and had very little experience. But because I had support from the condominiums, the race was competitive. For me, the key to winning the election was palm cards, small cards listing the recommendations of the leaders of each community. Each resident would get a palm card delivered to his or her door the night before the election. It would be headlined, for example, CENTURY VILLAGE DEMOCRATIC PICKS. The ability to turn out a substantial vote was what gave these communities political power. Residents often took these palm cards into the voting booth with them and almost always followed the recommendations. Years later, while I was running for Congress, I was able to joke that Hillary Clinton was only half right in the book she wrote—in my district, it takes a Century Village.

It was the responsibility of each candidate to get the palm cards printed and distributed. I had to print a different palm card for each community that supported me because they might be supporting different candidates in other races. So I had eighty thousand palm cards printed, and the day before the election I worked with volunteers to get them in the proper stacks to be distributed.

Meril Stumberger, a wonderful person and a close friend as well as a master of political organizing, was helping me. This is a person I have respected from the day we met and her help in my career has been invaluable. Also, unfortunately, she has a weak bladder. We were working so hard we were giddy, and late at night something happened that made us start laughing uncontrollably. Uncontrollable laughter is problematic for a person with a weak bladder. The palm cards were in a large cardboard box on the ground below where she was standing.

The realization of exactly what was happening was a moment I will never forget. My political future was in that box, that now-wet card-board box. How far will a politician go to win an election? I was about to find out. We laid out all the cards to dry, we used a hair dryer, we did everything possible to get those palm cards dry—and we agreed we wouldn't talk about this until after the election.

I still lost. I got beat 52.5 percent to 47.5 percent. I lost because I'd made too many mistakes. Since that time, I've watched people I greatly respect lose campaigns. I was right there with Al Gore and Joe Lieberman in 2000, and that was more than heartbreaking. That was devastating, because I knew that Al Gore had legitimately won the state of Florida, and that the consequences of that stolen election would have a profoundly negative effect on the entire world. My loss in this first race wasn't going to affect the world. It affected Laurie and me, but most other people didn't see much of a difference.

I was able to keep it in perspective. Obviously I was disappointed. I'd worked my heart out for sixteen months; I went to every meeting, I sat in every living room I could. The campaign had become my life. And then it was over.

The most difficult thing for me was to attend my Election Night "victory celebration." The next few weeks were also difficult. Almost everybody I met would lower their voice and offer condolences as if someone had died—particularly the older community leaders, who had become emotionally invested in my campaign. I'm sure they thought I was a lot more upset than I was; I had to cheer them up, reminding them that it was simply an election. Life goes on. Nobody's sick, nobody died. I wasn't trying to make them feel better, I was completely genuine; I was a young lawyer with a wonderful, pregnant wife. What she was doing, having a baby, was far more important than my election. Would I have preferred to win? Of course, but I'd lost. And the reality was that I'd learned a great deal more from losing than I would have if I'd won. Had I won, I probably would have believed that I knew what I was doing and should simply keep doing it. But my loss made it obvious that there were many things I should have done better. And in my next campaign, I did.

Two years later, when I ran for the state senate, those lessons proved invaluable. This was a strong Democratic district, so the party primary was really the general election. The incumbent was a very conservative Democrat, Don Childers, who had held the office for sixteen years. Childers was an old-school Deep Southern politician, a giant of local politics. I'll tell you how conservative he was: He had actually been George Wallace's campaign manager in Florida when Wallace ran for the presidency in 1972. Through the years, many people had tried to take him on and he'd beaten every one of them. He had almost total name recognition in the district, knew all the elected officials, and had all the corporate donations sewed up. The sugar industry supported him. The Jewish Democratic president of the state senate came to West Palm Beach, the heart of the district, to endorse *him*! Logically, it was a race I couldn't win.

I was the opposite of Childers in every way. He spoke with a Southern drawl; my accent was more southern Queens. I was pro-choice, he was pro-life. I was for gun control, he was against it. I was for universal health care; we had a quote from him saying seniors were a drain on the treasury. Where to build the trash site was an issue: I was firmly against putting it in Boca Raton, he didn't object to putting it there. The only slight chance I had was that the district had changed since he was first elected; the voters had become less conservative, while he really hadn't changed at all.

My opponent raised almost four hundred thousand dollars. I barely raised fifty thousand. It was a rough campaign. Several times pro-life people threw fake fetuses at me and called me a murderer. I raised enough money to take one poll, the very first poll of my political career. Polls done correctly tell you a great deal more than how well or poorly you're doing at that moment; they lay out the strengths and weaknesses of the campaign and provide a guide for your strategy. My one poll told me, basically, that there was no strategy that could help me win this election. Childers had close to 40 percent of the vote, I had 6 percent. My pollster's advice was succinct: "Have fun. You're going to lose." Although in fairness he did say that if I did a long list of things, I might have a slight chance. I might.

For the first time in my political career I went negative. Every politician is an expert on campaigns. We all believe we know what's best. The reality is we don't. It's very easy to point out after the election what a candidate should have done. In 2004, for example, it seems obvious that the Republican machine was successful in negatively defining John Kerry. It wasn't done in one day or two weeks, it took months, but Kerry's staff never figured out how to stop it, to change perceptions. They didn't know how to fight back. It was a fatal flaw and he lost because of it. There is a lesson to be learned there, although perhaps it should have been learned after it was done to Michael Dukakis. Bill Clinton was the master at punching back immediately; he set the standard in terms of how to respond quickly and effectively. The bottom line is, If you take an unfair hit, you can't assume voters will be able to differentiate the truth from political fiction. So if you're not punching first, you have to at least be ready to counterpunch quickly.

I hadn't learned how to do that yet. I had little money. I couldn't afford to run an advertising campaign. But one morning about two months before Election Day, my mother-in-law called me in my law office. She was furious. "Robert, did you hear that radio commercial?" she asked. Apparently Childers had run his first radio advertisement. I hadn't heard it. "It's an anti-Semitic commercial," she said.

Less than a minute later a reporter from *The Miami Herald* called. "Don Childers ran his first radio spot," he told me. "What do you think about it?"

What could I say? I hadn't heard it—but I took my mother-in-law's word for it. "I think it's an anti-Semitic commercial."

The reporter was Jewish and he sounded surprised. "Let me read it to you," he said.

As he read it I listened carefully. And I wasn't hearing anything that sounded anti-Semitic. But at the end he referred to me as a "loud, ex–New Yorker." In fairness, I am loud. In fact, in my first congressional campaign one older voter explained to a reporter that she had "voted for Wexler because he was the only one I could hear." And I am an ex–New Yorker, although I'd moved to Florida when I was ten years old and gone through the Florida public school system and graduated from the University of Florida. I was a full-fledged Floridian. So what was Childers really trying to say?

The inference was, Wexler's not one of us. He's one of those loud Jewish New Yorkers who think they can come down here and take over. The headline the next morning was something like "Wexler Claims Childers Is Anti-Semitic." Suddenly people who had never before paid attention to a state senate race got in touch with my campaign. In the next two weeks I raised about twenty-five thousand dollars.

Calling him anti-Semitic was perhaps overly negative, and he denied the charge. But I wouldn't have done it if I hadn't believed it was valid. I didn't know what was in his heart, but I knew his record. He had long associated himself with people like Wallace who were antagonistic toward African-Americans and Jews. In fact, within a few years he had switched parties and eventually became head of the Christian Coalition in Florida.

My campaign consultant, Tom Plante, an extremely bright and creative person, suggested that we use the money we'd raised to buy pot holders. Pot holders? Well, at least people wouldn't immediately throw them away. So we had WEXLER FOR STATE SENATE printed on thirty thousand pot holders. The pot holders came in three colors. I started knocking on doors, introducing myself, and offering the gift of a pot holder—matching the kitchen wallpaper—to the woman of the house. I handed out thousands of them. Then we did the one mailing we could afford, which included a comparison of Childers's positions and mine, and a pot holder.

We had several debates. During one of them, I said he had voted for the landfill and Childers denied it. I had a copy of the *Journal of the Senate* with me, so I was able to prove he was wrong. I hammered him with it and he got furious and called me a bald-faced liar. The next day the newspapers reported that the "young challenger" had gotten under the seasoned politician's skin.

I generally sleep well the night before an election. Not that election. No matter how I figured it, I couldn't come up with a reasonable scenario in which I got to 50 percent. I thought the election would be closer than most people predicted, but the best I thought I could do was climb into the mid-40s.

For a politician it's always about the numbers. Either you learn how to count votes early in your career or there is no late in your career. And no matter how dim the prospects of winning an election seem to be, I've never known a successful politician to give up hope. So I hoped, although no knowledgeable observer would have given me any chance at all.

On Election Morning I was standing outside the voting booths in Kings Point in Delray Beach when a station-wagon-type ambulance stopped in front of the building. The attendants opened the back and wheeled out an older man lying on a stretcher. He was attached to an oxygen canister. In a broken Eastern European accent—I will never forget this—he looked up at me and said, "Vexler, I came to vote for you."

At that moment I realized I had a chance to win this election. I had struck a chord. The turnout in those areas in which I was strong was enormous and in the rural areas, where I had calculated that at best I might get 10 percent of the vote, I received 35 percent. The hardest thing I had to do that night was look as if I wasn't shocked. As they counted the votes on Election Night I was certain they'd made a terrible mistake—I was winning. I won the election. It wasn't quite a landslide, but it was a political earthquake. Those pot holders had won the election for me. Voters carried them to the polls. Even today, two decades later, people tell me proudly they still have their pot holder.

Ambition is never a secret in politics. When you're running for an office, that office seems to be the greatest goal you will ever achieve, it's the holy grail—until the day after you're elected, in which case too often you immediately start looking up at the next level. It's said that every United States senator looks in the mirror and sees a president. So, long before the opportunity existed, I knew that I would run for Congress.

Early in my first term the state senate had to redraw the congressional district lines. Redistricting is one of those esoteric and complicated political tasks that few voters pay any attention to, but those lines may well determine which party controls the United States House of Representatives. The fact is that a pool of Democratic and Republican voters can be divided in an almost infinite number of ways to produce a desired election result. By overloading one district with voters of a minority party, for example, a state legislature can dilute the number of that party's voters in other districts, ensuring victory in all of those districts for the majority party. In 2002 the Texas congressional delegation consisted of seventeen Democrats and fifteen Republicans, but Republicans won control of the state legislature for the first time in more than a century. At the urging of the powerful conservative leader Tom DeLay, the Republican majority in the Texas legislature redrew the boundaries of the state's congressional districts, using a variety of legislative methods to create several new districts with a Republican majority. As a result, in 2004 Texas elected twenty-one Republicans and only eleven Democrats to the House, guaranteeing that President Bush would be working with a solid majority in the House. Proving that not all bad deeds go unpunished, a campaign finance investigation related to this scheme eventually caused DeLay to be indicted—and ended his own political career.

Former Democratic congressman Ronnie Shows was a casualty of reapportionment in Mississippi in 2001. "They just drew me out of my district," he explained. "My opponent's campaign manager was actually in the room with people on the state senate side as they drew the new lines. They left me with 35 percent of the voters that had elected me, and took out my Democratic base and moved it into an already strong Democratic district. I never really had a chance to win."

When we redrew the district lines in the Florida Senate in 1991—as we were required to do by the state constitution—I was already hoping to run for Congress someday in the distant future. In Florida, state senate districts are considerably smaller than congressional districts; Florida's 19th Congressional District, for example, was made up of two state senate districts, my district and a neighboring district represented by State Senator Peter Weinstein. Peter and I were friends, and we often worked together. When the legislature reapportioned the state, Peter and I worked out a trade. I wanted Century Village in Deerfield Beach, home to thousands of Democratic voters, which I knew would play a pivotal role in a congressional election, in my state senate district. Peter wanted a different retirement community in his district, one that was very important in state senate elections but irrelevant in the congressional district. Both of us got what we wanted.

This is the minutiae of politics. This type of work goes on in every district in every state in the nation. Most people believe it has no impact on their lives—but this route led directly to my participation in many of the significant political events of the last decade. The conservatives realized long ago the impact that local politics has on the national agenda and got their voters to participate in these local elections, a strategy that allowed them to gain power and legislate their beliefs into law.

Florida's 19th Congressional District was very well represented by Harry Johnston. Harry knew I intended to run for Congress when he retired or ran for another office—I would not have challenged him— and he told me that when he was ready to retire he would call me in advance of any announcement. Harry was very popular; he'd won four terms in the House and easily could have held that seat as long as he desired. One day in 1995 I was in Tallahassee, meeting in the state senate, when he called. "I'm keeping my commitment to you," he said. "I'm not going to seek reelection." He was going to announce it the next day and asked me not to say anything.

Keeping a secret in politics is like eating soup with a fork. Twenty minutes later Harry called back to inform me that someone had leaked the story to the press and he was going to make his announcement within the hour. My first phone call was to my wife, my second call was to Amadeo "Trinchi" Trinchitella. Trinchi was the Democratic leader of Century Village Deerfield. He was more than the leader, he was the quintessential, stereotypical condominium leader. Trinchi was "the man." His palm card was golden. Trinchi's endorsement was the most important factor in the election. No one commanded the respect that he did.

I flew home from Tallahassee that night. At eight A.M. the next morning I was waiting in his office; I remember looking at him and saying, "Trinchi, you've got the power to make me a congressman. If you're with me, I will be a congressman."

It took a few weeks, but eventually he decided to support my candidacy. Over the years we became very close; he was like an uncle to me. Trinchi passed away a few years ago, but his impact on me—and thus anything that I accomplish—will never be forgotten.

By that time I had been through four elections. My experience had taught me how to run a professional political campaign. There were no more dead dogs or soiled palm cards. I'd learned that winning an election requires individual discipline and a professional team, and putting together that team requires raising a substantial amount of money. You need a professional fund-raiser, a pollster, a media adviser, a direct-mail expert, a TV-commercial producer, a campaign manager, and all the other experts whose job it is to make a candidate look completely in command.

The fundamentals of a political campaign are essentially the same whether you're running for Congress or for a local office. You need a message and a candidate who is effective at delivering that message. You also need the resources to communicate that message, and you need some luck. Some of that luck you make, some of it just happens. And finally, there will be the unanticipated issues, and how you react will often determine whether you win or lose.

Because Florida 19 is strongly Democratic, Harry Johnston's seat would belong to the winner of the Democratic primary. I had two opponents for the Democratic nomination: State Representative Ben Graber was a doctor and State Senator Peter Weinstein was a lawyer. I was surprised when Peter announced his intention to run. We'd sat next to each other for several years during state senate Judiciary Committee meetings. He'd told me that his ambition was to become a judge, like his brother in New York.

On the issues, there was very little that would distinguish me from my opponents. Basically we had the same constituency and we had voted the same way on almost every issue. So there was little substantive reason to support one of us over the other two. That meant the campaign was about creating the right perception. Who was most honest, who was most likable, who made you feel the best? Peter and I started the campaign as friends, but by the end of it he was suing me for defamation of character.

My initial objective was to create the perception that I was the leading candidate. But early in a campaign there is only one real measure of success: How much money have you raised? In the first quarter I had eleven fund-raising events and raised $180,000. That was an enormous sum for that time and more than both my opponents combined had raised. That success made it appear that I was the front-runner, as well as gave me the resources to pay for a substantial campaign.

I assumed that both of my opponents were going to attack me. I'd taken off my halo and accepted that eventually I would have to respond in kind. I certainly did not go as negative as former Michigan congressman Mark Siljander (recently indicted for alleged money laundering), who compared his opponent in the Republican primary to Satan, but I did attack my opponents with claims that I thought were fair game. In one mailing, for example, I attacked Peter Weinstein as a threat to the security of senior citizens, since he had "supported Newt Gingrich's budget amendment—the cornerstone of the Republican agenda . . . an agenda that has targeted $270 billion in Medicare cuts." Graber was "a doctor who takes campaign MONEY FROM TOBACCO companies." Wexler? "Wexler passed Florida's toughest ethics laws . . ." Like it or not, that's what is known as politics.

Peter Weinstein raised two negative issues against me: First, he claimed that I had accepted too much campaign money from the sugar industry, which had long been accused of polluting the Everglades, and second, that in a race between three Democrats, I was the "Republican."

This is what I'd learned: During a campaign you have to be astute enough to recognize a problem before it becomes a bigger problem. The 19th Congressional District did not include the sugar areas. In fact, the district is historically the most pro-environmental, anti-sugar part of Florida. So when the sugar industry contributed ten thousand dollars to my congressional campaign, a huge amount of money for me, my opponents gleefully made it a major campaign issue. It was obvious that this charge had the potential to become a serious problem for me if it got traction. I spoke at a Democratic club meeting in Delray Beach, and several people challenged me about my support for the sugar industry. I didn't have to take a poll; I knew my constituents believed I was in the wrong place on the sugar industry. Often the facts are a lot more complicated than can easily be explained—even when you've done absolutely nothing wrong. The fact that they asked about it meant I had to respond. I had to defuse the issue.

Rarely can you turn a negative into a positive, so at least I had to neutralize it and better explain my position. I immediately reexamined some of the positions I'd taken regarding sugar industry issues and began emphasizing some votes I'd made that were not beneficial to sugar. I didn't change my position, just the emphasis.

Potentially more damaging in this district was the charge that I was actually the "Republican candidate." That could have been decisive. My opponents had their facts right: My campaign manager and eventually my chief of staff, Eric Johnson, had formerly been the head of the local Young Republicans—although he'd gotten disgusted with the party and become a very active and strong Democrat. And they also charged that I had taken a campaign donation from the former chairman of the local Republican Party. That was also true: The Republicans knew that this district was going to elect a Democrat and recognized I was the strongest candidate. Weinstein ran a TV commercial that showed money being passed from one hand to another in some sort of illicit way and then blared that "Wexler had hired the former president of the Young Republicans to be his campaign manager." It was intended to define me to the voters as the most conservative candidate in the race.

We decided to counter the charges by presenting me as young and aggressive and hardworking, ambitious in a positive way, and attuned to seniors and the issues affecting their lives. It was nothing fancy; the image was that I was very approachable, very much of the people. I could have been their son or grandson. To respond to the charge that I was too conservative, we ran a commercial in which we didn't even mention my opponents but stated flatly that I was tough enough to stand up to Newt Gingrich. We considered using a slogan, sort of a brand name, to help me create that image. Bob Graham, who served Florida as both its governor and senator, and who is a person I respect enormously, was a Harvard graduate and a particularly sophisticated man. To appeal to the conservative and more traditional voters of central and northern Florida, his supporters called themselves "Graham crackers."

The best image-making slogan was created by Florida senator and governor Lawton Chiles, who walked a thousand miles across the state during his 1970 senatorial campaign, and became known as "Walkin' Lawton." That slogan identified Chiles as a simple man, a man to be trusted, a man who was approachable, a walkin' man. It was a brand that stuck with him throughout his career, and he never lost an election. We debated creating a slogan, but we couldn't find exactly the right brand, so we never did it.

Eventually Peter Weinstein emerged as the more serious opponent. Arguably the biggest difference between Peter and me was our appearance. He was more than a decade older than I was, and bigger. He also weighed a lot more than I did. At the beginning of the campaign he went on a diet and lost a substantial amount of weight. I'm sure that was very difficult to do and he was justifiably proud of it. But when we sent out a mailer to one hundred thousand voters, we included a photograph from The Miami Herald that showed him at his former weight. We never believed that this was going to become an issue. We hadn't concocted a photo of him to make him look heavier. We didn't take a picture and blow him up an additional seventy pounds. That was him and it was a legitimate thing to do. During a campaign you're not going to ask your opponent for a flattering picture to use in a mail piece.

I have no idea how much of an effect this mailer had on the election. I think everything you do matters. Unless, like Senator George Allen, you make a huge mistake—like smiling when you racially insult a supporter of your opponent—you never know what issue, what comment, what tie you put on in the morning, is going to make the difference. I won the primary and then the general election. Actually, I spent less money in the general election than I had on winning the primary.

My friendship with Peter Weinstein was a temporary casualty of that election. Today we are good friends again, and Peter has become a highly respected judge. At the time, however, he was so offended that he sued me for ten million dollars, claiming we had altered the *Miami Herald* photograph we'd used. That was untrue. Eventually we went to arbitration and compromised.

He withdrew the lawsuit.

I was going to Congress. And this time my campaign manager had voted for me.

3

Mr. Wexler Goes to Washington

———————————

The husband is the boss—if his wife allows.

—Yiddish proverb

One of the very first pieces of legislation I had been involved with in the Florida Senate funded a system that enabled hearing-impaired people to use the telephone. This was an important bill for both the disabled and the senior communities. About sixty students and their teachers from a school for the deaf in Saint Augustine came to the capitol to watch as we voted. Knowing they were going to be in the gallery, I found a teacher and learned three sentences in sign language. After the bill passed I was going to look up at the kids in the gallery and, using sign language, tell them it would now be going to the governor for his signature and they should write or contact the governor's office to express their support. I practiced my sentences in front of a mirror for hours. This was going to be a great moment! A good bill and very good politics.

The bill passed easily. I looked up at the kids and proudly signed my three sentences. And then the kids started to laugh. As I discovered, I didn't get the sign language exactly right. What I signed to them was that the bill had passed and it would now be going to the governor for his signature and they should all contact the governor and tell him, "Up yours!"

That wasn't the last mistake I made. The fact is that when I entered the state senate, I had absolutely no idea how to be a legislator. But during my three terms there I learned how the system worked and how to work within the system. So when I was elected to the U.S. House of Representatives I believed—naively, as it turned out—that it would be more of the same, just on a bigger stage.

I was wrong. Congress is its own world, different on every level from anything I'd ever done before. Different pace, different intensity, different stakes, different everything. When most freshman members are asked before entering Congress what they intend to accomplish, they usually have a sensible political list. But when they're asked the same question a few months into that term, the answer undoubtedly would be simply, to survive.

For a newly elected member of Congress, there is no time after the election to enjoy your victory. A congressional office is like a small business—and you have about six weeks from Election Day until you're sworn in to get that business in operation. Among many other things, that means hiring a staff, renting office space in the district, setting up your office in Washington, lobbying for committee assignments—and finding a place to live within commuting distance of the Capitol.

The official orientation begins in Washington the Monday following the election. It's Congress 101. New members are briefed on everything from parliamentary procedure to where the bathrooms are. They receive *The New Member Handbook* from their party, which offers nuts-and-bolts instruction on how to run an office, hiring a chief of staff, dealing with constituent services and the media, mailing a letter, making a one-minute speech mostly for constituent consumption: "A Member does not actually have to deliver a one-minute speech. He or she can simply ask unanimous consent that it be placed in the Congressional Record . . ." "Members should not wear overcoats or hats on the Floor while the house is in session." "As a special service for freshmen Members, the Leader employs a television producer and camera operator who are available to videotape committee hearings . . . and stand-up interviews for use in producing video news releases." All this information comes at you in a blur of excitement.

Congressional offices are selected during that orientation, based on seniority. Two incoming classes are grouped together for seniority purposes—members in their fifth and sixth terms would be in one group, for example. Then each group has an internal lottery. It's like the NBA draft. Numbers get picked out of a hat. When your number comes up you get ten minutes to make your selection. There are three office buildings, Longworth, Cannon, and Rayburn. The Rayburn building is considered the most prestigious because most senior members are there and the offices are larger. The first office I had was on the sixth floor of Longworth. I remember the day I walked into that office for the first time. I was stunned. One-third of an entire wall consisted of a huge safe. Apparently before the first campaign finance laws were passed, political contributions were routinely made in cash. The amount of that contribution was usually determined by the importance of the committee on which you served and your seniority. A senior member might be given twenty-five hundred dollars in cash. On some days members received as much as ten thousand dollars cash money. And it was completely legal!

In an institution that so values tradition, you would think that members would have some sense of the history of each office: John Kennedy had this office, Tip O'Neill had that one, Gingrich sat here. But it doesn't work that way at all. Generally you know the last person who occupied your office, and then only because they are probably still in Congress. The one object I did inherit was a leather chair that legend has it was passed down by the last five congressmen who represented my district, a big monstrous chair called, for no reason I could determine, The Turkish Chair.

Eventually I moved into an office on the second floor of Cannon. I chose that office because it was a short walk to the Capitol. I often had to walk over there to vote several times a day, and being closer saved a great deal of time. Some of the older members choose offices close to the underground subway that transports members to the Capitol to vote. I like to walk over there, but this is far from uniform. Rep. Jesse Jackson Jr., for example, is known to ride a Segway to the Capitol.

Hiring a staff was actually relatively easy. Long before I was sworn in I was receiving résumés from experienced staffers. After every election there is a reservoir of people searching for jobs. But my predecessor, Harry Johnston, wanted me to keep as many of his staff members as possible. I did keep many of them. In fact, I desperately wanted to hire Suzanne Stoll to be my first chief of staff, because I knew I didn't have the slightest clue what I was doing. I figured somebody better know how all this worked. This turned out to be a wise decision. Suzanne was a wonderful chief of staff and remains a close family friend.

During that three-day orientation—sometimes even before that—new members begin lobbying for committee assignments. Nothing will be more important to a member of Congress than his or her committee assignments. As Florida congressman Alcee Hastings explained, "In this institution you can have the magic bullet that would cure all our domestic ills, but if you're not on the right committee it won't get heard." The real business of the House gets done in committee. There are twenty-five full committees and more than a hundred subcommittees. What happens on the floor—the debates and voting—is almost always scripted. It's a great show, but almost nothing takes place on the House floor that hasn't been planned by the leadership. It's in committee where legislation gets written, where real oversight takes place, where the agenda of the House is determined, that a member can have an impact.

Generally members will serve on two committees, although they can receive a waiver to be on a third committee. Obviously members want to serve on those committees that are relevant to their district. For example, Democrat Kirsten Gillibrand, who upset Republican veteran John Sweeney in 2006, has about eighty thousand military veterans in her upstate New York district, so for her it was imperative she get a seat on the Armed Services Committee. Agriculture is a main industry in that rural district, so she also landed an assignment on the Agriculture Committee.

At the beginning of each Congress, the Rules Committee determines how many members from each party will serve on a committee. The majority party always has the majority of the members on every committee, which ensures that they are likely to win every vote, but each party's steering committee actually makes the assignments. The size of the committees varies. There are about sixty people on Appropriations and only forty on Judiciary.

Obviously certain committee assignments are considered more desirable than others. Most people have no idea what the Ways and Means Committee is, for example, but it's probably the most powerful of all committees. Ways and Means has jurisdiction over taxation and major government programs like Social Security and Medicare. The Appropriations Committee controls government spending, determining how hundreds of billions of dollars are distributed each year. The Financial Services Committee, on which I serve, oversees all the nation's financial institutions, including the Federal Reserve, Department of the Treasury, and the banking, securities, and insurance industries. As a member from Florida, being assigned to this committee is very desirable because the soaring cost of home insurance is the number one issue in the state.

Getting on the committee of your choice is real inside politics. You begin by meeting with as many members of the steering committee as possible, telling them what assignments interest you and why you'd be a perfect fit. You also meet with the most senior member of your party on the committees of your choice, because he or she is the captain of that particular ship and has to want you on the committee. Generally Democrats select committee chairmen based on seniority, while Republicans under Gingrich and DeLay routinely passed over moderates with seniority to appoint less senior members who adhered to the right-wing agenda.

The two committees I wanted to join were Judiciary and Foreign Affairs. While these are among the best-known committees, they don't appropriate any funds, and they don't hand out large contracts (like Transportation or Armed Services). They offer very little help with fund-raising, and in fact I was warned that serving on Judiciary could hurt my career. I remember meeting with Minority Whip David Bonior during this process. Bonior is one of the most ethical men I've ever known. I didn't always agree with him on the issues—especially concerning Israel—but I always respected him. As we sat in his office, he pointed out that the Judiciary Committee is probably the most partisan committee in the entire House. It's the place where the most controversial social issues—abortion, school prayer, separation of church and state, the death penalty, gun control—are debated. "It's the center of political controversy," he warned me. "All the constitutional issues go there. You're constantly voting on the high-profile, gut issues. These are things people know about. You want to be a senator? You're going to take four hundred votes on prayer in schools, eight hundred votes on abortion. Believe me, if you win your district by fifty-two percent, you don't go on the Judiciary Committee."

I enjoy the controversial issues, I told him. Those things that make political blood boil are the most interesting and intellectually challenging to me.

And then he told me something I will never forget. "Look," he said. "It could be about a year down the road we have an impeachment, and that'll happen in the Judiciary Committee. Is that something you want to be involved with?"

Impeachment? Truthfully, I thought he was nuts. Impeach President Clinton? I laughed to myself. And I assured him I wanted to serve on the Judiciary Committee.

For most members of Congress, the Foreign Affairs Committee doesn't directly impact their district. Indiana Democrat Lee Hamilton, the former ranking member—the senior minority member on a committee—was probably the most knowledgeable and respected member of Congress in the area of foreign policy. "But you know what?" he said. "I never talk about foreign affairs in my district. That's not something that would do me any good."

Fortunately, one of the most important issues to my constituents was the security and well-being of Israel. So in my district, at least, foreign relations really matters. And Israel matters most.

I was very fortunate to be assigned to both the Judiciary and Foreign Affairs Committees. I think, like every other new member, I had great expectations. But as we all learn quickly, the realities of the job force us to move in unexpected directions. There is just no way of knowing what part of you is going to rise to the surface.

In addition to the official orientation, the Kennedy Institute of Government at Harvard offers a seminar for incoming members. It's essentially a civics lesson. At one time just about every freshman attended this meeting, but in 1994 Newt Gingrich dissuaded Republicans from going—these were Harvard professors, so they must be left-wingers—offering instead a seminar sponsored by different Republican think tanks, policy groups like the Cato Institute. While everyone is invited to all of these meetings, generally Democrats now attend the Harvard seminar and Republicans go to their retreat. So from the very beginning of their careers, representatives are divided by party loyalty.

These are nuts-and-bolts meetings, pointing out basically that new members know almost nothing about the system. Among the subjects covered are parliamentary procedure and ethics. Anyone who watches C-SPAN would believe that we understand parliamentary procedure, that we know those carefully followed rules of conduct. And that would be wrong. I'm often as confused by those rules as everyone else. I wouldn't want to be tested on them, because I wouldn't do very well. Maybe there are a half-dozen members who understand procedure completely, but the rest of us have only a rudimentary understanding. If I wanted to make a parliamentary objection, I would first speak with the parliamentarian, the person who really does know those rules, and find out the best way to proceed. While it's certainly possible to serve without understanding all the rules, knowing them is a distinct advantage.

Ethics are emphasized. Supposedly Will Rogers once boasted, "We have the best Congress money can buy." People believed that when he said it in the 1930s—and based on recent polling, many people still do. That hasn't been my experience, however. The bottom line taught at these seminars is simply that you can't use your public position to unduly benefit yourself in private. I've found that most members of Congress are inherently honest people, Democrats and Republicans alike. But when you have 435 people in any group, some will go astray. Unfortunately, one bad apple is a reflection on the entire orchard. Any lapse in ethics makes headlines—and is often then exploited by the other party for partisan reasons—and that reinforces any negative perceptions people have about Congress.

My experience has been that most members are careful about maintaining ethical standards. This is a very public business, and one wrong choice can quickly damage a career. This is how careful we have to be: Once a month a group of Jewish members used to get together with a rabbi. As Sam Gejdenson (D-CT), who was part of that group, remembers, "What happened was the rabbi would say something, and then each of us would tell him why he was completely wrong. It was a great intellectual exercise. For these meetings the rabbi would bring in deli food, mostly lox and bagels. But because he was supplying a meal, we had to get approval from the Ethics Committee. The committee examined the issue carefully and decided that real lox was too extravagant. So from that point on the rabbi could only bring in lox spread." Oy Congress! This might well have been the only time in history that lox was considered a potential bribe.

At each of the orientation seminars, one point is emphasized over and over: It's your name on the door.

After winning my congressional election, the first person I called for advice was Connecticut senator Joseph Lieberman. Before you begin dealing with the powers of state, before making decisions that will change lives and involve billions of dollars, you have to find a place to live. While many members don't bring their families with them to Washington, choosing instead to fly home each weekend, Laurie and I decided it would work best for our family if our three young children attended school in the Washington area. I called Senator Lieberman because he was an observant Jew like me and asked him about religious schools in the area. Joe Lieberman helped us get settled, the beginning of a relationship that became very close during the chaotic 2000 election.

Washington is a very expensive city in which to live. A congressman's salary is not nearly enough to pay for a mortgage in his or her home district and a comfortable place to live within commuting distance of the Capitol. There are many wealthy members of Congress, but there are probably an equal number who worry about paying their bills at the end of each month. Like me. Some members of Congress actually sleep in their congressional office rather than rent an apartment. But Florida congressman Ron Klein's experience is probably more typical: With two other members, he rented a two-bedroom apartment. A small two-bedroom apartment. To make it work, he explained, "We converted the dining room into a bedroom by putting up some doors. Truthfully, it isn't as glamorous as it sounds. My son is a senior in college. When he came up for my swearing in, he and my daughter thought it was absolutely hysterical that he was living in a nicer room in his college dorm than I was as a congressman."

Democratic representative Shelley Berkley from Nevada was luckier; she found a studio she could afford. "It had been years since I walked in the front door and saw my bedroom, kitchen, living room, and bathroom right in front of me. When my kids come to visit, we blow up an air mattress, although we have to step over it to get to the other side of the room. And I felt privileged to get this apartment at the outrageous price that I did."

At one time Senator Dick Durbin (D-IL), Senator Chuck Schumer (D-NY), Rep. Sam Gejdenson (D-CT), and Rep. George Miller (D-CA) shared an apartment. As the senior member Schumer could have had the upstairs bedroom, but because that was a little more expensive he stayed downstairs.

Members of Congress take the oath of office on the third of January, roughly seven weeks after the election. By that time, your offices in both Washington and your district have to be staffed and at work and you have to have found a place to live while Congress is in session. Sometimes the first opportunity you get to savor your victory, to take a deep breath, is the day you get sworn in.

Taking the oath of office is a moment no one will ever forget. As the late Rep. Tom Lantos from San Francisco described it, "It is an unbelievably magic moment. I was only one of 435 sworn in that day, and while I was standing there with my right hand raised I couldn't help thinking about the grandeur of this country. That I, who came here as a penniless immigrant with a heavy accent and no connections, could make it to the floor of the House of Representatives . . . There is no way to describe that feeling."

Actually, I almost didn't make it to the swearing in. My wife, Laurie, was pregnant with our third child, Hannah—and she was due to deliver in Florida the same day I was supposed to take the oath of office in Washington. And just to increase my anxiety, there was the potential that my vote could determine who became Speaker of the House.

These were my options: Be with Laurie when she was giving birth or help determine the history of America—and be in the doghouse at home for the next twenty years. Actually, it wasn't a difficult decision to make. Missing my child's birth was not an option. At that time the Republicans had a slim five- or six-vote majority. Newt Gingrich was expected to be elected Speaker of the House, but he faced some serious ethical issues, and several Republican members had said publicly they weren't going to vote for him. His margin was two or three votes, and it was rumored that other Republicans would refuse to vote for him. My nightmare was that Gingrich would be elected Speaker by one or two votes—and my missed vote would make the difference. That would then become the defining moment of my congressional career, even before it had begun.

One of the most difficult aspects of a politician's life is balancing your responsibilities to your constituents with those to your family. Right after the election I'd gotten a call from former Florida Democratic representative Dante Fascell, who'd served nineteen terms in the House. In Florida he was an icon. We had lunch, and in a two-hour span he told me everything there was to know about his experiences in Congress, most of which I've forgotten. But the one thing I do remember is him telling me, "The only regret I have is that I missed my son's childhood." That comment made an enormous impression on me. That wasn't going to happen to me, no matter what the consequences to my career, I promised myself at that time. And here I was, a few weeks later, facing the first real test of my commitment.

Laurie and I met in high school. She has never been the type of person to base her life on my schedule—let alone give birth on my schedule. But this time she decided to induce labor three days early, allowing me to be there when Hannah was born and then go to Washington.

I took my eight-year-old daughter, Rachel, and four-year-old son, Zachary, my parents, and father-in-law with me to the Capitol. The actual swearing in takes place on the House floor, and on this occasion members are allowed to bring their minor children onto the floor. After the ceremony the vote for Speaker takes place. This is the only time there is an actual roll call vote on the floor; otherwise all voting is done electronically. But for this vote they call out the names of each of the 435 members. As each name was called, the member responded either "Gephardt," the Democrats' choice, or "Gingrich," the Republicans' choice. The roll is called alphabetically, and it can take as long as two hours. Wexler, obviously, is near the end. I didn't care. I didn't mind waiting. This certainly was one of the most exciting moments of my life. I was looking around the chamber, feeling the extraordinary history that had taken place there, thinking about the great men and women who had served there long before me, waiting as the *T*s were being called, when my son looked up at me with pride and love in his eyes and said those words known to every parent, "Daddy, I have to go the bathroom."

This was another moment of decision. "Let's go," I said, grabbing his hand and leading him off the floor, trying to listen to the names being called. We raced to the men's room. I recall it taking longer than I expected. In my memory it took him about nine years. We rushed back to the floor with a few seconds to spare, in time for me to cast my first important vote as a congressman, for Dick Gephardt to be Speaker. Of course, he lost. Welcome to the minority.

Although the official ceremony takes place on the floor, freshman members are also invited to be sworn in individually by the Speaker. Most members do it. It's taped and makes a nice picture for the local media in your district, but it has no legal meaning. After his election in 2006, Congressman Keith Ellison (Democratic-Farmer-Labor-MN), the only Muslim member of congress, decided to use the Koran when he was sworn in by Nancy Pelosi, causing some right-wingers to complain.

According to *The New York Times,* conservative radio talk-show host Dennis Prager told his audience—as usual completely inaccurately—"The act undermines American civilization."

In reality, Ellison raised his right hand with all the rest of us and was officially and legally sworn in on the House floor. Thus apparently saving American civilization. When I was sworn in by Newt Gingrich I brought my own Bible with me. It was the Old Testament because I'd been told that the Speaker had only the New Testament. While I was being sworn in, I couldn't help thinking about the man I'd met during my campaign who told me, "I hope when you get to Washington you'll punch Newt Gingrich in the nose."

To which I had replied, "You bet. That's the first thing I'll do." I can still hear myself saying that. And today I see myself in a photograph hanging on my office wall, standing right next to Gingrich and smiling broadly. Newt Gingrich personalized politics to a terrible extent and was a ruthless leader; at the same time he is an intellectually energetic man who invigorates a debate, sometimes in a constructive fashion, although I rarely agree with him. At that moment, though, he was representing the institution, not himself or his political party. So I didn't punch him in the nose.

Shortly after the swearing-in ceremony, the House takes a two-week break before returning to Washington for the president's State of the Union address. During those first few days we're in session, it's common to see new members wandering around the halls trying to find a cafeteria or a shop or, on occasion, their own office. While it may take a few weeks to become accustomed to the place, the work starts immediately. This is one of the few jobs in which the decisions you make on your very first day matter. There is no period of adjustment. I had been in office less than four months, for example, when President Clinton began teaching me how the real game of *Mr. President* was played.

4

Oval Office Politics

———————————

Why do we expect our presidents to control destiny, when they cannot even control the House of Representatives?

—Russell Baker

While in the state senate, in 1992 I had been an early supporter of Bill Clinton in his run for the Democratic nomination. I was tired of losing presidential elections and convinced we needed a southerner to lead the ticket. I thought he was charismatic, very smart, and electable, so I organized a large rally for him at a Delray Beach synagogue before the Florida primary. It attracted more than a thousand people. I entered Congress at the beginning of President Clinton's second term. Legislation had been proposed that gave him authority to negotiate trade agreements with other nations. This was my first controversial vote in Congress, and much as I respected Bill Clinton, I intended to vote against him. The unions in my district, which had supported me very strongly in the election, were against it, and I trusted their views on the impact this legislation would have on working men and women.

The vote was going to be close. Clinton needed five or six more votes to get the bill passed, and those votes weren't going to come from the Republican side. So the White House focused on a small group of Democrats who might be persuaded to change their minds and their votes. In my initial conversations with the president, I explained that this vote was politically difficult for me. I had just been through a tough primary election in which I had been accused of being the Republican in the race. Many of the voters in my district really didn't know me. I didn't want their first impression to be that I was someone who voted against their interests.

"Why don't you come on over," Clinton said. He asked me to bring tapes of the commercials that had been run against me. "Maybe we can figure something out."

When the president of the United States invites you to the White House, it is unheard of to refuse the invitation. (Although, truthfully, that's exactly what I did throughout George W. Bush's first term. After the U.S. Supreme Court selected Bush to be president in 2000, I made a pledge to boycott the White House for the next four years.) When I got to the White House I saw it was ringed by union members watching to see which members of Congress went in to see the president. I noticed a sign indicating that someone from the local in my district was there. So they knew I was in play.

I brought Suzanne Stoll and Eric Johnson with me. On the way over, Eric warned me that Clinton was going to put tremendous pressure on me. "Don't get charmed by him. I don't care if he is the president. Don't cave," he admonished me. "Don't cave."

Ten seconds after Clinton began speaking, I glanced at Eric, who was clearly in awe. He was sitting there nodding his head. Caved.

Clinton was eager to see the commercials we'd brought with us. He seemed to love the challenge of dissecting a political race. He led us into a small room, put the tape in the VCR, and pressed Play. Nothing happened. He pressed a few more buttons, tried a few other things, and still he couldn't get the monitor to play. Eric and I tried to help him figure it out. Wow, I thought, this is just like being on the audio-visual squad in high school. Clinton bent down behind the monitor and played with some wires. Finally, after several painful moments, we got it to work. One of the spots showed a picture of Eric while a narrator said ominously, "Wexler hired the former president of the Young Republicans to be his campaign manager . . ."

My best ally disappeared completely when the president told Eric, "Why, I'd be honored to have a handsome fella like you working on my campaign . . ."

Afterward Clinton critiqued the commercials, digesting the political dynamic. He understood my predicament. "If you're gonna vote against the unions," he asked, "what can I do to counteract that vote?" In other words, how can I help you help me? Bill Clinton is one of the brightest men I'd ever met. He was well known even then for his ability to make each person he spoke with feel as though they were the only person in the room, but what particularly impressed me was his grasp of details about things I should have known well, but that he had no reason to know at all. During this meeting he made a compelling argument for my support, reminding me that as a Democrat he was a friend of working Americans and promising that if he won the authority to negotiate trade deals, he'd protect labor and the environment. He emphasized that in order for him to remain a strong leader, he had to win votes like this one; otherwise, he'd be a lame duck for the next four years and be powerless to help Democrats in Congress—or the unions on other matters.

I'd been in Congress less than four months and was sitting in the White House with the president of the United States, being told that the success of his second term might depend on my vote. As I explained to him, I had mixed feelings. I wanted to support him, I just didn't see how I could do it without compromising the interests of the people I cared about at home. The meeting ended without any resolution.

The White House kept the pressure on me. On a Sunday afternoon, Laurie and I and our three children were with friends at a pizza restaurant near Dupont Circle when the White House called and asked us to come over to meet with the president. Believe me, as much as I try to keep things in perspective, when you're sitting at lunch with friends and you have to explain, "The president wants us to come over to the White House," it's a pretty heady feeling. Few things impress Laurie, but this time she really wanted to go—even though she was dressed in overalls. We had another pleasant meeting, and once again I explained why I couldn't support him on this issue.

But he persisted. The third time I was invited to the White House I brought several members of my staff with me. When a White House assistant explained politely that the president would see only "the congressman" in the Oval Office, I responded that in that case we would just need to meet elsewhere. My staff still uses this as an example of the sense of camaraderie in our office. In reality, I just wanted support around me when I turned down the president. Eventually they let us all in.

At this third meeting we discussed those things he might be able to do to help me politically if I agreed to vote with him. We discussed Alzheimer's research, which was important to the senior citizens in my district, and he told us about his uncle who had suffered from that terrible disease. We talked about the schools in my district and what he could do to help me there. And finally we talked about the Middle East, about Israel in particular, and he said, "You know, maybe I can get you involved in some things that would be interesting for you, things you'd enjoy." If I could play a role in U.S.-Israeli relations, I would not only enjoy it, but it would be very important to my constituents.

That meeting continued late into the night. The president liked to talk politics. He wore me down. I agreed that if he needed my vote to ensure passage of the bill, I would vote yes. But if my vote wasn't absolutely necessary, I would be free to vote against it. I didn't believe I was voting against my conscience or my district. There were positive aspects of the bill. And I was learning about the absolute importance of party unity in Washington. Ultimately, President Clinton was most persuasive when he outlined the potentially negative consequences to his administration if he lost the trade vote. I finally decided I would not be serving my district well, or the country, if I had a hand in compromising Clinton's standing and effectiveness.

It was this type of personal charm that enabled Clinton to be persuasive with other members of Congress as well.

In 1993, for example, when the president was looking for votes to approve his controversial North American Free Trade Agreement, he invited freshman Alcee Hastings to the White House. According to Hastings, "I went over to the Oval Office and he gave me a cup of coffee and put his hand on my knee and said, 'Alcee, I need you to do this.' Considering that my parents had worked as live-in domestics to save enough money to pay for me to go to college, the fact that I was sitting in the White House and the president of the United States was asking for my vote was pretty impressive. Naturally I agreed to support his position.

"On the floor of the House a week or so later Pete Visclosky from Indiana asked, 'I heard you're voting for NAFTA. What'd you get?'

"'What did I get?' I said. 'See, I'm new here. I didn't get anything. What are you talking about?'

"Pete joked, 'Why didn't you at least ask him for a bridge?'

"I laughed at that. 'Well,' I explained, 'see, in my district we don't have a river.'

"Pete didn't even hesitate. 'Then you should have asked him for a river.'"

Just as with Alcee, there was no deal made for my vote. No quid pro quo. And as it turned out, my vote was not needed. The White House never found the other votes, and the bill was never brought to a vote. But Clinton did not forget our conversation. Several weeks later I received an invitation from the State Department asking me to join Secretary of State Madeleine Albright on a trip to Europe to meet then Israeli prime minister Benjamin "Bibi" Netanyahu and PLO chairman Yasser Arafat. Sometimes people ask me why Democrats remain so loyal to Bill Clinton. There was no benefit for him to include me on this trip, but for me it was vitally important. The fact that he remembered our conversation was tremendously impressive, and a small example of why he is such a remarkable politician and commands so much loyalty.

At that time, my daughter Rachel loved the movie *Prince of Egypt*. As I boarded the Air Force flight to Europe, having now been a congressman for almost four months, I kept thinking about a key line from that soundtrack: "You're playing with the big boys now." This was the first time I'd been on an executive branch flight. The feeling was much greater than being a kid in a candy store. I had no idea what I was doing there, so I just enjoyed it. The thing that most impressed me was that there was a large office copier on the airplane. In fact, they had a whole press room, but I'd never seen a copy machine on a plane before.

This was my introduction to the world of real politics. Admittedly, I wondered what value I could add to these meetings. I was a freshman congressman with absolutely no power in Congress. Few members even knew who I was. But if I could play even the most minor role, it could be the beginning of a larger role for me in foreign policy.

In addition to the secretary of state, there were six assistants and myself on the plane. For me, the hardest part of the trip was not showing my excitement. We met with the Israeli delegation in a London hotel. While Albright was with Netanyahu I waited in another room with several of her assistants. At one point she came into that room and discussed the progress of her meeting. Eventually she looked at me and asked, "Would you be willing to say this to the prime minister?"

For an instant I wondered if she was talking to me. I was floored by the concept that she was asking me to play a role in these talks. Truthfully, I don't remember my lines, I don't remember the substance of what I was to tell him, just that it advanced the American negotiation position and it was a position with which I agreed completely. No one ever explained to me precisely why I was asked to do this, but I can assume that they felt these words might be meaningful coming from a very pro-Israel Jewish member of Congress. After I agreed, they put me in position in the hallway, where I would be certain to meet Netanyahu. Like an actor standing backstage when the curtain is about to go up, I stood there going over my lines in my mind, waiting for this "accidental" meeting to occur.

Suddenly the door opened and the prime minister was standing in front of me. The heavily guarded floor had been cordoned off, so he knew I was part of Madeleine Albright's party. He just looked at me and asked, "What are you doing here?" It was a serious question. Bibi understood that I was there for a reason and wanted to know what it was.

My honest answer would have been "I have no idea." Instead, I delivered my lines. He listened, and shrugged. I don't remember his being particularly receptive.

When I reported this to Madeleine Albright, she shook her head, commenting that he was being very stubborn. She was going to have to rethink her approach to the Israelis.

We flew from London to Bern, Switzerland, to meet with Arafat. Before the flight, I had a few free hours in London, so I went shopping for my kids, buying a large toy typewriter for my son and big dolls for my daughters. I was carrying them in huge bags. On a commercial flight my bags would have taken up several seats. As I got on board, Secretary Albright gave me a quizzical look, clearly wondering, Who are you to come on board with those packages? I don't know what possessed me, but I said to her, "Just be thankful I only have three children."

On the flight to Switzerland I remember thinking, When I call Laurie, how can I possibly explain any of this? It seemed surreal. And then, as we were waiting for the elevators in Bern, I found myself standing four feet away from Yasser Arafat, dressed in a kaffiyeh and full garb. He'd stopped to speak with members of our delegation. I'd seen Arafat on television many times, and here I was standing close enough to him to notice that his hands were shaking as if he had Parkinson's disease. Within a few years I would be sitting with the leaders of several Arab and Muslim nations, I'd carry messages between them and Israel, I'd arrange very private meetings between their representatives and Israelis, but I was still new enough to the world of international diplomacy to wonder if this trip might end up being the highlight of my entire political career. I had no way of knowing the events that lay in the future.

5

How the Gingrich Stole Congress

When we got into office, the thing that surprised me most was to find things were just as bad as we'd been saying they were.

—John F. Kennedy

I was elected to the House of Representatives in 1996, one term after the beginning of the so-called Republican Revolution. I knew what I was getting sworn into. I knew how tough it was going to be dealing with the Republican majority. The House wasn't designed by the Founding Fathers to be a place of peace and harmony. It has always been a rough place to do political business. The fact that members have to fight for their political careers every two years makes it a much more confrontational body than the Senate. It's always been that way. According to the *Annals of Congress,* a predecessor of the *Congressional Record,* in January 1798 Vermont Republican representative Matthew Lyon got into a loud argument with Roger Griswold, a Federalist from Connecticut, which ended with Lyon spitting tobacco juice into Griswold's face. After an attempt to expel Lyon from the

House failed, Griswold attacked him on the House floor, beating him on the head and shoulders with "a large yellow hickory cane." Lyon grabbed tongs from the fireplace and fought back. Eventually the two men were separated, but throughout that day other members fought with fists and sticks all around the House.

In 1996 the House was under the close-to-dictatorial control of Speaker Newt Gingrich and Majority Whip Tom DeLay. DeLay was known as "The Hammer," which was about as close as either of them came to actually picking up a weapon. The weapon they used to consolidate control was their new majority, which allowed them to change the rules under which the House had operated for decades. By stacking committees with a larger majority of Republicans than had been usual under the Democratic majority, and by selecting the chairman of each committee mostly by loyalty to the conservative agenda and the ability to raise money rather than by seniority as it had always been done, they ensured that their political allies would control those committees. By controlling the committees, they controlled the fate of every piece of legislation. By controlling the Rules Committee, which establishes the rules under which each piece of legislation is considered, Tom DeLay controlled the floor of the House. By controlling the Appropriations Committee, DeLay controlled every member's budget and earmarks. By working closely with Republican lobbyists, he guaranteed that the large Washington firms and national corporations would hire only Republicans and listen to their advice—and that these firms would assist Republican fund-raising efforts.

While the Republican strategy was admittedly effective, it was harsh and, at times, repulsive to any sense of decency. Most important, these brass-knuckled "take no prisoners" tactics perfected the politics of personal destruction that so poisons Washington today. It is this extraordinary vindictiveness that startles many new members of Congress when they arrive.

Many people who have been in Congress for a long time can remember similar excesses by the Democratic majority. But what made the Gingrich-DeLay 1994 takeover so unusual, according to Sarah Dufendach, who served as chief of staff to David Bonior, was that:

They knew they had to burn the place down to get back control and they were willing to do it. The only way they could get control was to attack the House as an institution and they did it.

They moved in like an occupying army. As soon as their transition team moved in they sent out an edict that no boxes would be permitted to leave the building without being inspected by the Capitol Police, that papers could not be shredded, and that computers would be confiscated. Supposedly we no longer had access to files.

I told them, "Go ahead, make my day. The police will search my property over my dead body." But I could take care of myself. What was really unnecessary was that at the same time they began attacking the most defenseless people working on the Hill: the police officers, the maintenance people, the people who worked in the cafeteria and the mailroom. They cut jobs and salaries, they outsourced the cafeteria and the mailroom. These were the very people they would need to enforce these policies. So many of the things they did were so petty. They took away reserved parking spots. There was an old tradition, dating back I'm sure long before Washington had air-conditioning, that each summer morning a bucket of ice would be delivered to each member's office; they took away the ice. Once a week members were allowed to request flowers for their office from the botanical garden right across the street. They took away the flowers.

They changed the tone of the House. Experienced members told me that when Tip O'Neill was the Speaker of the House, he and Minority Leader Bob Michel would fight all day and then go out and have a drink together. Members from both parties played golf together, and on occasion they socialized. Certainly the House was run on a partisan basis, but it wasn't cutthroat politics. There was a certain amount of civility. That changed with Gingrich and DeLay.

Maybe people weren't hitting each other over the head with hickory sticks, but the civility disappeared. Democrat Eliot Engel of the Bronx remembers a confrontation he had with Republican Duke Cunningham of California—currently serving time in prison for accepting bribes—that exemplified the new regime. "At one point we kept hearing that Albania was involved with terrorist groups, which I believed was false. Cunningham disagreed with me. I invited the FBI to come to a closed hearing and give us an intelligence briefing. At the end of that hearing Cunningham comes over to me and out of the blue said, 'You're an asshole. A liberal asshole.' It wasn't 'I disagree with you' or 'I have some questions.' This was long before anyone knew Cunningham was a crook. I thought he was just a nasty guy."

That was the level of debate to which Gingrich and DeLay reduced the House when they gained control.

Some of the actions taken by the right-wing majority were not just petty, they were totally counterproductive. At one point a bill was being debated on the floor, for example, and Los Angeles congresswoman Maxine Waters was speaking. She was allotted two minutes for her remarks. The reality is that whatever she said, it wasn't going to change any votes. The Democrats were going to lose; the Democrats always lost. But at the end of her two minutes she hadn't quite completed her statement so she asked for an additional thirty seconds. This is just the ordinary way of doing business. It happens all the time. But this time a Republican objected to giving her those extra few seconds. The Democrats became infuriated and we began invoking parliamentary procedures to prevent any business from being done. We basically shut down the House. This was all being broadcast on C-SPAN. A simple request for the courtesy of an additional thirty seconds to speak resulted in the House being deadlocked for several hours. Who benefited from such shenanigans? Certainly not the American people. I wish I could say that only the Republicans engaged in such childish behavior, but that would be distorting the truth. It's just that they did it so much more often. After this particular episode lasted too long, a Democrat renewed the request for an additional thirty seconds. This time no one objected. In response, the Democrats started cheering. We so rarely won anything that our reaction to this meaningless victory made it seem as if we had successfully reenacted the New Deal.

The Republican leadership routinely denied the Democrats access to rooms in which to hold meetings and hearings. At one point Minority Leader Dick Gephardt was actually forced to hold a meeting out on the front lawn. The ranking member of the Judiciary Committee, John Conyers (D-MI), learned an important lesson: When requesting a room for a meeting, he would always specify a room with catering—not because he wanted catering services, but because those were the largest rooms.

The rancorous attitude got much worse in the 109th Congress, when Republican Ways and Means chairman Bill Thomas actually called the Capitol Police to forcibly remove Democratic members of that committee from a room. Thomas, who had been elevated over a more senior Republican, introduced a revised version of a pension bill at midnight and tried to push it through the committee the following morning. Democrats demanded time to read the ninety-page bill, but Thomas refused to delay the vote. To protest, the Democratic members marched out of the room into a nearby library. Thomas then proceeded to call the police and asked them to clear the library. As Charlie Rangel (D-NY) remembered it, "The sergeant of arms came and said he was advised by the Capitol Police that the chairman of the Ways and Means Committee asked that we be removed from the room. And I said we were not going to be removed. And the sergeant of arms said he thought that was an issue that should be resolved by members of Congress and members from the committee."

A few days later Thomas tearfully apologized on the floor—but he also refused to reconsider the pension bill.

Gingrich and DeLay made a formidable team. I didn't get to know either one of them personally; there was very little connection between the Republican leadership and Democratic members. Newt Gingrich was a man of ideas, ideas that I vehemently disagreed with, and he was needlessly nasty, but at least he had an intellectual foundation for his actions. DeLay was far less concerned with ideas; rather, he was focused on doing whatever was necessary to win. Former Mississippi congressman Ronnie Shows remembers a vote on renewing a trade agreement with China that had devastated the textile and furniture industries in North Carolina. The Republicans wanted this legislation to pass—but a Republican congressman from North Carolina intended to vote against it. It was a terrible bill for his district. As Shows recalls, "After this member voted against the bill, I watched DeLay walk up to him on the floor and force him to change his vote. The man literally was crying as he cast his vote. DeLay stood right behind him until he changed his vote. The leadership controlled so much money, and the network they built was so efficient, that if anybody dared go against them they called them a bad Republican and threatened to run a more loyal Republican against them. That's how they maintained party discipline."

The one place in the House that generally had remained free of partisan politics was the gym in the Rayburn building. Members who worked out together, or who played basketball, tended to get along. But after a workout one morning Shows looked up while shaving and DeLay was standing next to him. "Ronnie," he told Shows, "I'm doing an experiment. We're trying the tactics we intend to use in other races against you."

"I didn't know what he meant," Shows remembered. "So I kind of laughed it off. But a couple of days later I was walking through the tunnel to my office and Republican congressman John Sununu passed me. I knew him a little, although we'd never had a real conversation. 'How you doing?' I said to him. And he said to me, basically, 'We're going to crush you.' Just like that. 'We're going to crush you.' And they did. That's the way they operated." During redistricting, the Mississippi Republican legislature sliced up Shows's district, handing it to Republican Chip Pickering.

After having been in the minority for so many years, it's easy to understand the Republican desire for payback, but Gingrich took the use of power to new levels. For example, there is time set aside at the end of each day for members to make statements or speeches on the floor primarily for the consumption of their constituents. This time is called Special Orders. As they stand at a podium and speak, the camera focuses directly on them, and when seen on television the impression given is that they are addressing the full House. In truth, the House is empty, with the possible exception of the next speaker waiting to address an empty chamber. What Gingrich would do when he was speaking was point across the aisle as if there were a Democrat sitting there, then challenge that nonexistent Democrat to explain why he made a certain vote that day. The silence was supposedly proof that the Democrat could not defend his or her vote.

One day, though, a C-SPAN director had enough of those theatrics.

When Gingrich pointed across the aisle and issued his challenge, the director panned the camera in that direction—and it was revealed to viewers that Gingrich was accusing an empty seat.

Even before Gingrich swore me in, Democrats had filed seventy-six ethics claims against him with the Ethics Committee. Eventually that bipartisan committee recommended that the House publicly reprimand him for failing to seek proper tax advice concerning a course he taught at tax-exempt colleges that he used to support his political action committee. In fact, the second vote I cast in the House was to support that recommendation of the Ethics Committee—which was accompanied by the largest fine ever levied against a Speaker, three hundred thousand dollars.

Throughout my career in the Florida Senate, Democrats and Republicans had worked well together. Certainly we were partisan, but we were Floridians first. In fact, among my closest friends was the future Republican governor, Charlie Crist. Charlie has always taken great pride in being respectful to Democrats and inclusive of all points of view.

But that certainly was not the way the Republicans ran Congress. While I was aware that Gingrich and DeLay had marginalized Democratic participation, until I actually got to the House I couldn't fully comprehend how completely they had taken over the legislative process. I don't know of a single piece of meaningful legislation proposed by a Democrat that got out of committee without a Republican putting his or her name on it, although in many instances the Republicans did allow the Democrat on the bill as a cosponsor. For example, when Ronnie Shows learned that as veterans turned sixty-five, the Department of Defense was taking away their military health care and substituting Medicare, he filed the Keep Our Promise to America's Military Retires Act, which guaranteed that veterans would receive the military health care they had been promised. The late Charlie Norwood (R-GA) cosponsored it. But the Republican leadership refused to consider the bill. It didn't matter that it was great for veterans, they just didn't want Shows to get credit. Instead, they changed the name to Tricare for Life, changed a few of the provisions, credited a Republican as the author, and passed it.

If legislation did reach the floor, its fate was determined by Republican leadership. The key number on the House floor is 218. It takes 218 votes to pass legislation, and the Republicans controlled more votes than that. They didn't need the Democrats to pass their agenda and they knew it. As the director of floor operations for Majority Whip Roy Blunt (R-MO) once admitted, bluntly, "For my purposes, they [Democrats] are irrelevant."

"The Republicans perfected the marginalization of the minority to a science," Eliot Engel remembers. "Speaker Dennis Hastert wouldn't allow legislation to get to the floor if it required Democratic votes to pass. He used to say he wouldn't put legislation forward unless he had a majority of the majority."

They didn't negotiate with Democrats; instead they imposed their agenda on Democrats. That's the way it worked. Nowhere was this more blatant than in conference committees. For legislation to become law, it has to be passed by both the House and the Senate in the exact same language; usually the initial versions passed by each body are substantially different, so appointed representatives of the House and the Senate meet to negotiate the final language. The legislation that may become law is hammered out in this conference committee. During this process drastic changes can be made; new provisions and amendments can be introduced, and others can be eliminated. Only after agreement is reached on the specific language does exactly the same piece of legislation go back to each body for an up-or-down final vote. Conference committee reports cannot be amended.

Usually each party leader is permitted to appoint a certain number of members to the conference committee. It's a desirable assignment. Once, when the Democrats held the majority, Duke Cunningham challenged former congressman Ron Dellums (D-CA) to a fight because he hadn't been put on the conference committee negotiating a defense bill important to his district. Dellums said that he would be happy to fight him, but even if Cunningham won, Dellums couldn't put him on that committee. Because it was a defense bill, the senior Republican member of the Armed Services Committee—the committee where the bill originated—appointed all the Republicans to the conference committee.

The situation got so bad that in many instances the Republicans refused to allow Democrats even to attend conference committee meetings. Sometimes they wouldn't tell Democrats where and when these meetings were being held. On occasion Democrats were told not to bother showing up. A Democratic member recalls being told by Republican leadership, "You guys can come to the conference committee if you want to, but we're not going to do anything until you leave." In fact, when the conference committee met to consider President Bush's Medicare bill, conferees Charlie Rangel (D-NY) and Marion Berry (D-AR) were physically prevented from entering the room.

Apparently the Democrats had run the House differently when they held the majority. Not necessarily because Democrats are more civic-minded or bipartisan, but rather because of the nature of the two parties. Traditionally the Democratic Party has been a coalition of members whose beliefs and interests could be widely divergent, ranging from Northeastern liberals to Southern conservatives. That made it very difficult for the leadership to impose party discipline, to convince members to vote the party position rather than their own interests. The Republican majority elected in 1994 was dominated by right-wing conservatives who willingly used hardball tactics—like eliminating seniority and rewarding loyalists with committee chairmanships and cutting funding for local projects—to maintain control.

Predictably, since the Democrats regained a majority in 2006, the Republicans have hypocritically demanded fair treatment—although one thing I haven't heard a single Republican ask for is the same treatment they gave Democrats.

Every action taken by Gingrich and DeLay was intended to build an enduring Republican majority. These new Republican members believed that Democrats weren't the loyal opposition, they were the enemy. Tom DeLay's K Street Project essentially required lobbyists to isolate Democrats, in terms of both legislation and campaign financial support.

Seemingly there was little the Democrats could do in response to the right-wing revolution. The most we could do was try to block the most heinous legislation. Minority Whip David Bonior organized a parliamentary group to figure out legal ways to tie the place up in knots: in a sense, parliamentary guerrilla tactics. At one point when Republicans tried to force debate on an issue, the Democrats refused and kept the House open all night. All through the night members stood up and talked about their districts and why they came to Congress. The Republicans tried to turn out the lights, but a Democratic member found the switch and turned them back on. Obviously these antics didn't affect anything. Democracy in Congress is simple—the side that has the majority of the votes wins. And the Republicans had those votes.

So I entered the House at a particularly contentious time in its history. I had to learn how the system worked for a member of the minority, how to get things accomplished in a hostile environment.

6

House Rules:
How a Bill (Rarely) Becomes a Law

It is amazing what you can accomplish if you do not care who gets the credit.

—Harry Truman

In order to truly understand the damage that George W. Bush and his neocon cohorts have done to our government, it's necessary to know how the process really works. Not how the system is described in textbooks, but rather how it has been perverted for extreme right-wing gain. No one would claim that Democrats aren't partisan, but the extreme measures taken by the right wing to try to consolidate its power are unlike anything seen before in Congress.

Most Americans believe that making laws is the most important function of the Congress. Article 1, Section 1 of the Constitution states firmly, "All legislative powers herein granted shall be vested in a Congress . . ." In the more than two hundred years since passage of the first major bill, the Tariff Act of 1789, only a small fraction of the bills proposed have actually been signed into law. It can take years for a proposal to go through the entire legislative process, and should it actually be passed, it'll probably bear only a slight resemblance to the original bill.

There have been several hundred books titled *How a Bill Becomes a Law*. Sometimes there are variations, *How a Bad Bill Becomes a Law*, or *Congress in Action—How a Bill Becomes a Law*. But all of these books have one thing in common: Not one of them has ever been made into a major motion picture. None of them has even made the *New York Times* Best Seller List. And there's a reason for this: It's really boring. It's a complicated, cumbersome process, a process that isn't even as exciting as, say, the complete history of zoning regulations. The manual of House rules (*House Rules and Manual*) is more than a thousand pages long—in addition to twenty-five volumes of precedents. A bill can go through more than a hundred different steps before it becomes law. Truthfully, though, most lawmakers don't know all those specific parliamentary steps.

Having served six years in the Florida Senate, I was a realist when I came to Congress. I didn't have great expectations, I had moderate expectations. Illinois senator Paul Douglas once said that when first elected to the Senate he had hoped to save the world. After several years he still hoped to save the country. And by the time he was leaving office he would have been very happy just to save Indiana Dunes National Lakeshore. I was even less fortunate than Douglas—I was in the minority when I entered Congress. Any legislation I filed, I did so with the assumption that it was very unlikely to become law. Nevertheless, I continued to file bills that met the needs of my constituents—for example, fixing Social Security—and I worked the floor of the House trying to convince skeptical Republicans to give my legislation a chance.

Among those bills I filed was the Restore the American Dream Act, which would have allowed young people to contribute to a tax-free home savings account rather than a traditional retirement plan. Still a good idea, it went nowhere. Or the Full Time for Violent Crime Act of 1997, which would have closed a legal loophole through which more than a thousand violent felons were released because of prison overcrowding. It went nowhere.

On average, approximately four thousand bills are filed annually in the House, and fewer than one of ten ever becomes law. But all of this failed legislation I filed served at least one very important purpose: I was doing the work my constituents demanded of me. They elected me to represent their priorities and I was determined to do that. Never mind that Newt Gingrich and his Republican majority swatted me away like a troublesome fly. At least my constituents were aware that I was working on their behalf, even if they rarely saw any concrete results. These weren't frivolous bills; in each case it was something in which I believed, something I thought would have been worth pursuing, but it just wasn't going to happen.

Minority members file a lot of bills to make substantive or political points, even though they have little chance of being passed. In the summer of 2007, for example, Republican representative Steve King of Iowa filed an amendment to an appropriations bill to prohibit the Speaker of the House, Nancy Pelosi, as well as other members, from using State Department funds to travel to Cuba, Iran, North Korea, Sudan, or Syria. The actual purpose of the bill was to highlight conservative complaints that Speaker Pelosi had dared travel to Syria. Of course these same Republicans ignored the fact that several Republican members had traveled to Syria just days before the Speaker's trip to Damascus. Did King really believe the Democratic majority was going to decide, Wow, what a great idea, let's attack our leader for attempting to create a dialogue with a rogue leader who was supporting insurgent forces in Iraq and sources of international anti-American terrorism such as Hezbollah and Hamas? Why didn't we think of that? This proposed amendment didn't have the slightest chance of moving forward—even without the embarrassing coincidence that the day it was filed, Bush administration officials happened to be in North Korea—but the fact that it was filed was carried by newspapers around the country and focused attention on this conservative whining point. Undoubtedly, it earned King praise from his conservative Iowa constituents and attention from the talk radio hosts. For King, this was an effective piece of legislation. And it actually moved the debate by getting that attention.

I had learned how the legislative process is supposed to work for the benefit of society while serving in the Florida Senate. Few people appreciate the degree to which the state legislature affects their everyday lives. Whether it's the educational system, health care, environmental policy, taxes, transportation, or law enforcement, state legislatures often determine the controlling rules and regulations. In the Florida Senate I actually could propose legislation and get it passed, even when I was in the minority. Most of the time I was there, the senate was divided equally between Democrats and Republicans, or the Democrats were one or two votes short, so the only way anything ever got done was by bipartisan cooperation. And we cooperated, we worked together. Working with Republican members I successfully passed a great deal of legislation through the senate.

The Florida Senate operated very differently from the United States House of Representatives. Unlike the House, in which members spend their days continually going back and forth between their offices and committee meetings and then go to the floor to vote, in Florida each of the forty state senators had desks on the floor. Most of our voting in the state senate was done the last two weeks of the session and we stayed on the floor all day, from nine o'clock in the morning till late at night, five days a week. When you spend that amount of time on the floor, you get to know most of the other senators quite well. There was a comfortable leather couch against the wall where I would sit with the current Republican governor, then state senator Charlie Crist, talking for hours while debates were taking place. At one time we were cochairmen of the Criminal Justice Committee, so we worked together on several pieces of legislation—and got them passed.

Which is how I gained the name Castration Bob. This began when a federal court ruled that Florida's prisons were overcrowded and the prisoner population had to be reduced significantly within ninety days. That meant tens of thousands of prisoners would have to be released, among them hundreds of repeat violent sex offenders. After hearing from many criminologists and psychiatrists about recidivism and the lack of effective treatments, I proposed a bill to chemically castrate some of these offenders. Obviously this was not a bill that would endear me to liberals, but even now I have no regrets about it. I believed that based on the situation we faced, the possible consequences of putting thousands of violent sex offenders on the streets would have been disasterous. The American Civil Liberties Union responded by calling me "Ayatollah Wexler." The lead editorial in the *South Florida Sun-Sentinel* suggested that a more appropriate medical procedure would be "a lobotomy for Wexler." And in other papers I became "Castration Bob."

Politically this did not hurt me at all, even in the liberal district I represented. In politics, you can't be too tough on crime. Personal safety and security is not a partisan issue—although the Republicans have tried to make it one. People of all political ideologies are sickened by repeat violent sex offenders. Society has the right—the obligation—to offer protection from these felons.

I also proposed writing a bill to bring back chain gangs. At that time the perception was that Florida prisons were like country clubs, prisoners had cable TV and workout rooms, and sentences were being reduced. Chain gangs were meant purely as a punitive measure: Crime doesn't pay. But after all the attention I received for my chemical castration proposal I decided it probably wasn't such a great idea to go forward with this one. Instead I brought it to Charlie Crist, suggesting, "You might want to consider doing this." In fact, he filed the bill and thereafter became known as "Chain Gang Charlie," a nickname that didn't hurt him at all in Florida.

The Florida Senate passed both bills, although my castration bill was defeated in the Florida House. Since then, though, a chemical castration bill has passed the Florida legislature in a somewhat different form. The point is that in the state senate I learned how to write bills, maneuver them through the process, and get them passed. When I had a good idea, there was the distinct possibility that it could become law, regardless of which party was in the majority.

Unfortunately, little of what I'd learned in Florida applied in the U.S. Congress.

Every bill in every legislature begins the same way: with an idea. It does not have to be a good idea, just an idea. Throughout history a lot of wacky ideas have become law. In Kansas, for example, if two trains meet on the same track, neither can proceed until the other has passed. In New York, it's illegal to jump off the Empire State Building, and a marriage can't be dissolved for irreconcilable differences unless both parties agree to it. My state of Florida prohibits rats from leaving ships docked in Tampa Bay. And in the U.S. House we passed a resolution protecting Christmas—even after its Republican sponsor, the late Virginia congresswoman Jo Ann Davis, refused to offer the same protection to Hanukkah and other holidays. A group of Jewish representatives were discussing the hypocrisy of this particular bill and wondering if we should vote against it when Massachusetts congressman Barney Frank, one of the smartest members of the House, asked sarcastically, "How can the people of retail be against Christmas?"

I thought the resolution was absurd, and eventually I voted against it. As far as I could determine, Christmas wasn't in any danger and didn't need Congress to rescue it. The idea for this resolution came from conservative talk-show radio hosts, and once again the conservative members in Congress obediently carried out their wishes. After I had voted against that resolution, the conservative outlet Newsmax included me in an article it headlined "22 Congressmen Hate Christmas." Bah! Humbug!

So any idea, no matter how absurd, can become a bill. Although most people refer to all legislation passed by Congress as bills, there are actually several different forms it can take. Generally, legislation that enables the government to take an action, authorizes spending, or mandates some activity is a bill, while a resolution is a statement regarding a specific issue or legislation concerning the operations of Congress. The primary difference is that for a bill to become law it must be passed by both the House and the Senate—the same bill, word for word—while a House resolution needs only the approval of one house. Privatizing Social Security is a bill. Recognizing and congratulating the University of Florida for winning consecutive NCAA basketball championships is a resolution. Transferring jurisdiction over comatose Terri Schiavo from the Florida court system to the federal system required legal action to be taken, so it was a bill. Criticizing the prime minister of Malaysia for what I believed was an anti-Semitic statement expressed the opinion of Congress without making changes to U.S. law, so it was a resolution.

This was one of the first resolutions I filed in Congress. At that point I didn't truly appreciate the impact a freshman congressman could have around the world. Since then I've learned that outside the United States, statements by members of Congress are often mistakenly believed to be the position of the entire government. When the prime minister of Malaysia, Mahathir Mohamad, claimed that the economic crisis in his country was the result of a "Jewish agenda" and was specifically caused by Jewish financier George Soros, adding, "When a person of Jewish origin does this kind of thing [currency speculation], the effect is the same as when a Muslim carries out something akin to terrorism," I felt I had to respond.

These comments were barely reported in the United States. They didn't cause much of a ripple. But I knew that the prime minister had a history of making anti-Semitic remarks and felt this one called for a response. Working with members of my staff, I drew up a resolution demanding that the Malaysian government condemn these remarks and that the prime minister apologize or resign for what I described as "hateful bigotry recalling the horrors of Nazi doctrine and history's darkest moments." After all, Malaysia is a significant nation in the world, and its prime minister was blaming his country's economic problems on a conspiracy of Jewish financiers. I didn't ask the House to impose any penalties or take any action; it was simply a resolution, a statement by Congress repudiating an anti-Semitic proclamation by a world leader. Two members of Congress, Tom Lantos and Gary Ackerman, signed on as cosponsors.

Few Americans were aware that this was taking place. But throughout Malaysia and the Far East it was front-page news. The UMNO, Malaysia's ruling political party, met and condemned "Wexler's Resolution." Apparently thousands of Malaysians gathered outside the American embassy in Kuala Lumpur to protest. The prime minister suggested that the resolution was an American attempt to control him and used it for his own political purposes. Our State Department, caught in the middle, said that the resolution could be "counterproductive" and sent "mixed signals" to the Malaysian government.

The magnitude of the reaction to my resolution was very surprising. But as the newspapers in my district and my constituents agreed, I was right. Prime Minister Mahathir needed to be chastised. So in response to his dismissive response, my office asked members of the House to sign a letter we'd written expressing "shock and outrage" at the prime minister's anti-Semitic comments. Counting the members who had signed the original resolution, we had thirty-six signatures, or, as was reported in Malaysia, "36 U.S. Lawmakers Demand Apology from Mahathir."

WHEN THE BUSH administration outlined its controversial plan to privatize Social Security by allowing recipients to invest a percentage of their current savings individually, the Democratic leadership decided to let it sink of its own weight. In our caucus, our party meeting, we were told that our strategy was to point out all the defects in the president's plan but not to respond with our own plan. In fact, the Democrats did an excellent job of highlighting the numerous problems with the Bush plan, but the Republicans always responded by asking, logically, I thought, We hear what you don't like about the president's plan, so let's hear your plan to save Social Security. If we were honest, we had to admit we didn't have a plan.

In my district that wasn't good enough. I represent more people on Social Security than any other Democratic member of the House. More than 180,000 of my constituents receive Social Security benefits. So this is *the* bread-and-butter issue in my district. All the publicity the Bush plan received caused them tremendous anxiety. Many of my constituents depend on their monthly Social Security check for a substantial portion of their income. They were not interested in any changes. They believed correctly that by privatizing Social Security we were gambling with their future. In my district, if I was asked about saving Social Security and all I could say was, The other guys' plan stinks, I'd look like an idiot. I would lose all my credibility. Clay Shaw, the

Republican congressman then representing the adjoining district to mine, had a plan. And like other Republicans, he was continually trying to goad the Democrats into proposing a counterplan to take some of the heat off Bush. Shaw warned Democrats, "You're not going to be with us on landing if you're not with us on takeoff."

To which Ben Cardin (D-MD) pointed out, "I'm not so sure I want to be there on the takeoff if you're going to have a crash landing."

Finally, when a popular Palm Beach County civic group called the Forum Club invited Clay Shaw and me to jointly appear there to debate the issue of Social Security, Eric Johnson pointed out correctly that I couldn't possibly show up without my own Social Security plan—unless I intended to be humiliated. So that's when it became obvious that I had to stray from the Democratic Party position and risk angering Nancy Pelosi and my party's leadership by filing my own plan to save Social Security.

The fact that this plan would never be considered by the Republican-controlled committee didn't matter. This was something I had to do. I also believed completely that the president was engaging in a legislative debate on an issue about which Americans inherently trusted Democrats to protect their interests. We were the party that created Social Security and have always supported it; if it needed to be fixed, we needed to be the party to fix it.

We invited several senior advocacy groups to meet with us, including the National Council of Senior Citizens, Families USA, and Alliance for Retired Americans. We spoke with lobbying groups such as the National Committee to Preserve Social Security and Medicare. We had numerous meetings with Democratic think tanks—groups that research policy issues and make recommendations, such as the Center on Budget and Policy Priorities. We even considered the viewpoint of Franklin Roosevelt's grandson.

On paper, our plan was very effective. It accomplished our goal of putting Social Security on solid financial ground without cutting benefits, raising the retirement age, or using a treacherous scheme such as privatization. On paper, we saved Social Security. Real life was considerably more complicated.

Very basically, to fund the Social Security trust fund, 6.2 percent is deducted from the first $90,000 of each person's earnings, and his or her employer matches that contribution. After that an individual can earn anywhere from $90,001 to a billion dollars and never pay another cent. So people who earn less than $90,000 are paying Social Security taxes on 100 percent of their income, while people who earn more are paying a smaller percentage. Unless something is done to change the system, there will be a financial shortfall. After considering all the options, we decided to remove the $90,000 cap and tax additional income at half the tax rate. That was it. No privatization, no cut in benefits, no increasing the retirement age.

You learn a lot about real-world politics and the fine art of compromise when you're drawing up legislation. For example, how could anyone be against a bill protecting Flipper? If there was ever a slam-dunk bill, it had to be the Save Flipper's Life Act. Everybody loves dolphins. Unfortunately, certain forms of tuna fishing result in the killing of dolphins. Sam Gejdenson wanted to pass legislation that protected dolphins. "It was impossible. The environmental groups wanted one hundred percent protection, never-in-a-million-years-could-you-kill-one-dolphin legislation. And absolute pure wasn't going to happen," Gejdenson told me. "The fishermen liked the existing system because it was no hassles for them. The economic consequences were just too much for other nations to agree to. So we ended up in a situation where nothing was doable. The environmentalists were angry because they felt I was copping out, the fishermen were angry because they felt I was favoring the environmentalists, and as a result, nothing got done."

Bills can be almost any length, from a few pages to thousands of pages. The Patriot Act was almost a thousand pages. Appropriations bills can be several thousand pages long. Our Social Security bill was only six pages long.

Filing our Social Security bill was complicated. Nancy Pelosi did not want me to file it. I mean, she really did not want me to do it. As I later told reporters, "It's certainly fair to say that Mrs. Pelosi did not encourage me to do this." Nancy and I had several conversations about it. My relationship with Nancy has always been excellent; there was no friction between us. Nancy is a very respectful person. She doesn't threaten. She states her position firmly and eloquently. And I very much respected her position; she was doing exactly what the Democratic leader should have been doing, trying to maintain party unity.

The Republicans play tough with their members. When Republicans split from the party line, if they dared vote their conscience or their constituents' interest rather than following party dictates, they were subject to losing their committee chairmanship or other party position—and their chances of ever being given a valuable job became pretty slim. For example, ten-term Connecticut congressman Chris Shays, a moderate Republican who has repeatedly broken with his party to represent his constituency, has been shut out of a favorable committee assignment. He finally got so fed up that in 2007 that he warned his party leadership that he would not run for another term or would resign from Congress if they did not support his bid to become the ranking Republican on the Oversight and Reform Committee. But Nancy never threatened me with any kind of penalty. She didn't agree with what I was doing, but there would be no reprisals.

Republicans made sure my bill never saw the light of day, but it was a success because it received a great deal of national attention, thereby providing a genuine progressive alternative to Bush's reckless Social Security privatization scheme.

TRADITION IS THE superglue that holds the Congress together. Very often things are done the way they are done because they have always been done that way. Certainly there are simpler ways of doing certain tasks, but following long-established procedures is a means of continually reminding members that we are part of a historic tradition, tradition that our actions need to respect. To file a bill, someone has to carry it physically to the office of the Clerk of the House and hand it to him, or it can be dropped in a box called the hopper. The hopper is a mahogany box on the rostrum in the House chamber. That's the way

John Quincy Adams did it, that's the way we do it. Although usually we have one of our office interns do it.

Now, I'm aware that the general perception in the country is that Democrats and Republicans rarely speak to one another and never cooperate. Sometimes the media make it seem as if we're only a few steps away from pistols at dawn. There are problems; there is bitterness; but on a day-to-day basis most members do work together.

The reality is that no matter how much I may disagree with some Republicans about their political beliefs, there are specific issues on which we will agree. When I decided to offer legislation urging the European Union to add Hezbollah to its terrorist list, an action that mandated serious economic measures to be taken, I asked moderate New Jersey Republican Jim Saxon to cosponsor it with me. Jim Saxon is pro-life and against stem cell research, but he also supports gun control and campaign finance reform. From conversations we'd had on the floor while awaiting votes, I knew that he was very interested in counterterrorism issues, and members of our staffs were friendly. So I asked him if he would be interested in joining me to sponsor this legislation. There was no question whose name would go first on the bill. I initiated it, but he was in the majority; it became the Saxon-Wexler bill.

There are many Republicans with whom I've had very public disagreements. There was tremendous bitterness between Democratic and Republican members of the Judiciary Committee during the Clinton impeachment process. Yet I have taken several trips and cosponsored legislation with Steve Chabot (R-OH) and now Senator Lindsey Graham (R-SC), both of whom were active members of the impeachment panel. While I disagreed about as strongly—and admittedly as loudly—as it is possible to disagree with anyone during the impeachment process, personally I enjoy their company and respect both of them a great deal. I think they're completely wrong in their politics, but they're earnest and dedicated public officials. Only months after our impeachment battles, then Congressman Lindsey Graham called and asked me if I would work with him on a bill that would cut taxes by $345 billion over ten years. The Democratic and Republican leadership each held strong positions on a tax reduction bill, and we drew up a bill that included the best of both positions. This was a compromise bill, calling for a larger tax cut for the less wealthy than the Republican Party wanted. The Small Savers Act, as we titled it, moved millions of middle-class workers into the lowest tax bracket, increased the amount of money that could be put in IRAs, and lowered capital gains taxes. As Graham explained, "I got to know Mr. Wexler through the hearings because we sat there for months yelling at each other. We were on every show but the Food Channel together. The fact that we're working together will make news." I think a good part of the reason we worked together is that we both knew our collaboration would get some attention. If that guy Wexler and that guy Graham could work together, well, anything might be possible.

THE FATE OF legislation in committee is determined by the committee chairman. When Lee Hamilton was a freshman member, he joined a small group in filing a bill that would have increased the term served by House members from two years to four years. Hamilton asked the powerful chairman of the Judiciary Committee, New Yorker Emanuel "Manny" Celler, how he stood on the bill.

"I don't stand on it," Celler replied politely. "I'm sitting on it. It's right under my fanny and it will never see the light of day." And that is probably the best summation of the power of a committee chairman that I've ever heard. If the committee chairman—for whatever reason—doesn't want the legislation to be considered, he tables it, which means he doesn't do a thing with it. He just doesn't call it up for consideration, so no one ever has to go on record as voting for or against it. It disappears without a trace.

When the AARP, the American Association of Retired Persons, supported President Bush's prescription drug bill, I was furious. This was a bill written by lobbyists for the pharmaceutical industry. It actually prohibited the federal government from negotiating lower prices directly with the drug manufacturers. It was, according to *The Miami Herald*, "an unmitigated disaster." The AARP exists to represent the interests of retired Americans. Yet it endorsed this bill. So I drew up a nonbinding resolution that condemned the AARP's support for this legislation. I had several sponsors. The resolution generated media coverage in my district and my constituents were very supportive. It also sent a strong message to the AARP from legislators who normally support them, which probably made them more careful in the future. Because the Republican majority supported this legislation, however, my resolution disappeared in committee, never to be seen or debated.

It's in committees and subcommittees that the actual work of legislation gets done. A fair amount of true debate actually takes place in committee. It's in committee that amendments are added, hearings are held, and witnesses testify. When you see a congressional hearing on C-SPAN, it's taking place in a committee or subcommittee. During my career I've questioned or met with an extraordinary range of witnesses, from the commissioner of baseball to Secretary of State Colin Powell. In fact, I remember during my first term, Democratic members of what was then called International Relations met with Yasser Arafat. For some reason this meeting was held in a windowless room in the basement of one of the office buildings. There were about thirty-five people in the room, including five or six of Arafat's aides, sitting around a U-shaped table. Arafat was sitting in the center of the U; the ranking members of the full committee and Middle East subcommittee, Lee Hamilton and Gary Ackerman, were sitting on either side of him. Meetings with high-ranking officials take place all the time.

At this time Arafat was visiting the Clinton White House on a regular basis as the administration tried to forge a Middle East peace agreement. The PLO was also receiving aid from the United States, so Arafat really had to show up. This meeting was just getting under way when the lights in the Capitol went out. Because we were in a room with no windows, it was absolutely pitch-black. We sat in the darkness for about a minute, but it seemed much longer. When the lights went on, Gary Ackerman reached his hand to his back pocket, then looked at Arafat and said loudly, "You stole my wallet!"

Arafat, who conveniently understood English when doing so was to his benefit, looked totally perplexed. So much for the peace process.

Everybody was laughing. Well, at least the Americans were laughing.

It's in committee that legislation is considered, debated, and amended, a process known as the markup. Amendments can be added to legislation either in committee or when it is considered on the House floor. Each proposed amendment has to be debated and voted on independently. Amendments are supposed to be germane to the subject of the bill, meaning that they have something to do with it, but that definition often gets stretched. Amendments are the Silly Putty of legislation—they can be pulled and pushed and pounded and can completely change the bill.

As Shelley Berkley explained it, at the end of the 109th Congress in 2006 the word on the floor was that the Republicans intended to attach an amendment banning Internet gaming to the defense bill. I doubt if even the great Sherlock Holmes could find a connection between national defense and gambling on the Internet. To prevent that from happening, several Democrats pointed out how offensive it would be to the troops fighting in Iraq and Afghanistan to delay funding for the war in order to slip a ban on gambling into the bill. Having been caught, the Republicans didn't do that—instead they slipped it into a bill funding port security, knowing how politically difficult it would be for anyone to vote against a bill that supposedly protected our ports against terrorists.

The Republican majority was skilled in the political use of amendments. The Democrats, for example, continually tried to pass legislation raising the minimum wage, which the Republicans did not want to do. But they didn't want to be seen as the party that prevented the working poor from earning an additional dollar an hour. So what they did was attach an amendment raising the minimum wage to legislation providing a substantial tax cut for businesses. For a lot of Democrats that tax cut was a poison pill; there was no way they could vote for that bill. It was defeated as the Republican leadership knew it would be, as they intended it to be, but it allowed Republicans to claim that they had proposed an increase in the minimum wage and the Democrats had voted it down.

Throughout my career in Congress, I had become accustomed to the Democrats losing every meaningful vote. I remember the day that changed, the first meeting of the Judiciary Committee following the 2006 election in which Democrats regained control of the House. During this meeting we were discussing a piece of legislation and a Republican member offered an antiabortion amendment. It had no relationship to the bill, it was just the usual way Republicans had been running the House for the previous twelve years. It was almost as if he didn't know any better. Rep. Steve Cohen (D-TN) remembers it very well: "Whatever we were doing, they had tried to tie some sort of abortion measure to it, even if it was obtuse or irrelevant. In this particular case Steve King, a conservative Republican from Iowa, proposed taking money out of an international program because it might be used to communicate information about abortion. So I asked him, 'Has this money ever been used that way in the past?' 'It hasn't,' he admitted. 'But it could be and we don't want that to happen.' To which I responded, 'So you're offering this amendment as a prophylactic measure?' I'm not certain they understood it."

This time, for the first time, the Republican proposal failed. It was the first abortion vote we'd taken that we had ever won. None of the Democrats cheered, but I know we were thinking the same thing: Sensibility has returned. Then we went on with our business as if the world hadn't turned upside down.

When legislation is voted out of a standing committee, it goes to the Rules Committee. The Rules Committee sets the agenda for the House. It decides what's going to be discussed on the House floor and when that's going to happen; it decides how much time will be allowed for debate, whether or not amendments can be added to a bill, how many amendments, and then specifically which amendments will be allowed to be put up for a vote. Just as the chairman controls what happens in a committee, the Rules Committee controls what happens on the floor of the House.

"Most of the time when the Republicans were in the majority, we had a closed rule which meant we were not allowed to put an amendment on the floor," Eliot Engel said.

If the Republican leadership knew that if an amendment reached the floor it would pass largely with Democratic votes but with some moderate Republicans voting for it, they just passed a closed rule. They used it to give their people cover. Say, for example, that we wanted to add an amendment that would be popular with the public, like providing millions in funding for research into children's asthma, to a health care bill. The Republicans knew that if it reached the floor it would pass—believe me no representative wants to go on record as voting against children with asthma. In fact, a number of Republicans probably would get up and state, "I'm for increasing funding for asthma research and I intend to vote for it when it gets to the floor," knowing that it was never going to reach the floor. The Rules Committee would simply propose a closed rule, and those same people would vote for the rule. That allowed them to say accurately that they had never voted against the amendment, that it had failed on a technicality. Nice, very nice.

One of the best things Speaker Pelosi and the Democratic leadership did when we took power was to eliminate the corrupt Republican rules system. This is one of the most important reforms that can be made because it affects every bill we consider in Congress.

Today we can't meet without the participation of minority members; every member has time to read a bill before voting on it, and the length of a vote is determined by a clock, not by however long it takes to get the majority's desired outcome.

After twelve long years, fairness and democracy have returned to the people's house.

7

Rhetorical Wars and
the Tragedy of Terri Schiavo

The religious right is neither.

—Bumper sticker

For the most part the debate in the House is a grand show. Once a bill reaches the floor, almost every member knows how he or she will vote. The decision to vote yea or nay on legislation has been made long before the debate begins, and no matter how articulate the arguments or how powerful the ideas, minds are already made up. Several years ago, *Congressional Quarterly* published an article in which the editors divided up the different roles members of Congress can play and picked out the members they felt were the most successful. No one can play all these roles, because members have very different skill sets. One of the roles is legislator, a person who drafts legislation and creates the strategy necessary to get it through the process, or conversely, stops the other guys from getting their legislation passed. Another role is party organizer, the people who run the party. And then there are the rhetorical warriors, those members who by virtue of advocacy, by speaking and using the media and other forms of communication, influence the debate in the country. Probably because of my active involvement in the Clinton impeachment fight, and maybe just a little because of my loud voice, I was named a rhetorical warrior.

My wife laughed.

But in at least two instances I remember in the House, rhetoric actually influenced votes during the debate on the floor. The first was during the Terri Schiavo debate, when the House considered whether or not to allow the federal government to get further involved in what was clearly a family matter, even after the state of Florida had concluded its own judicial review. Unlike most matters that reach the floor, this one presented no clear political position for Democrats to take. While the Republicans attempted to make this a moral issue, too many people in this country, even some of those on the floor of the House, had wrestled with a similar decision in their own lives: When is it time to allow a loved one to die? When do you remove a feeding tube or a breathing apparatus? It was a terribly sad choice that never should have reached the Congress. I know a lot of members felt extremely uncomfortable about it. But the Republican leadership, for whatever political gain there might be, desperately tried to portray it as a right-to-life issue.

The speeches that night were impassioned, about life and death. I don't believe many members of the House had the time to determine how their constituents felt about the issue. For me, it was particularly difficult because so many of my constituents are senior citizens. As usual, I was sitting with the Democrats and it was clear when the debate began that several members had not yet reached a decision. There were several Democrats who had flown back to Washington for this vote thinking they would probably be voting for the Republican position. Republicans weren't uncomfortable enough to change their votes, but after listening to the debate, many Democrats were persuaded to vote against allowing further federal interference. For Democrats, it had become a vote of conscience.

The facts were pretty simple: The husband of a brain-dead woman wanted to finally allow her to die, while her parents wanted to keep her on life support. It's a horrendous situation for any family to have to endure. I can't begin to imagine how terrible it was for all of them, her husband, parents, and brother. And there was no easy solution. So the best thing to do is to follow the existing law. The law is meant to arbitrate between competing claims. Florida governor Jeb Bush had made numerous attempts to get the state courts to intercede on behalf of her parents. The case had been tried by six different courts, and nineteen judges had concluded that this was a family matter—and that Terri's wish would have been to remove life support. When after more than a decade on life support, Terri Schiavo's feeding tube was finally removed, Speaker Denny Hastert called us back into session the weekend of Palm Sunday to pass legislation that would ignore the decision of the state courts and permit federal court intervention. The fact that this violated the core Republican belief in states' rights didn't even slow them down. They saw this as a cultural winner. Who would want to go on record as voting against feeding a helpless, disabled woman?

Republicans decided to frame this as an issue concerning "the sanctity of life." There was a religious undertone to it, too; all the right-wing Christian groups were praying for her. DeLay actually said, "One thing God has brought us is Terri Schiavo." And they were being egged on by Republican doctors like Senator Bill Frist, who was able to "diagnose" Terri Schiavo from videotape, and Georgia congressman Phil Gingrey, who was trained in obstetrics and gynecology and claimed, "The tragedy of the situation is that with proper treatment, now denied, Terri's condition can improve." The fact that six court-appointed doctors had examined her and concluded that she had no cognitive ability didn't stop them from substituting political theater for medical knowledge. After her death an autopsy confirmed that Frist and Gingrey were completely wrong and their long-distance political diagnoses were extraordinarily irresponsible. There had been hundreds of cases similar to this one in Florida, but what made Terri Schiavo different was the national media attention. The GOP used a brain-dead woman as a political pawn. For DeLay and Hastert, this was the perfect wedge issue.

Unless it is an extremely pressing issue or votes are required, I don't work on the Jewish Sabbath. From sundown Friday to sundown

Saturday I'm with my family. But Nancy Pelosi was polling Democrats on a Saturday to see where we stood, and my office contacted me. This was an important issue for my constituents. Living wills are widely used in South Florida, and most of my constituents feel very strongly that the government should stay out of urgent family matters. I believed that what the Republicans were doing was shameful. Disgraceful. And I wanted to confront them. They intended to overturn two hundred years of judicial independence for a short-term political victory.

I met with Terri Schiavo's husband, Michael, in Washington. He was incredulous that the most difficult decision he had ever faced had become a matter for public debate. Ironically, DeLay had faced a similar situation several years earlier, when his father had been put on life support after being injured in an accident. When it became apparent that there was no hope of recovery, DeLay had permitted his father to be taken off a respirator—precisely what he was trying to prevent Michael Schiavo from doing.

Democrats in the Senate decided this was an issue they couldn't win—they didn't have the votes—so they didn't bother returning to Washington. With only a few Republicans present, the Senate passed the legislation by a voice vote. In the House I worked with a handful of my Democratic colleagues to force a debate. This time I wanted to put the right wing on record. Even Tampa Bay Republican Ginny Brown-Waite, who represented the district in which Terri Schiavo was hospitalized, courageously asked for time to speak on the floor.

"This is a very difficult decision that I know does not come easily for any member of this body," she said. "It is gut wrenching and reaches deep into our hearts. My daughter, who was born five days after Terri Schiavo, is a health-care professional who, when I asked if she would want me to battle to keep a feeding tube in if she had not signed a living will . . . her response to me was sufficient to help me make up my mind. She said to me, 'No, Mom. If you really loved me, you would want me to have rest and meet the Lord.' "

The Republican leadership was furious that she was going to vote with the Democrats, but there was nothing they could do.

As it turned out, the Republicans won the vote but lost the political war. While this fight pleased some conservative voters, polls indicated that by a huge margin Americans wanted the government to stay out of their family affairs. Eventually the decision of the courts was upheld and Terri Schiavo was removed from life support and died peacefully.

I ALSO BELIEVE that the debate in March 2007, when the Democrats attempted to use an emergency funding bill for the war in Iraq to set a timetable for withdrawal, influenced several votes. I have no way of knowing this for certain, but I do know that several members were undecided about how they would vote when they walked onto the floor that night. In particular I listened carefully to the remarks of freshman Rep. Patrick Murphy (D-PA), the first Iraq War veteran to be elected to Congress. He said, "You know, a few blocks away from this great chamber, when you walk in the snow, is the Vietnam Memorial, where half the soldiers listed on that wall died after America's leaders knew our strategy would not work.

"It was immoral then and it would be immoral now to engage in that same delusion.

"That's why, Mr. Speaker, sending more troops into civil war is the wrong strategy. We need to win the war on terror, and reasonable people may disagree what to do, but most will agree it is immoral to send young Americans to fight and die in a conflict without a real strategy for success. The president's current course is not resolute, it is reckless."

That vote passed with the minimum 218 votes.

But those debates were certainly the exception. The floor of the House might be the place where C-SPAN has had its most significant impact. What happens in the House no longer stays in the House but instead is broadcast to almost every other house in the country that has cable TV. As a result, most representatives know precisely where the camera is when they speak, hoping the voters back home in the district are watching or that the local news station might use a clip. If any minds are going to be changed, it'll be those people watching at home.

The amount of time allotted to the debate is limited by the rules.

Maybe we'll vote an extra several billion dollars to keep troops in Iraq, but we can't afford to spend too much time debating it. Generally the majority and minority are each given one hour, occasionally longer, which the party leaders divide among those members who request time to speak. If a controversial issue is being debated, you may get a minute or two at most, sometimes as little as thirty seconds. Go ahead, try to make a lucid argument about how to secure Social Security in thirty seconds. Try to convince someone that American soldiers should stay in Iraq or be withdrawn in one minute. Conversely, if the debate concerns a noncontroversial matter and you don't want to speak about it, you can probably get all the time you don't want. You may be allotted as much as half of the entire twenty minutes given to debate.

There are some incredible extemporaneous speakers in the House, and it's magic to sit listening to the beauty of the English language as used with great power by men like John Lewis of Georgia or Barney Frank of Massachusetts. But most members prefer the security of prepared remarks, maybe not an entirely written speech but at least a list of the talking points they want to hit. Unless the subject matter is extremely technical—in which case I will read my speech—usually before going onto the floor I'll review the remarks my staff has prepared for me and then incorporate the ideas into an extemporaneous speech.

Speaking on the floor of the House of Representatives is a privilege—and it's exciting. No matter how many hundreds of speeches I've given, I'm acutely aware of where I am every second. Now, if I'm making a thirty-second statement about an issue of minor significance, I don't worry about my speech for hours or rehearse it, but when I am going to speak about a meaningful issue, I will reflect on it and gear up for that moment. There is a lot of pressure knowing that any sentence that comes out of your mouth that is poorly chosen or inappropriate can come back to haunt you in a very significant political way. Remember, one poorly chosen word ended Senator George Allen's political career—and may have changed history. Had he been reelected, he would have been a strong contender for the Republican presidential nomination in 2008—and who knows what might have happened? Without written notes to refer to, I may forget two of the four points I want to make, or stress the wrong point. And even with notes I may butcher a word or, worse, invent a word, or even use a wrong word, which is embarrassing. Once, on CNN, for example, I referred to the well-known Kyoto Treaty as the "Coyote Treaty." Maybe not up to the level of George W. Bush's malapropisms, but close.

Democratic Whip David Bonior is a smart man, but as his former chief of staff, Sarah Dufendach, remembers, his staff lived in fear every time he had to speak: "I was standing in the back of a committee meeting, and he wanted to talk about promoting microorganisms. *Microorganisms*. Unfortunately, he began talking about promoting the use of microorgasms.

"I thought, Please, Lord, let me fall right through the floor now.

"On another occasion David was invited to speak to the Tiltrotor caucus, which consisted mostly of executives from Lockheed-Martin. In preparation for this speech we'd learned that apparently there is a type of helicopter that utilizes a tiltrotor. We struggled to write that speech and we rehearsed it and then he went off like a trooper to give it. And he gets up there and looks at these top executives of a major defense corporation and tells them how pleased he was to have been invited to address the Roto-Rooter caucus. And for the rest of that speech, this was the Roto-Rooter caucus.

"Once," she went on, "I wrote a speech for him and included instructions in it. In big capital letters, inside parentheses I would write (PAUSE FOR APPLAUSE) or (MAKE THIS POINT FORCEFULLY). And, perhaps I should have predicted this, he read them out loud. He read them without pausing: 'And I want to say right here that this has been a tremendous group effort, pause for applause, and we should all be very proud, stop.' "

Personally, I'm not seeking to invent new words, but sometimes, for no apparent reason, I'll just use a word that doesn't appear in any dictionary. It's close to a word, it sounds like a word, but it isn't a word. Usually the people listening to me know what I mean, but that doesn't mean the word exists in the known language.

It isn't just on the floor that I'll butcher the language or forget something, it's a habit I've had my entire career. Same thing with names.

Politicians need to remember names. It's one of the basic job requirements: Remember the names of those people who support you. At the end of every political speech I'll stand in the back and greet people, many of whom I've known since my first election. Once, I had finished speaking at a large condo and was standing in the back greeting a lot of old friends. A woman I had known for years approached me and I became very excited because I remembered her husband's name. Unfortunately, I didn't remember hers. But I figured I could fake that. I shook her hand confidently and asked, "So? How's Louis?"

"Robert," she said, "Louis passed away."

"Oh," I said, and meaning it, remembering what a wonderful man he was, "I'm so sorry."

She looked at me with surprise. "Robert, you were at the funeral."

Now, what do you say after that? *Have you tried the rugelah?* There's nothing that can rectify that, it's horrifying. And it has happened to me, and probably every other politician, often enough for me to know that I should use notes when I speak on the House floor.

And perhaps whenever I'm on national television. Especially when that national television program is *The Colbert Report*.

8

The Colbert Report:
It's a Fun Thing to Do

The worst sin in politics is being boring.

—Richard Nixon

It is well understood by members of Congress that the press is not always your friend. Both print and electronic journalists are busy trying to perform their own jobs and advance their own careers, not ours. The competition in their business is as rough as it is in politics, so they are always looking for a story that puts them on the front page or earns them a few more seconds of airtime. There has always been an uneasy relationship between politicians and journalists, and with the tremendous proliferation of Web sites and cable channels in the last few years it's become even more strained. As the very surprised former Republican senator from Virginia George Allen learned in 2006, when he offhandedly used an ethnic slur to insult a young college student in front of a friendly out-of-the-way rally—an ethnic slur that most people didn't even know was an ethnic slur until the media pointed it out—anything you say anywhere at any time to anyone might end up in print, on the air, or all over the Internet. And as in Allen's case, that one word could cost you a legitimate shot at the presidency.

For politicians, television, more than the print media or even the Internet, is the benevolent monster. It can just as easily make you a political star as an out-of-office politician. Because I've been involved in several major national events, I've been invited to appear on numerous political talk shows. So when comedian Stephen Colbert invited me to be featured on the "Get to Know a District" segment of his comedy program, no red lights started flashing warning signals in my head.

In fact, I'd never seen the show, although I had heard very good things about it from those who had. But when the invitation was extended by the show, my staff became unusually excited. They urged me to do it. In fact, I watched the show several nights before taping my interview and thought it was funny and witty, so I knew what it was. I wasn't blindsided.

Essentially, on his show, comedian Stephen Colbert—whose character is a staunch conservative—cleverly puts people in awkward situations. For example, when Georgia Republican Lynn Westmoreland appeared on this segment, Colbert began by establishing the fact that he had sponsored a bill requiring the display of the Ten Commandments in both the House and Senate. Westmoreland proudly wondered what better place might the Ten Commandments be displayed than in public buildings?

Colbert agreed: Where else might the Ten Commandments be displayed? But then Colbert blindsided him by asking him a trick question: Name the Ten Commandments.

Westmoreland looked stunned. "All of them?" he asked. He got three of them before admitting he couldn't do it.

Steve Cohen is a Jewish member of Congress who represents a Tennessee district with a majority of black voters. As Cohen remembers it, when Colbert wondered if he was not only the first Jewish congressman from Tennessee, but the first Jew from Tennessee, "I told him, 'There are several Jews in Tennessee.' Then he asked me, 'So what did you do after you got elected? Did you have a bar mitzvah?' 'No,' I said, 'You only do that after you've been here for thirteen terms!' "

So I knew exactly what I was in for when I accepted this invitation. At least, that's what I thought. The reason for doing a show like this is that it is extremely popular with an audience that doesn't necessarily watch politicians in the mainstream media. This audience doesn't just watch the show, they are true fans of the show. They're fanatics. Other members who had done the show told me that after their interview was broadcast they were recognized by people who otherwise never would have known them. So this show gives you the opportunity to reach an audience you otherwise would never meet. For example, Congresswoman Eleanor Holmes Norton, who represents the District of Columbia, has appeared on the show four times. Eleanor is a nonvoting member of Congress. D.C. doesn't have a vote—and she has been lobbying to change that throughout her eight terms. "Colbert had me on because he wanted to make fun of D.C. trying to get a vote in Congress," she said. "And he did. But my appearances on his show have gone further to spread the notion that there are six hundred thousand people living in the District of Columbia, second in per capita federal income, who have no vote, than all of my speeches on the floor and all of the work that organizations have done. It has popularized a very serious issue that needed to get national attention that we could not have gotten any other way. Nobody could have afforded that type of advertising."

It seems to me that those members of Congress who refuse to go on this type of show are missing a significant shift in American politics. Younger Americans get their political news and form their political views from programs like this. Maybe before I did the show I agreed with those people who dismissed it for not being serious enough, but I learned differently. Shows like *The Colbert Report* are actually quite sophisticated; it's political comedy laced with a great deal of information and sarcasm. "I'm going to nail you here," Colbert accused Norton. "I've checked your voting record. You've not voted once while you've been in office. You want to defend that?"

To which she responded, "Our government is imposing taxes on our residents without giving us a vote in the House or Senate."

You can't find *The Colbert Report* funny, or *The Daily Show,* or even Bill Maher's show, without knowing what's going on in the world.

After I agreed to appear on Colbert's show, my staff reminded me that I was on the show to be the straight man and I shouldn't try to be funny. They warned me that he was certainly going to ask me outrageous and embarrassing questions, so the last thing I should do is be offended. I'd seen some members appear on the show and become upset when Stephen said something ridiculous. I mean, this is a man who combed the mustache of my friend Rep. Eliot Engel, who handled the situation wonderfully. So I was ready to play along.

He's the comedian, he's the one who gets paid to be funny. Not being funny was easy for me; that's something I do naturally. Most important, my staff told me, don't take yourself too seriously. If I was going to try to be serious I would look ridiculous and be well advised not to go on the show. "It's on Comedy Central," Eric Johnson reminded me. "It's not CNN. So relax."

There was no way for me to prepare for this appearance other than by watching previous shows. My interview lasted more than an hour and a half, and was edited to about three minutes. As Steve Cohen recalls about his appearance on the show, "In five minutes you could take a game between the New England Patriots and Florida International and edit it down to make it look like Florida International won, so it's always a danger." I had no say about the way the show was edited. If you've seen my appearance, you certainly know that's true. But I must admit that *The Colbert Report* was totally fair with me. When I sat down with Colbert, or *col-bear,* as he pronounces it, although Eleanor Holmes Norton calls him "Col-*bert,*" I had no idea that this was about to spark the largest personal controversy in which I had ever been involved.

I'd dealt with Syrian president Assad, with Yasser Arafat, but nothing really prepared me for Stephen Colbert. At one point in the middle of the interview, Colbert noted that I was running unopposed in my next election and suggested, "Let's have some fun. Let's say a few things that would really lose the election for you if you were contested, but remember, you're not contested. There's no way you can lose. I enjoy cocaine because?"

I repeated the setup. "This would *lose* me the election?" Colbert repeated that it would lose me the election if I said this.

"I enjoy cocaine because . . . ," I began and then started laughing.

I was laughing because it was funny. Colbert stopped me. "Just say it without laughing because then people will think it's a joke."

Okay. Although it was a joke. "Um, because it's a fun thing to do."

Colbert wanted me to say the entire sentence, in fact he said it for me, "I enjoy cocaine because it's a fun thing to do."

And I repeated it. "I enjoy cocaine because it's a fun thing to do." When they broadcast the program the audience was hysterical at this point. Point of fact, I don't enjoy cocaine, I've never tried cocaine, and I certainly don't think it's a fun thing to do. I think it's awful. This was obviously a joke. I was joking about things that would surely cause me to lose an election if they were true. I was the butt of this joke and I didn't mind.

The joke wasn't quite over. With a straight face Colbert continued, "I enjoy the company of prostitutes for the following reasons."

I suspect you can imagine what happened next.

Yes, that's exactly what happened.

Many people have asked me exactly what I was thinking when I said these things. The answer's simple. This is a comedy show. What separated me from a lot of journalists is that I realized it was a joke. Particularly when Colbert emphasized that it was just a joke. A joke.

Unfortunately, not all journalists understood that. Or perhaps they didn't care. The next day the Associated Press carried a story reporting that a congressman had admitted to using cocaine and frequenting prostitutes. It wasn't until the middle of the story that they mentioned it was said on a comedy show on the comedy channel. Even then, Eric Johnson had to fight with them to correct their story. The *Today* show showed a clip and treated it as serious news. Fox News . . . well, Fox News is Fox News. They have their own conservative agenda. My reaction was a certain degree of disbelief. *The Colbert Report* was on a comedy channel. Every show on the channel was a comedy show. I assumed that people would understand that a show appearing on Comedy Central would be a comedy show. No one would take it seriously, right? Well, one of the worst things a politician can do is underestimate the impact of an event. The morning after my segment was broadcast, some newspapers and TV stations treated it somewhat seriously. Then I began to be concerned—had I made a serious political mistake?

In an unprecedented step, the night after my interview ran—and the controversy erupted—Colbert actually stepped out of his character to report on the reporting on *The Report*. He showed representative clips of the type of absurd and silly news reporting these so-called legitimate news shows had done; for example, he showed a clip of a *Today* show reporter sitting in a rowboat reporting on a flood—as two men wearing boots walked by in front of her—revealing that the floodwaters were only inches deep. Colbert concluded his rebuttal and extraordinary defense of me by telling people how nice it was to find a politician with a sense of humor—and finished by urging listeners, "Vote for Wexler!"

Years ago this appearance would quickly have been forgotten. Those people who hadn't seen it wouldn't have access to it. But we're in a brand-new political world. Almost immediately the clip was posted on YouTube, and hundreds of thousands of people viewed it on the Internet. I suppose I should have known that in this type of political environment you shouldn't say anything, kidding or not, that can be used against you. In fact, when Ben Graber announced in early 2007 that he would run against me again in the Democratic primary—and was contributing two hundred thousand dollars of his own money to his campaign—he lambasted my appearance to a reporter from *The Hill* newspaper: "There are many ways to look at it. Maybe he was shocked and the truth came out."

At least now my constituents know that my opponent also has a sense of humor.

9

Voting in Congress:
The Hill Has "Ayes"

I have been thinking that I would make a proposition to my Republican friends . . . that if they will stop telling lies about Democrats, we will stop telling the truth about them.

—Adlai Stevenson

Voting on proposed legislation is certainly one of the most important things we do in the House. There is a clock on the wall of each member's office surrounded by a ring of colored lights that correspond to a code: One light indicates the House is in session, other lights indicate what type of session or whether or not a vote is going on. Blinking lights, I believe, have some other meaning. The clock is a relic, an attractive relic that still lights up, but I have no idea what all those lights mean. I don't think anybody does.

Members are allotted fifteen minutes to vote the first time a bill is voted on, and that fifteen minutes can be stretched if the leadership needs more time to round up votes. The Democratic caucus contacts every Democratic member by special beepers to alert us that voting has started, then again with ten minutes left, again with five minutes, and finally the classic two-minute warning. During a vote the traffic on the busy street between the Capitol and the House office buildings is frozen for the last few minutes of each vote; the traffic lights stay red to allow members to walk safely—or, on occasion, run—from their offices to the Capitol. Unfortunately, several times I've been in a car racing back to the Capitol for the vote and gotten caught in the traffic jam. Once the lights are frozen, traffic doesn't move. Each time I've been caught in this situation I've had a member of my staff with me, so I've been able to jump out, screaming, "Take the car," and start running the half-mile up the hill, waving my member's card to get past security.

On the floor at the end of every other row of seats there are electronic boxes. Members cast their vote by putting their official card in this box and pressing the aye or nay button. It's somewhat similar to using an ATM. There are actually four voting options: yes, no, present, and just not showing up. Present means you're there, you've voted, but you don't want to go on record as voting for or against something. Out of many thousands of votes in my career, I've voted present only three or four times. I voted present when President Bush wanted to declare a day of prayer and fasting in 2003. It was ridiculous, it was like trying to legislate Yom Kippur. Generally I take a position and deal with the consequences, but when the Republicans were in charge, they continually put up bills like this one designed primarily to embarrass Democrats into voting against something that sounds harmless, but was really quite silly. So rather than vote against it and subject myself to political attacks—Wexler votes against prayer!—I voted present because I didn't want to give them the satisfaction or the benefit of my voting for them. It was my way of registering an objection without voting no.

On the wall high above the Speaker's podium is a colorful electronic tote board on which votes are registered; a green light indicates an aye vote, a red light is a nay. It's a way of making sure you voted the way you intended to vote. If you accidentally press the wrong button, or if you change your mind, you can change your vote at any time until the time expires. It happens to the best of us. We also have voice votes on the floor, usually for noncontroversial legislation. Both the advantage and the disadvantage of a voice vote is that there is no record of how each member voted.

So the act of voting is easy. It's deciding how to cast your vote that—at times—is hard. Probably the question I'm asked most often is how do I decide which way to vote on an issue. That's like asking me to name the worst member of the Bush administration. (Oh, wait, that one *is* easy—Dick Cheney.) The answer is that there is no single answer. Deciding how to vote is a balancing act between the needs of my constituents and the needs of the nation as a whole, my personal beliefs, and political reality.

As we learned so incredibly painfully in 2000, every vote matters. I know it sounds melodramatic, but it is absolutely true: One vote can end a political career—one vote can change history. In 1993 President Clinton submitted the Omnibus Budget Reconciliation Act, which also became known as the Deficit Reduction Act. This was Clinton's attempt to balance the budget by raising taxes on the wealthiest 2 percent of taxpayers. So it was a tax increase on the richest Americans, but it was designed to eliminate the deficit and reduce the federal debt. In 1993 the Democrats still had a slight majority. In the Senate the vote was evenly split and Vice President Al Gore had to cast the deciding aye vote. In the House every Republican voted against it as did several Democrats. It finally came down to one member, freshman congresswoman Marjorie Margolies-Mezvinsky from Pennsylvania. This is every member's nightmare—a hugely important political issue comes down to his or her vote. As she cast her vote, Republicans were chanting "Bye-bye, Marjorie." Rep. Margolies-Mezvinsky voted for the bill, enabling it to pass 218 to 216. History shows it was an excellent vote; it enabled Clinton to balance the budget and turn the national debt into a billion-dollar surplus. It began a period of fiscal responsibility and historic economic growth. But in the election of 1994, in which the Republicans took control of Congress, that vote probably resulted in Margolies-Mezvinsky losing her seat.

I recall one time when my vote made a difference in the outcome, and that was during my first term in the Florida Senate. We were supposed to be in session for two months, but because we couldn't pass a new budget or a reapportionment bill, we stayed in Tallahassee for six months. So I was away from home much longer than my family had anticipated. Several months earlier Laurie and I had made plans to go to Disney World to celebrate my mother's sixtieth birthday, never expecting that the senate would still be in session. Finally, the senate passed the last bill, a budget bill. There were forty senators and one of them wasn't there, so it passed 39 to 0. Under the rules, though, we had to wait twenty-four hours and pass it a second time. That was the only vote left before we adjourned. So I went to the president of the senate and asked permission to leave one day early. Go, she said, there's no issue.

We were going to Disney World! I flew from Tallahassee home to Boca Raton, packed up the car, and we took off for Orlando.

What I did not know was that as we were driving, all hell had broken loose in Tallahassee. The compromise that kept the divided senate functioning had broken down completely. The Republicans refused to vote for the budget bill, committee chairmen were being switched, deals were being made, the president of the senate was being challenged. And without my vote, the Democrats were one vote short of stopping the chaos. This was long before the widespread use of cell phones, and we were unreachable. In fact, as we drove into Orlando we went right past Sea World and I saw there was a Flipper show starting in about twenty minutes. "Come on, let's go see it," I said.

Laurie wanted to check into the hotel first. I was standing in front of the registration desk in shorts and a T-shirt and handed the clerk my credit card. "Oh, Mr. Wexler," he said, "we have some messages for you." Some? He handed me a stack of maybe twenty-five messages, from the governor, the president of the senate, from everybody.

I immediately called the president of the senate. "We sent a plane to West Palm Beach to get you," she said. "And no one could find you." If I came back right away, she told me, I could have a committee chairmanship. She would send the plane to Orlando.

A committee chairmanship? That was great, but all I could think of was how unhappy my family was going to be when I told them I had to leave. This was not going to be easy. "I don't care about a chairman-ship," I said. "There's only one thing that matters. I have to be back in Orlando tonight. I don't care what it takes, a bus, a car, but you have to get me back tonight."

I didn't even have a suit with me. I flew back to Tallahassee and got to the capitol about six o'clock in the evening. The entire state senate was gridlocked and awaiting my vote. I will never forget what State Senator W. D. Childers said to me as I rushed onto the floor of the sen-ate. "Robert," he drawled, "it's a good thing you were with your wife." I cast the deciding vote, then got back on a plane and flew back to Orlando.

The reality that votes have consequences was really brought home to me when I was still in the Florida Senate. I introduced and we passed the first mandatory Medicare assignment bill, legislation that limited doctors' fees to the Medicare assignment allocation. It meant that sen-ior citizens wouldn't have additional out-of-pocket expenses. The way I wrote it also saved the state and seniors a substantial amount of money. Senior citizens loved my proposal. In fact, it became federal law a few years later. At that time most doctors in Florida were doing exceptionally well financially, but naturally they despised the bill. To them it was socialism, the worst form of governmental regulation. As far as doctors were concerned I was public enemy number one. They even put material in their waiting rooms attacking me. There were doc-tors in our synagogue who refused to sit next to me. The ones who were really angry wouldn't sit in the same row. But it became personal when my daughter Rachel got hurt. She fell into glass and we rushed her to the hospital and a doctor refused to treat her because he hated me so much. I was furious, absolutely furious, but there wasn't much I could do. Eventually another more responsible doctor took care of Rachel. So I learned early in my career that my vote really does affect people—including me.

In the U.S. House of Representatives, most votes can be categorized either as interest group versus interest group, or core values. An interest group vote might be the dairy farmers of Wisconsin as opposed to the dairy farmers of New England, or the cable company against the phone company. These bills are the kind of standard legislation we deal with every day, usually without much publicity. Core values are those subjects that boil the blood, the issues that divide the country and keep right-wing radio in business: the rights of gun owners versus the danger and harm guns pose to the public, reproductive choice, gay rights, the separation of church and state, the death penalty, the war in Iraq, impeachment, and the privatization of Social Security. Both types of votes affect tens of millions of people, but it's the values votes that tend to garner the most attention and affect political careers.

The first thing I consider before voting is, How does the proposal affect my district? There's a phrase we use to describe representatives who vote against the interests of their constituents: former members. We're called representatives because we're supposed to represent our constituents. I've never voted against my conscience, but generally I'm very much in accord with the people of my district. That's obvious: Members think like the people who elected them or they wouldn't have been elected in the first place. The one promise I reiterate time and again when I speak to my constituents is that I will dance with the one who brought me.

There are several things I do when I want to find out how my constituents feel about an issue: We hold town meetings. I read the editorials in the local papers as well as the letters to the editor. The number of phone calls, letters, and e-mails we get in my Washington office as well as in the district is a good barometer of both the way people feel and how intensely they feel it. Sometimes less formal interactions are the most revealing. If I'm in the supermarket or a local restaurant and two or three people come up to me and say the same thing, odds are thousands of people are thinking it. I often take a cab to the airport, and cabdrivers are the best natural pollsters in the world. They're talking to people who live and work in the district all day, so they get a good sense of local opinion.

I'll also periodically call a number of community leaders, many of whom I've known since I first sat on their couches two decades ago. I'll just call them out of the blue to ask them what they think about a national event or a local story or even local politics. Many of them are in their late seventies and eighties now, and I respect their life experience. These are wise people and they have learned so much by living life that I would be foolish not to pay close attention to what they have to say. I remember when the Republicans got serious about impeaching President Clinton. At first I had no idea how my constituents felt about it. I have a large number of very patriotic veterans in the district. And while they may be politically liberal, for the most part they have traditional, conservative lifestyles. These are definitely not wild and crazy people. And there was all this talk about how Bill Clinton's actions had demoralized the military and dishonored the presidency.

I went out on a limb very early in opposition to impeachment. I believed I was defending the Constitution, but many people would say that I was defending Bill Clinton. Generally I have a strong feeling about the consensus in my district, but this time I didn't. I had no polling. I didn't know how the people sitting around the pool playing mah-jongg, or in the clubhouse, felt about the president's indiscretions. I went home the weekend after prosecutor Ken Starr's revealing and salacious report was made public. It was awful reading. I appeared on several talk shows, so people knew where I stood. I faced my voters for the first time when I made a speech at a synagogue in Century Village in Deerfield Beach. When I finished I waited for the reaction. I was bracing myself for anything. A man I had known for a long time came right up to the stage. He was a World War II veteran, a man who had landed on Normandy Beach in the first wave. That experience had shaped his life. He was so angry his face was red and he was literally shaking. He looked up at me and said, "I want to tell you something, Robert. I didn't go climbing up those beaches in Normandy so these bastards could do this to the president of the United States." I knew right then how my district felt about impeachment.

It's true that all politics is local. It all begins in the home—although in my case it often begins in my mother-in-law's home. I've known my mother-in-law since I was seventeen years old and I think the world of her and my father-in-law. She's not an overtly political person, but her instincts and opinions reflect those of the overwhelming majority of the people who live in my district. I'll speak with her often, and as any son-in-law knows, I'm getting the unadulterated truth from her. The Terri Schiavo situation, for example, was a big issue in Florida. When I spoke with my mother-in-law I discovered that she agreed completely with my position—and as it turned out, so did the overwhelming majority of people in the district. So I often use my mother-in-law as a barometer of public opinion in the district. It's certainly not scientific— but it works because it seems that everyone's mother-in-law lives in my district.

Almost always my vote will be in accord with the beliefs of my constituents, but there have been exceptions. Probably the one that did surprise me was my vote to give President Bush the authority to use our military in Iraq. That was the most difficult vote I've ever cast. I didn't vote for that resolution because Saddam Hussein was a brutal dictator; there are a bunch of brutal dictators in the world. And it wasn't because he was paying twenty-five thousand dollars each to the families of suicide bombers in Israel, although obviously that disturbed me a great deal. It was because I believed the military and intelligence officers who told the Congress that Saddam Hussein had weapons of mass destruction.

The Bush administration and its right-wing supporters have said many times that Congress had access to the same information as the president. That's an exaggeration. Both in committees and in closed, classified sessions we were briefed by high-ranking government and military officials. When the Joint Chiefs of Staff appear before you in Congress they don't come as Democrats and Republicans, they come as military experts, and I believed them.

Only after we'd won the military battle and failed to find any WMDs did it become obvious that throughout the entire process the administration had provided selective intelligence to us, that they failed to provide us with all the information and intelligence. The truth is that Bush and Cheney were plotting to attack Iraq long before 9/11 and they manipulated intelligence and evidence to justify their course. A study by two nonprofit journalism organizations published in January 2008 counted 935 false statements made by the administration in the two years following the attacks on 9/11, concluding that these statements "were part of an orchestrated campaign that effectively galvanized public opinion and, in the process, led the nation to war under decidedly false pretenses."

On at least 532 occasions the president and administration officials stated unequivocally that Saddam Hussein possessed WMDs, or was trying to get them, or that Iraq had connections to al-Qaeda. And those were just public statements.

It has always bothered me that long before it became apparent that Hussein did not have WMDs there were people who were smart enough, intuitive enough, lucky enough, whatever the combination, to know it. That would have been a leap of faith, too, but they were right. I wish I had been one of them. But among those people who believed my vote was wrong were the majority of people in my district. We took a poll after the vote, and I was surprised to discover how strongly my district was against going to war. This was one time I'd voted against the prevailing sentiment, although when I'd voted I didn't know the true strength of that opposition. Maybe I should have; many of these people had been to war, they knew the horror of it, and they didn't trust George Bush. So they didn't like my vote. Basically, the pollster reported, I had a reservoir of credibility because of my other votes and positions, so they gave me a pass on this one—but don't make another vote like this again.

I remember exactly when I found out how strong the opposition to the war was. I went to a condo meeting after the vote and a woman I'd known my entire career, a woman who still had her pot holder, yelled at me. I can close my eyes and hear her: "Robert!"—never Wexler, never ever Congressman—just "Robert! What were you thinking voting like that!" It was not a question, it was a strong rebuke.

So the first rule of voting is obvious: Support your district.

The second rule is equally obvious: Support your party.

The key number to remember is 218. That's the number of votes needed to pass legislation. It doesn't matter how you get there—they might all come from the majority or it might be a bipartisan vote—but 218 is the number legislation lives or dies by.

The ability of either party to get to that number is the measure of its power. And getting there requires party unity. On a great number of votes, procedural votes or votes in which my district has absolutely no stake, I'll vote the party line. Many times members won't even know all the provisions of the bills on which we're voting. Often the system makes it impossible. The rules dictate that members should have forty-eight hours to read a bill—but the rules also allow rules to be suspended or ignored by declaring a bill an "emergency measure." In 2003, for example, the Republicans declared 57 percent of all bills emergency measures and cut the time allowed to read them. In 2005 the Republicans gave us one hour—*one hour*—to examine the three-thousand-page budget bill that would determine how the government spent one trillion dollars. One hour for one trillion. In the House, the majority can do anything it desires.

The Patriot Act, arguably one of the most important pieces of legislation in recent history, a document that interfered with our cherished constitutional rights, that permitted the government to spy on American citizens, was made available for us to read the night before we had to vote on it. It was more than a thousand pages long. It was an absurd way to adopt such important legislation.

When a vote is in progress, the first thing I'll do when I walk onto the floor is look up at the tally board to see how the other Democrats from South Florida are voting. Alcee Hastings usually votes early, so I'll look at his vote. I trust him a great deal. Most of the time we're in accord, but not always. If Alcee or Florida congresswoman Debbie Wasserman Schultz have voted differently from what I intend to do I'll find out why. I want to make sure they don't have different information than I do.

When you're in the minority, there usually isn't much pressure to go along with the party. The majority has to maintain discipline; they have to win votes. The party leadership always knows what every member is doing. There is an old system in place to count votes. It begins with party whips. The Republicans introduced the whip system to the House in 1897 as a means of keeping track of how their members felt and intended to vote about each issue. The term *whip* is English and refers to the "whipper-in," the person on a fox hunt responsible for keeping the dogs close to the pack.

The majority has great power to punish its members who don't go along with the party line. The ultimate penalty is the loss of a committee chairmanship or assignment. Moderate Republican Chris Shays, for example, lost out on the chairmanship of the House Government Reform Committee because he insisted on enacting campaign finance reform against DeLay's objection. When New Mexico conservative Heather Wilson dared challenge a Republican amendment to the Medicare bill, she was forced to give up her spot on the House Armed Services Committee. In addition to committee assignments, the party can limit your appropriations—the projects you bring home to your district—and in other ways make it difficult for you to be an effective legislator. It's a delicate balancing act. They need to do enough to keep you in line, but they can't punish you so much they risk losing your district.

Without a doubt the best-known example of a party exerting pressure on its members to follow its leaders was the infamous November 2003 vote on the four-hundred-billion-dollar bill to add a prescription drug benefit for seniors. What happened in the House that night was unprecedented. North Carolina Republican congressman Walter Jones called it "the ugliest night I've ever seen in politics in twenty-two years."

There were many reasons for Democrats to be against this plan: It didn't extend care to those senior citizens who needed it most, and it handed huge profits to the pharmaceutical and insurance industries. But many conservative Republicans who preached small government were also against it because of the huge price tag. So when the bill finally came to the floor, the Republican leadership couldn't get those 218 votes. When the allotted time for the vote expired, the tally was 218 against and only 216 for. That's when they went to work.

Technically the rules say that no member may have less than fifteen minutes to cast his or her vote—but they don't say anything about more than fifteen minutes. It wasn't that unusual to extend the clock. In the past the Democrats had done it. When then Speaker Jim Wright (D-TX) once allowed a vote to last an hour while he rounded up votes, for example, the Republicans were furious, describing it as an abuse of the process. The prescription drug vote began about three o'clock in the morning, a good time to start a vote if you don't want America to see what you're doing, and lasted two hours and fifty-one minutes. It was the longest roll call vote in the history of the House of Representatives. The Republican leadership was obviously so embarrassed by what was taking place on the floor that C-SPAN, whose cameras normally pan the floor, was not allowed to show the Republican side.

This was a bill the Republican leadership had to deliver to the pharmaceutical industry, at whatever the cost. This was the hardest of hardball politics. No one will ever know completely what threats were made on the floor that night to ensure passage of the drug bill, but a few days after the vote, retiring representative Nick Smith (R-MI) wrote on his Web site, "members and groups made offers of extensive campaign support and endorsements for my son, Brad, who is running for my seat. They also made threats of working against Brad if I voted no . . ."

Smith had been specifically targeted by both Denny Hastert and Tommy Thompson, Health and Human Services secretary, who defied tradition by actually coming onto the House floor to lobby. They sat on either side of Smith like bookends, increasing the pressure on him.

Additionally, according to conservative columnist Robert Novak, "Business interests would give his son $100,000 in return for his father's vote."

To Smith's credit, he resisted these threats and voted no. After which, Novak continued, Duke Cunningham and other Republicans taunted him that his son was "dead meat." Months later Brad Smith was defeated in the Republican primary, and eventually Tom DeLay was admonished by the nonpartisan House Ethics Committee for offering political favors—his support for Brad Smith's campaign—in exchange for Nick Smith's vote.

While much of that story is known, we Democrats fought our own party battles that night. The bill could not have passed without some Democratic votes, and Nancy Pelosi fought hard to maintain party discipline. There were several Democrats who had strong political reasons for supporting the bill, and that was understood. That's the reality of politics. But there were several others whose reasons for supporting the bill weren't immediately obvious. I'm someone who has voted against the party on important votes, so I understand the pressure people feel, but in this case there was tremendous resentment toward those members. There weren't many important votes that we actually could have won—but this was one of them. And defeating this bill would have been a meaningful victory.

One of the Democrats feeling the pressure was Oregon's David Wu, a moderate, who supported the bill because he felt it was better than what already existed. But Wu did not want to defy party leadership. When the vote was stuck at 218 to 216, he was the 435th vote. He simply refused to vote. Apparently he had decided that, whatever happened, he would not be the vote that allowed the bill to pass. So he waited, and waited.

Democrats gathered around Wu and tried to convince him to vote no. The House had been in session most of the night. People were exhausted and irritable. Some members who were worried about being pressured had gone back to their offices, not wanting to be found. Eventually, former president John F. Kennedy's nephew Congressman Patrick Kennedy (D-RI), at the suggestion of Mississippi Democrat Gene Taylor, suggested on the floor of the House, "Ask not what your country can do for Wu, but what Wu can do for your country!"

Nobody knows how long the Republicans would have kept the vote open, but at about six o'clock in the morning, two conservatives finally agreed to switch their votes, and the prescription drug bill was passed. The final vote was 220 to 215. Wu voted with the Republican majority. And while there were some hard feelings, after the Democrats took control of the House in 2006, he was given a waiver at his request to serve on three committees.

Both parties try to protect their members whenever possible. The primary objective is to keep your members in office so that, if their votes are not needed, members are not pressured to vote the party position. When the Republicans were in power, very often you'd see the northeastern Republicans waiting until the party got its 218 votes before casting their votes. Once that number had been reached, the final tally didn't matter to the party, so the members could cast it according to their own political needs. Angry that they were able to get away with this so often, a veteran Republican once told me, "The Republicans show their compassion by shooting the wounded after the battle."

The larger the majority, the easier it is to maintain that majority, because the party has more votes than it needs to pass legislation and can let members cast the politically smart votes more often. But even then, those members may pay politically for the party position. For example, when the Democrats were trying to pass a crime bill in 1994, among the many provisions was a ban on assault weapons. "That was crazy," remembers Neil Abercrombie, who was there. "I stood up in the whip meeting and I told them, 'Look, I'm in a district where I could vote for a bill that says my wife gets to decide who can have a gun in this country and I can get away with it. But what about all the people for whom this is going to cause great problems? Forcing them to vote on assault weapons is handing an issue to the NRA. They could lose elections.'

"I suggested they make that a separate vote, so those members could vote for the crime bill and against that, and it was pointed out to me that on its own it wouldn't pass. So I asked, 'Well, what does that tell you?' We were putting our own members in political jeopardy. If they voted against the bill, their opponents could criticize them for voting against the crime bill, for being soft on criminals. But if they voted for it, their opponents could go after them for voting to take away people's guns. The leadership just didn't get it. And because we did things like that, we lost the majority. Even Tom Foley, the Speaker of the House, got beat. Imagine that, the Speaker being defeated. It's because we put people in precarious positions with votes like that."

Abercrombie was referring to members like Minnesota Democrat Collin Peterson, who represents a very conservative district and of necessity often crosses party lines. Peterson is part of the Democratic Blue Dog Coalition—named in honor of the paintings of blue dogs by Cajun artist George Rodrigue that hung on the walls of coalition founders Jimmy Hayes and Billy Tauzin, both from Louisiana and both of whom eventually switched parties. As Peterson told *Washington Post* reporter Juliet Eilperin, "In my district if you're not pro-gun and pro-life and pro-snowmobile, you can't talk to them."

The most difficult bills to vote on are those that are written specifically to appeal to competing constituencies, the bills that make bad law but great election fodder. The Republicans were extremely clever at drawing up legislation that split the Democrats. When Tom DeLay thought he could peel Jewish voters away from the Democrats, he introduced a foreign aid bill that cut aid to Africa and Latin America—and so did nothing for the poorest people in the world—but increased aid to Israel. As an example of wedge legislation it was brilliant, and typical of the despicable tactics that made DeLay infamous.

It was obvious that this was an awful bill. The Republicans believed that Jewish members in particular would have to vote for this bill or be charged in their next campaign as being weak on supporting Israel, while African-American and Latino members would have to vote against it. Eventually what we did was get all the Jewish members together, and about half of us agreed this was wrong. While we knew we couldn't win the vote on the floor, we also knew that President Clinton would veto it, and that the Republicans could not get the two-thirds majority necessary to override that veto. They couldn't pass it without us. Oh, they tried, they just didn't have the votes. Eventually the Republicans caved in and restored debt relief for Africa and funding for Latin America.

The Republicans were always trying to get the Democrats on record as voting against what they perceived to be the basic moral issues in this country: patriotism, prayer, motherhood, and apple pie—while voting for gay rights, stem cell research, and abortion. They were trying to divide America at the lowest common denominator. Those were their most cherished political issues.

For example, when a federal district court judge ruled that a 2.6-ton monument inscribed with the Ten Commandments had to be removed from the Alabama State Supreme Court building, the Republicans thought they had another one of those great wedge issues. They weren't concerned about constitutional principles such as separation of church and state; they wanted to get Democrats on record as voting against the Ten Commandments. This was the ultimate moral issue for the Republicans: Are you for or against the Ten Commandments?

Believe me, no politician wants to face voters as the person who voted against the Ten Commandments. Barney Frank played a major role in the debate. He even followed up with a brilliant motion, suggesting that we vote on each commandment separately. His explanation was that he might be in favor of some of the commandments, but not all. He wanted to put everyone on record on each of the commandments to see if their personal behavior comported with the specific commandment. I believe he said something about particularly looking forward to voting on "Thou shall not commit adultery."

School prayer was another issue the Republicans always saw as a winner for them. They liked to be able to portray Democrats as the people who voted against God. This is an issue that particularly bothers me because it translates into little children all across America being made to feel different, being made to stand up and say, "I don't want to participate in this prayer. Treat me differently." In the House I resent it because it's an attempt to force the Jewish members to stand up and object. Fortunately, there are many brave Christian members who also stand up for principle on this issue. But there's no reason for this legislation. The reality is that religion is flourishing in this country. People can pray wherever they want to, and I would argue that it's because of the separation of church and state, not in spite of it. For me, this is an easy vote. I don't believe prayer should be mandated by the state. And there will be few repercussions in my district for voting against it. But for Texas Democrat Chet Edwards, this can't be anything but a political nightmare. My respect for him is enormous—every time this issue is raised he objects to it.

Almost always, we know what the outcome is going to be before we vote. But even so, the time spent on the floor of the House during the actual vote is invaluable. One thing rarely figured into the political equation is how technology has changed the system. Before air-conditioning, for example, Washington, D.C., was unbearably hot and humid in the summer, so Congress adjourned and members went home, often by horseback or wagon. Now, of course, the temperature indoors is easily controlled and the sessions can last well into the summer heat. Jet travel also made a huge impact on Congress. In years past it took members too long to get back to their districts for a weekend, so when Congress was in session they stayed in Washington; people on both sides of the aisle got to spend considerably more time together than they do now. They got to know one another, and some friendships developed, which tended to encourage compromise. Now, with easy jet travel, most members return to their district just about every weekend.

With members traveling so frequently, the floor of the House is about the only place you meet and talk with people. When we're in session I'll spend hours on the floor. A lot of business gets done while we're waiting and voting. There are no assigned seats on the floor; people sit wherever they wish. Generally the Democrats and Republicans gather on their own sides. A group of Blue Dog Democrats like to sit in the middle, toward the back. I like to stay in the back, so I can make a fast exit. Jack Murtha always sits in one back corner. Everybody knows that is Jack Murtha's seat, and there's a regular flow of people lined up by his seat waiting to speak with him. Jack is an old-fashioned congressman; he knows the behind-the-scenes processes and he's very influential.

Members do a lot of lobbying for their legislation on the floor. They'll give a quick explanation of their bill or resolution to try to round up support. Some vote trading takes place there, too; members will trade their votes on issues that have no local impact for a commitment to vote their way on issues that matter to them. Sarah Dufendach remembers David Bonior desperately trying to gather votes for a billion-dollar bailout for Chrysler: "Not letting Chrysler fail was essential to Michigan, but the Southern guys all said, 'What do we care if Chrysler fails, we don't have any Chrysler plants in our districts. Free market. Free market.' Bonior then said the magic words to them: 'Tobacco subsidies.' So they voted for the bailout that saved Chrysler and thousands of jobs, and David ended up voting for that tobacco subsidy year after year after year, until he finally decided the debt was paid, and he just couldn't morally vote for tobacco anymore."

For a bill to become a law, the identical language has to be passed by both the House and Senate. Generally, after both bodies pass their versions of the legislation, members from the House and Senate meet in a conference committee to hammer out a compromise bill. House members of this conference committee are appointed by the Speaker and are usually members of the standing committee that has jurisdiction over the bill.

The way it's supposed to work is that appointed representatives meet and negotiate a compromise bill, which is then sent to the House and the Senate for ratification or defeat. But that certainly isn't the way it actually works. Each chamber determines the number and party membership of the conferees, but the majority party always has the majority of the members. In fact, when the Republicans had majorities in both the House and Senate, as I've said, their leadership didn't care if Democrats participated or not and at times even tried to lock them out of the room.

There wasn't much anybody could do about it. Conference committee meetings are private. There are no recorded minutes. Conference committees meet in secret, and they can do just about anything they want.

The truth is that conference committees are often referred to as "the third branch of Congress." Like a handkerchief that went into the magician's top hat and emerged a dove, bills that come out of a conference committee may bear little resemblance to the legislation that went in. New legislation is actually written in these committees by a small group of people who work in private. Then it goes back to the two houses of Congress for a straight up or down vote, no amendments. When the House passed an energy bill in 2003, for example, the Senate responded by passing an old Democratic bill that had long been ignored. That was not exactly an attempt at bipartisanship. Passing that bill allowed the Republicans to go into a conference and write a completely new energy bill. As New Mexico senator Pete Domenici told reporters, "I will rewrite this bill."

Michigan Republican Fred Upton, then the chairman of the House Telecommunications Subcommittee, actually admitted at a telecommunications industry forum that the Senate needed to pass "anything to get us into committee" so they could write new legislation.

"It happens in the dead of night," explained California Democrat

Pete Stark. "Lobbyists get a [Republican legislator] in a corner and say, 'We've got to have this.' Suddenly a tax break for a corporation or an obscure provision that benefits a single company or a grant of money to an industry that no one knew anything about appears in a bill—and because everything is done in private, there is absolutely no way of knowing who got it put there. Most of the time those things get caught before the bill is returned to Congress for a final vote—but not always. I think it's accurate to say we often vote on legislation we don't even know is in a bill."

Provisions don't just get added in conference, they also get eliminated. Although both the House and Senate had included language in an emergency supplemental appropriations bill for Iraq that specifically prohibited any of that money being used to establish permanent bases, the bill that came out of committee simply eliminated that restriction. It wasn't there, so it wasn't mentioned in the media. Addition by subtraction.

If a compromise is finally reached and a bill is reported out of the conference committee, the newly rewritten bill is voted on once again by the House and Senate. If both houses pass it, it goes to the president to be signed into law. If the president vetoes it, the bill is returned to Congress, where each house can attempt to override his veto—turning it into law without his approval—by passing it again with a more than two-thirds majority. But assuming the president does sign it, he'll often invite key legislators to the White House for a signing ceremony.

It's a big deal getting invited to the White House. No matter how jaded you might be, no matter where else you've been in the world, it is the White House. Don't believe anyone who tells you their heart doesn't beat just a little faster when they walk through the front door. I had been to the White House several times during Clinton's presidency, but I had refused to go during President George Bush's first term. After the election of 2004 I did go there for an awards ceremony that was the result of my legislation, the Leonard Kravitz bill.

When the family of rock star Lenny Kravitz informed my office that his uncle had been denied the medal he'd earned by saving his entire platoon during the Korean War because he was Jewish—in fact, as we learned, very few Jews or African-Americans were awarded combat medals in Korea or during World War II—it was obvious we should file a bill to rectify that.

Vietnam War hero and then Georgia Democratic senator Max Cleland sponsored it in the Senate, and it was signed into law by President Bush. It enabled many American heroes to receive their long-overdue honors. I was invited to the White House to see the first Medal of Honor awarded, although it did not go to Kravitz's uncle. The recipient was Tibor Rubin, a Holocaust survivor and World War II hero. This man is the embodiment of a patriot. He was recommended four times for this honor and was passed over each time because of anti-Semitism in the military. It was a very impressive ceremony. The entire Joint Chiefs of Staff were there, several senators were there, Bush and Cheney, and at the center of it all was a soft-spoken, unassuming man and his wife and children and grandchildren. The couple were both in their late seventies or early eighties and obviously people of modest means. This man escaped the horrors of the Nazis, fabricated his age to get into the army, and then risked his life to save his fellow soldiers.

Before the ceremony began, one of the people who had come to the White House with Mr. Rubin approached me. This was an elderly man and I thought he was going to say something about the feeling in the room. Admittedly, it was impressive. We were in the White House with several of the most powerful men in the world, about to see a humble man receive the honors he'd won on the battlefield decades earlier. I thought he would be in awe. Instead, this man leaned over to me, tilted his head toward the president, and whispered in an accented voice, "Does he really have to receive the medal from that son of a bitch?"

10

Have Passport, Will Travel:
Foreign Policy in Action

All politics is global.

—Thomas Friedman

I suspect that many Americans were greatly surprised by the Tom Hanks movie *Charlie Wilson's War*. Not the fact that Congressman Charlie Wilson could almost single-handedly raise the funds to provide the arms Afghani rebels needed to fight and defeat the Soviet Army, but that one member of the House could have that kind of impact on world events.

That's not the way people generally think about the House of Representatives. In fact, the Republicans have made a strong effort to reduce the amount of travel done by members of Congress—even bragging in 1994 about how few of them possessed passports. They bragged about it; how telling.

The fact is that Congress has a unique constitutional role to play in foreign policy: Congress declares war, Congress appropriates all foreign aid, and Congress—the Senate, actually—ratifies all treaties. The decisions we make are directly related to America's interests in the world and the security of every one of our citizens. The idea that Congress should make these decisions in a vacuum, without traveling abroad and gaining firsthand knowledge, is utterly irresponsible.

As a member of the Foreign Affairs Committee I feel very strongly that it benefits the nation when our elected officials meet with world leaders. It's not possible to understand the ramifications of our foreign policy without visiting other parts of the world. You can't fully understand the opinions and views of the governments and community leaders of other countries if you don't go there and talk to them yourself. You can't understand the complex realities of the Middle East unless you've been in Israel and Egypt and Jordan and Saudi Arabia, the Gulf States, and even Syria.

The belief that you can learn these things from a book or a report is ludicrous. For example, when Madeleine Bordallo entered Congress as the nonvoting representative from Guam in 2003, she was surprised when a Republican member told her he thought Guam was part of Hawaii.

How valuable are these trips? In 2004 I visited Israel with then representative Ted Strickland, now the Democratic governor of Ohio; Democrat Luis Gutierrez from Illinois; and Republicans Steve Chabot of Ohio and Ileana Ros-Lehtinen of Florida. While we were there we had a long and extremely detailed briefing by the Mossad, Israel's intelligence agency, about the Iranian nuclear program that was far more specific and useful than any information we'd received in closed hearings in Washington. And it wasn't even classified. But this information enabled me to properly weigh the value of claims about the progress of Iran's nuclear program being made by the Bush administration.

Because I have always been deeply involved in the Middle East I had tried several times to meet with Syrian leaders. They wouldn't give me a visa, not necessarily because I was Jewish—I'd been to most of the other Arab countries without any problem—but because I was one of the early sponsors of the 2003 Syria Accountability and Lebanese Sovereignty Restoration Act, which demanded that Syria end its support for terrorists, take its troops out of Lebanon, and stop its development of weapons of mass destruction. That legislation imposed economic sanctions on Syria. Furthermore, I had written a scathing letter to President Assad criticizing an offensive speech he delivered when the Pope visited Syria in 2001.

Ultimately, President Assad decided he needed to improve relations with America. When I mentioned to California Republican Darryl Issa, who was scheduled to go to Syria, that I'd wanted to visit that country but had been turned down several times, he told me there'd been a change of feeling within the Syrian regime and they might welcome me.

If not welcome, at least meet with me. As it turned out, the Syrians wanted to meet with those legislators who were particularly adverse to them. That was me. I went to Syria with the intention of telling Assad he needed to shut down Palestinian terrorist organizations based in Damascus. Assad knew I would be going from Damascus directly to Jerusalem to meet with Israeli prime minister Ariel Sharon.

I was vehemently opposed to the Assad regime, but I believed that part of my job included meeting with people I despised. In Beirut once, I'd met with a Lebanese government official who I suspected had been involved in the kidnapping of an Israeli Air Force officer and was most likely the person who handed him over to the Iranians. I had nothing but contempt for him, but in order to try to ascertain the status of the missing Israeli, I needed to meet with him. I felt the same way about Arafat, a truly heinous person. I imagine it was the same kind of feeling people had when they met with Lenin or Stalin. Meeting somebody like Assad was that type of thing for me—in this world we often have to deal with people we despise.

We met in Assad's office in the presidential palace. The U.S. ambassador to Syria was there, as well as several top officials of that government. Once the protocol was out of the way, it became a fairly confrontational meeting. I brought up the speech Assad had made, which was among the most vitriolic anti-Semitic speeches a modern world leader had ever made. Assad was very defensive, claiming that my translation of that speech was wrong, he'd never said those things. Then we talked at length about Syria's involvement in international terrorism.

Bashar Assad is an interesting man. He had been trained as an oph-thalmologist in London and never expected to become a world leader. He probably never expected to come back to Syria. His older brother was supposed to succeed their father, but he'd been killed in a car acci-dent. Assad had married a British-Syrian woman; his father-in-law is a surgeon in England. But what so struck me at that meeting was that for an intelligent man, he was so ill-informed about the United States. What truly frightened me was that his ignorance about this country's objectives and goals would lead him to make decisions that were based on false assumptions, and the results could be devastating.

President Assad knew I was going directly to Israel to meet with Prime Minister Sharon, and it was clear he was saying things that he expected me to report to Sharon. I've found that to a certain degree many Arab leaders think all Jewish people talk to one another and if you tell one thing to this Jewish person, inevitably he's going to repeat it to that other Jewish person. But one of the things that Assad told me, which I don't think is necessarily credible, is that he wanted to negoti-ate with Israel. It was clear that he was afraid Israel would make progress on some type of peace plan with the Palestinians and leave Syria out of the mix. And when I met with Sharon about seven hours later in Jerusalem, that's exactly what I told him.

As the meeting with Assad ended, he said a strange thing to me: "Please do come back to Syria and please come with your wife." I didn't respond and he repeated it. "Please come back with your wife. My wife very much enjoys the opportunity to meet with Western-educated women." It was surreal. Here am I, standing with this heinous character who violates every principle of life that I believe in and care about as an American and as a Jew, and I thought, Are you suggesting we go out on a double date? I couldn't wait to get back to the hotel to call Laurie and tell her, "Guess who we're going out with four Satur-days from now? The Assads. It'll be fun, we'll go to dinner, maybe a movie."

But it wasn't that question that made me pause for a moment and wonder how to respond. That had come earlier in our discussions, when Assad asked me, "Is George Bush crazy?"

What he meant was, Is George Bush actually crazy enough to attack me, so I really have to listen to the United States?

When I travel overseas I am careful to limit my criticism of Bush administration policy, which is not a particularly easy thing for me to do. But I do it. I always defend America and respond immediately and sharply to any undue criticism of our nation. I may point out that I have a different perspective than the administration, but I try to temper my remarks. I don't want to be overly critical. Critical analysis, yes; partisan attacks, no.

But is Bush crazy? Here was my dilemma: If I defended him and said the president of the United States was not crazy, Assad might assume Bush would act rationally. But if I agreed with him that Bush was crazy, he might hesitate about taking some action at some point in the future, or he might respond to an American action out of fear of the crazy president.

The last thing I wanted to do was put Bashar Assad's mind at ease. My sense was that this was a situation in which having a leader who supports terrorist activity and some of the worst regimes in the world, having him think that the president of the United States was just crazy enough to do something a little out of the box, that was a good thing. I told Assad that he needed to understand that George Bush is capable of taking actions other presidents might not contemplate. So, yeah, Bashar Assad, you need to shape up because this isn't an instance where you can rely on diplomacy to prevent something real bad from happening to you. I left that meeting thinking, this is one instance where George Bush's unpredictability may be a virtue.

I had applied for a seat on the Foreign Affairs Committee at the beginning of my first term primarily because of the importance of Israel in my district. The Foreign Affairs Committee is the oldest standing committee in Congress, going all the way back to 1775, when the Committee of Correspondence was formed "for the sole purpose of corresponding with our friends of Great Britain, Ireland, and other parts of the world." The first chairman was Benjamin Franklin. The name of the committee has changed many times throughout our history, as has its effectiveness.

In trying to demonize the foreign travel done by congressmen, Republicans, aided by mainstream media outlets, have successfully planted the impression in voters' minds that we're flying around the world to exotic locations on taxpayer dollars, living in plush hotels and having a great time. Alcee Hastings in particular has been unfairly criticized for being one of the most traveled members of Congress. But the reality of these "junkets" is very different. When Hastings went to the Sudan, for example, he recalls:

> We landed on an airstrip in Uganda and drove for nine hours in a Catholic Relief Services convoy to a refugee camp in the southern Sudan. We were permitted to bring in supplies to the camp because the people there were starving. While I was there we stopped at a hospital which had been bombed, and I watched a surgeon from Doctors Without Borders do an appendectomy without the patient having any anesthesia, and the only light he had was about a fifteen-watt bulb. To be in that camp and see three people starve to death was mind-boggling. On that trip we were also in Somalia and our helicopter was shot at . . .
>
> In Bosnia we stayed in a Holiday Inn with no windows and sheets over the door . . . and from my hotel I could see people being shot at while they were praying at a grave site.

In December 2004, Hastings went to the Ukraine to act as an international observer to ensure that elections were conducted fairly. As Hastings's chief of staff, Fred Turner, pointed out after complaints about that trip were made, "I don't think anyone would argue that going to snowy Eastern Europe and missing Christmas in Florida is a vacation funded by taxpayers." Hastings was the first American to be elected president of the Parliamentary Assembly of the fifty-six-nation Organization for Security and Co-operation in Europe, the largest regional security organization in the world.

I've also traveled extensively to remote locations and witnessed the kind of poverty that no words can accurately describe, complete devastation from war and natural disasters. These aren't the kinds of places I would choose to go on vacation, and I would hardly describe them as junkets.

But the value of these trips is undeniable. Most Americans don't think of members of Congress as major national figures. In fact, the average citizen probably can't name more than his or her own representative and a handful of others. But in countries around the world, members of Congress are considered prominent representatives of the United States government, and what we say and do is often believed to be the American position. Our visits are major news. The people may have never seen an American government official, and we become the embodiment of America for them. They don't quite understand how our government works. There's no difference in their mind between a member of the House or Senate and a member of the executive branch. A lot of times people have said to me, "When you talk to the president, would you tell him . . . ," as if it's something I do every day.

Occasionally, members of Congress do have access to the president, but we always have access to the State Department. Most foreign leaders understand and appreciate the power that one member of Congress, particularly a member of the Foreign Affairs Committee, can have in highlighting an issue or a problem. We can get the attention of our government focused on it. For instance, the small nation of Oman, on the Arabian Peninsula, has great strategic importance for American forces. We launched air raids from U.S. military sites there on Iraq during the Persian Gulf War and on Afghanistan and al-Qaeda after 9/11. It's a progressive Arab nation ruled by Sultan Qaboos, who is a moderate. I had the opportunity to meet with him in a tent in the desert during Ramaddan and he is an impressive figure, a man who has insisted on greater equality for women in a part of the world where too many women remain in oppressive conditions. Oman has been a valuable American ally for several decades. The Omani government very much desired to have a free trade agreement with the United States, but as a condition of that deal, we insisted that Oman not participate in the Arab boycott of Israel. Things were on track until *The Jerusalem Post* ran a story accusing Oman of stopping a shipment of Israeli goods. That was exactly the kind of thing that could have sidetracked the agreement. Because I'm known as a staunch defender of Israel, as well as someone who respects Oman, this was an important issue for me.

To try to get the whole thing straightened out, I wrote a letter to the Omani ambassador in Washington requesting information—and he responded to that letter with urgency, as if it had come from the secretary of state. Within days we met in my office, and Oman recommited itself not to boycott Israel. President Bush signed the trade agreement in 2006.

Foreign affairs is an area in which members of the House, even members of the minority, can have a tremendous impact on American economic as well as security matters. There are very important things happening behind the scenes every day—things that few people ever learn about—that can make a difference in countless lives. I had been working for several years, for example, to facilitate a relationship between Israel and an important country I can't name, a country that has never recognized the existence of Israel. Gradually there had been an interest, that interest evolved into a conversation, and in 2006 high-ranking officials from Israel and that nation met in my office for what was one of the first substantive face-to-face meetings between government officials from those nations in their history. It is a beginning.

Congressional travel plays a pivotal role in building stronger relationships with nations that are crucial to America's security interests. These congressional relationships are all the more important considering how badly the Bush administration has allowed our relationship with several nations, such as Turkey, to deteriorate. Turkish officials have a sophisticated understanding of world affairs, but that hasn't been appreciated by the Bush government. In fact, had Bush listened to the advice of experts in the Turkish Foreign Ministry before launching the Iraq War, it is quite possible we wouldn't be facing the chaos we've created now. Before the war the Bush administration requested land access through Turkey to open a northern route into Iraq. That was a very sensitive issue for the Turks because it amounted to allowing us to use Turkish territory to launch an attack on another Muslim country. The Turkish Parliament had been debating the issue, and we didn't know which way it would eventually vote. A refusal would make it necessary to substantially change our military strategy. Turkey had fully cooperated and participated with us in the first Gulf War, and as a result it had paid a terrific economic price for which it was never compensated.

The Turkish people and politicians were hesitant to disrupt their tenuous economy again.

Several weeks before the Turkish Parliment was scheduled to vote, I met in Ankara with Ambassador Ziyal, who was the Turkish under secretary for Foreign Affairs. He was a wise man, and in his career had smoked many cigarettes with the most knowledgeable and powerful diplomats in that region. He had an uncanny understanding of the realities of that part of the world and should have been a valuable resource for our government. He explained to me—and I know for a fact that he gave the same advice to the administration—that as bad as Saddam Hussein was, he was successfully containing the various sects in Iraq, and that if he were deposed, those interests would be free to fight among themselves. He warned that chaos would replace despotism and wondered whether America had fully contemplated all the consequences of the impending invasion. As we sat together before the war, he laid out the whole scenario that has taken place since then. Under Saddam, he said, there were people who suffered and people who benefited greatly. Once we got rid of Saddam and his army, all that would change. He wasn't arguing against the war, he was pleading that we be prepared to contain the sectarian violence after the invasion. American soldiers are not going to be met with roses, he said, and Iraq will not be able to pay for this war from its oil revenues. Essentially, he predicted everything that has happened.

Ziyal made a convincing case to me—and to the Bush administration, which ignored him. The arrogance of the administration in dealing with foreign nations is counterproductive and has set back American foreign policy for decades. Trying to convince Turkey to let us launch attacks from its territory, Deputy Secretary of Defense Paul Wolfowitz gave them an ultimatum: Either you're with us or against us. Given that Turkey, a staunch NATO ally, had twice led international forces in Afghanistan after 9/11, that was a horrific statement. Anyone with even the most elementary understanding of Turkish culture knows that pride plays an important role in its politics. Let me be more specific: You will never successfully persuade a Turkish political entity, whether it's an individual or the Turkish Parliament, by first demeaning them. Even if your logic is correct, and they should take certain steps, if you belittle them, they are not going to give you what you want. Wolfowitz should have known that. So the Turkish Parliament turned down the Bush administration request that forced the Pentagon to prepare a whole new plan only weeks prior to the invasion.

U.S.-Turkish relations went into a free-fall, and members of the Republican Party set out to punish Turkey. Their naive concept was that any nation that did not agree with the Bush administration was against us, and therefore decades and decades of alliances that had been built and carefully fostered just didn't matter. Even against the wishes of the White House and the State Department, some House Republicans tried to cut one billion dollars in loans to Turkey; one member even went so far as to claim that Turkey had American blood on its hands for failing to allow tens of thousands of American troops to use Turkey as a launching pad to invade northern Iraq. Ironically, after we'd failed to find any weapons of mass destruction, President Bush would argue that we had invaded Iraq to promote freedom and democracy—while several House Republicans were intent on punishing Turkey for exercising that same freedom in their moderate Muslim, majority democratic nation.

The relationships formed by members of the House who traveled to Turkey proved very important at that time. I've been to Turkey seven times. In November 2002 I introduced a resolution in the House supporting Turkey's application for membership in the European Union, which barely made a ripple here but was front-page news throughout Turkey. My wife jokes that I could run for prime minister of Turkey because I'm almost as well known there as I am in my own district. When I'm in Turkey, there's no difference between my schedule and that of Secretary of State Rice or other top administration officials. I meet with the Turkish prime minister and the defense and foreign ministers. If I make a speech there, it's generally well attended. I maintain a strong relationship with both our ambassador to Turkey and the Turkish ambassador to the United States. So as much as any American representative, I have a long and positive relationship with the Turkish government.

I went to Turkey in March—with Republican Ed Whitfield of

Kentucky—and in April 2003 to try to mend our relationship. I met with Prime Minister Recep Tayyip Erdoǒan and Foreign Minister Gul, mostly to have a conversation about the impact of the war on the region, and the future of American-Turkish relations. At the end of the meeting the prime minister and I affirmed that Turkey and the United States were "indispensable partners."

The important thing was that an American government official whom they knew, and from past experiences trusted, had made two trips to Turkey and would accurately report their point of view to Congress. It was not a matter of defending or criticizing the Turkish government, but rather an effort to figure out how to maintain a reasonable dialogue during a difficult period.

I've been back to Turkey a couple of times since. The biggest issue dividing our countries now is the failure of the United States to take any action against the Kurdish terrorist organization, the PKK. In 2006 I wrote a letter to President Bush—which was also signed by Representative Whitfield—demanding that the president begin to focus on stopping the PKK operations emanating from northern Iraq and, at a minimum, close down that terrorist organization's infrastructure. There are PKK training camps and offices in Iraq that are actively supporting murderous acts in Turkey. The simple act of writing that letter was widely praised by the Turkish ambassador, and my decision to hold a Europe Subcommittee hearing to focus attention on the terrorist activities of the PKK was also positively received in Ankara. Additionally, I introduced a resolution condemning the PKK and urging the U.S. and Iraqi governments to dismantle their operations.

Every congressman gets to choose those areas in which he or she intends to have an impact. Some members have no interest in international affairs—maybe their focus is on the environment or energy or economics—but those who do can have a dramatic effect on American foreign policy and the way America is perceived around the world. Maybe because there are often no immediate tangible results, this work doesn't receive as much attention as high-profile legislation or getting government money for local projects—everybody who has ever heard of the PKK raise your hand—but it is a fundamental part of the job.

One of the frustrations we face in Congress is that our shortcomings become much more widely known than the positive work we do every day. When Republican congressman Randy "Duke" Cunningham went to jail for accepting millions of dollars in bribes, it was in the news every day. When Democratic congressman William Jefferson of Louisiana was indicted after ninety thousand dollars in cash was found in his freezer, it was on every front page. Those issues are very serious and unfortunately reflect poorly on Congress, but what is irritating is that we do so many more important things that actually affect the future of our nation and few people ever hear about them. Corruption makes news. But in terms of national security, in terms of our children's future, it doesn't mean anything at all. For example, I doubt if many Americans know that the country with the largest Muslim population in the world is Indonesia. And what will matter most to our national security in the future is our relationship with countries like Indonesia.

You can make a strong argument that Indonesia is one of the most significant nations on earth, for a variety of reasons. Indonesia is an emerging democracy with 234 million people, mostly of the Muslim faith. Do Americans want to win the war on terror? Do we really want to win the hearts and minds of Muslims throughout the world? About two-thirds of all Muslims live in non-Arab countries. If we're going to win the war against terrorism, if we're going to defeat the forces of Islamic extremism, it's going to be done in Indonesia, Turkey, Azerbaijan, and Kazakhstan, maybe more than in places like Saudi Arabia.

That is why I was so motivated in 2004 to help form the Indonesia caucus. The idea came from Republican Dan Burton of Indiana, a conservative with whom I agree on almost nothing. But when he approached me I thought it was a great idea. It's the kind of bipartisan cooperation that should get publicity, but doesn't. A member of Burton's staff was deeply interested in Indonesia, and it was his motivation that caused Burton to get involved. Burton's chief of staff and Eric Johnson went to Indonesia first, where the idea was born. That's a perfect example of why foreign travel is invaluable. When Eric got back, he explained to me that Indonesia was changing, that it was no longer

ABOVE LEFT: My daughter Rachel Wexler, one year old, holds the Wexler pot holder during my successful state senate campaign in 1990.

ABOVE RIGHT: My son, Zachary, pictured at age six, and I sit on the steps of the Capitol building.

BELOW: The Wexler family in Boca Raton, Florida. From left to right: Zachary, Laurie, Hannah, Robert, and Rachel. *(Photograph by Jeffrey Tholl)*

Rep. Bob Barr (R-GA) and I go head to head on *Meet the Press* over the Clinton impeachment in 1998. *(Photograph courtesy of* Meet the Press*)*

"Wake up, America, they are about to impeach your president!" Here I am delivering a speech before the Judiciary Committee opposing the Clinton impeachment.

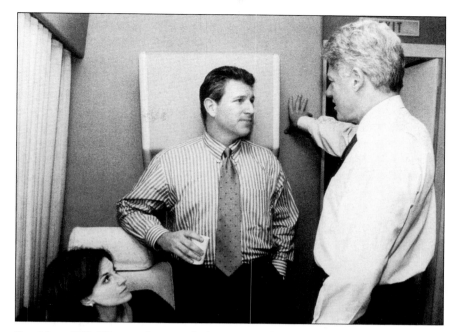

President Bill Clinton shares a light moment with my wife, Laurie, and me on *Air Force One*. *(Official White House photograph)*

Presenting First Lady Hillary Clinton with the famous Wexler pot holder during a fund-raiser she hosted for me in 1999. *(Photograph by Joseph Reilly)*

As I aggressively questioned Attorney General John Ashcroft during Judiciary Committee hearings on the Patriot Act, my daughter Hannah, age eight, colors in the foreground.

My loyal staff on the roof of the Hay-Adams Hotel following a fund-raiser for me hosted by President Bill Clinton. From left to right: me, Jonathan Katz, Suzanne Stoll, Eric Johnson, and Josh Rogin. *(Photograph by Peter Cutts)*

Greeting my friend Shimon Peres, president of Israel. *(Photograph © 2000 John Harrington)*

In Indonesia my son, Zachary, and I delivered soccer balls to children whose lives were devastated by the tsunami.

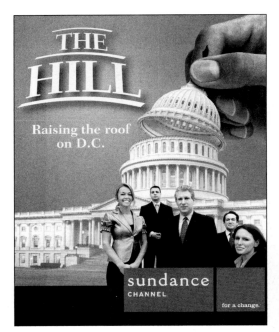

RIGHT: After Republicans claim Democrats are fabricating voter confusion on Election Day 2000 in Florida, I hold up the "smoking memo" that Palm Beach County elections supervisor Theresa LePore issued on Election Day in an attempt to prevent continuing voter errors due to the butterfly ballot. *(Photograph © Gary I Rothstein)*

LEFT: I spent years fighting for a voter-verified paper trail following the debacle in Florida following the 2000 presidential election. Here Florida governor Charlie Crist, an old state senate colleague and close friend of mine, signs legislation mandating a paper trail for the State of Florida. *(Photograph courtesy of Uma Sanghvi/Palm Beach Post/ZUMA Press)*

Here I give a stinging rebuke to President George W. Bush while introducing Democratic presidential nominee John Kerry at Florida Atlantic University in my district during the 2004 election. *(Photograph by J. M. Ristow)*

Stephen Colbert came to Washington to interview me for *The Colbert Report* in 2006. Although my appearance on the show only lasted minutes, the interview itself took over an hour and a half to tape.

The Republican Revolution is over! Speaker of the House Nancy Pelosi swears me in for my sixth term in January of 2007.

Huddling with Senator Barack Obama moments before I introduce him at the AIPAC 2007 annual conference in Washington, D.C. I was an early supporter of Obama during his 2008 presidential run and serve as chairman of the Obama '08 Florida campaign. *(Photograph by Joseph Reilly)*

the autocratic nation that it had been under the authoritarian ruler Suharto. The country was being transformed into a democracy and it was vital that America become involved in assisting that transition. It's a battle. I've now been there twice, and during one of my visits as many as fifteen thousand pro-Hezbollah Indonesians were protesting America's support of Israel in front of our embassy. The bad guys have plenty of support there, too.

But it is vital to our interests that America have an active presence in Indonesia, and as part of my responsibilities as a member of Congress I've had the opportunity and the power to get involved there. Not too long after the tsunami devastated the territory of Aceh on the Indonesian island of Sumatra, wiping away entire towns and killing tens of thousands of people in minutes, like so many Americans my son, Zachary, wanted to do something to help. For his bar mitzvah he wanted to participate in a charitable project and came up with a creative idea: He would donate one thousand soccer balls to the children of Aceh. Soccer balls were probably the last thing adults were thinking about—these people needed supplies to ensure their survival—but Zack reasoned that kids like him had lost everything, absolutely everything, and lacked the one piece of equipment that would enable them to play, to have a little fun in a desperate situation. He wrote letters to Nike and followed up with phone calls—and he managed to convince Nike to donate the soccer balls. That was positive for Nike's image, too, as it had been accused of using sweatshop labor in that part of the world to produce its products. Nike also arranged for the balls to be shipped from Pakistan, where they were made, to Aceh. Zack and I worked in concert with the United States Agency for International Development, which agreed to help distribute the balls.

Zachary and I flew for more than twenty-four hours to Indonesia. My family paid for Zack's travel. We landed in the capital, Jakarta, and the next day we flew to Aceh. We met with several top government officials, including the president.

I've seen extreme poverty in many places in the world. In India, for example, I can never forget the thousands of destitute young children who were living in a railroad station. I've visited disaster areas, but I'd never seen anything like this. It was a total void, great stretches of emptiness. For miles all we saw were cement foundations where homes once stood. Occasionally a floor had survived. On what must have been blocks of homes, people had staked out areas and posted signs with their family name so others would know it was their land. There was a mountain probably two miles inland that had been sliced open, as if by a giant knife. In many communities the only structure left standing was the mosque. It stood, we were told, because for generations people had cheated on following the building codes for their homes, but never for the mosque, because that would have been cheating on God. We heard about a huge electrical barge that had been the power source for an entire town. It was a power plant the size of a supertanker, and it had been carried inland six miles by the huge tsunami waves. This barge was much too big to move, so it was repaired and hooked up and was being used to provide power to another town. And then there were the mass graves, graves in which the survivors had quickly buried bodies to avoid disease, ten thousand people there, and over there.

I wondered whether my twelve-year-old son could grasp the horror of it all, because so much of what we saw was a washed-away surface. Then we met two boys about Zachary's age and through an interpreter they told us their stories. One of them described his mother and father and four sisters being lost, and how he lived afterward in a tent by himself for weeks and weeks. At that moment both Zack and I began to fully comprehend the magnitude of the loss.

When we were distributing the balls, we were surprised when a young boy didn't take one. He didn't want the ball, he told us, because he had no sneakers and couldn't play without them. Talk about ripping your heart out. I spoke with the local UN representative and said, "Listen. We've got to buy him sneakers. I'm not leaving here until he has sneakers."

The representative said that was fine, but we couldn't give sneakers to one child without giving them to all the children.

Fine. I don't know exactly, maybe twenty or thirty kids had survived in that town. I guessed it would cost about four hundred dollars.

But we were able to buy good sneakers for all the kids for a hundred dollars.

A soccer ball costs so little, yet to see the reaction of these young people when they held it and started kicking it was an incredibly powerful experience. Seeing them smile, seeing them be kids, was something I will never forget.

And they knew Zack and I were Americans and we were there. So many of those people told us that without American efforts after the tsunami they would not have survived. Our military supplied clean, fresh water that saved lives. Aceh is not only predominately Muslim, it is the most religious area of Indonesia. I remember seeing a sign, a white bedsheet on which someone had written by hand in paint and magic marker, "America is here. Where is Bin Laden?" I stared at that makeshift sign and understood its profound significance: This is what America needs to do. We can win the hearts and minds of Muslims.

After delivering the soccer balls, Zachary and I went back to Jakarta, where we met with Indonesia's democratically elected president, Susilo Bambang Yudhoyono. Yudhoyono wants greater political and economic ties to America and is progressive in many other important ways. He's an extraordinary man. I felt as if I was sitting with the Thomas Jefferson of Indonesia. He took out a map to explain how America fails to recognize that the most valuable tool we have in engaging with China is all the democracies and emerging democracies that surround China, including Japan, Taiwan, South Korea, Thailand, and Indonesia. All of them have their bumps and starts, but basically it is a Pacific rim of democracies and emerging democracies. It was a fascinating explanation from someone in that part of the world about what America might do to have a more constructive relationship with China.

The president held a televised press conference with Zachary standing next to him and told the story of the soccer balls and explained that it represented a bond of kinship between American and Indonesian children. Parts of the press conference were televised on the nightly news. It was on the front page of the major newspapers. The impact of what he'd said became obvious when we got back to our hotel. The workers couldn't pronounce the letter Z so they called my son Jack. They had seen the press conference and over and over were thanking "Jack." At the airport the next day people recognized him and stopped him to express their gratitude. When we finally got home, the American ambassador to Indonesia told me that we had done a wonderful thing for American-Indonesian relations. "Just fantastic," he said.

But evidence that many Americans have little understanding of the value of these trips, and in fact believe the Republican message, came in a letter published by the *Boca Raton News*: "I read the brief article about Rep. Wexler's visit to Indonesia this week to distribute soccer balls . . . Question: How much did this boondoggle cost? How many people went—wife, children, staffers, etc.? Did he consider UPS to ship the soccer balls? Did he consider sending food, clothing, etc?"

So while the Duke Cunningham scandal fills pages of newspapers, this is what Congress does of absolute value to the country. It actually went further than that. While I was in Indonesia I learned that President Yudhoyono had engineered a peace treaty between the central government and the rebels in Aceh, ending a thirty-year civil war in which fifteen thousand people had died and more than five hundred thousand people had been displaced. Among the privileges of being a member of Congress is the right to nominate people for the Nobel Peace Prize. Most people don't know that. Admittedly, I was one of those people—until we checked. So I did it, nominating him for the 2005 Nobel Peace Prize. I sent a long letter to the committee pointing out that Yudhoyono and his government should be commended for remaining firmly committed to addressing the country's political, economic, and humanitarian needs. "In working to resolve the dispute in Aceh, President Yudhoyono . . . helped resolve an armed conflict through a negotiated agreement that incorporates arms control and disarmament. Furthermore, he has helped to restore to the province of Aceh their human and political rights for representation in governance."

Outside of my office and the State Department, I doubt that anyone in the United States knew about this nomination. But in Indonesia it was a major event. An American government official had nominated the president for the most prestigious award given in the world! When I was interviewed by the newspapers from that part of the world, I explained that I had nominated President Yudhoyono, but actually I was nominating the people of Indonesia for being the one bright spot in the world in terms of creating peace in 2005.

The Nobel Prize nomination initiated a major debate in Indonesia about whether or not the president was worthy of the honor. A truly raging debate. It created a tremendous amount of publicity. Yudhoyono had been a military commander, and the Indonesian media went to the areas he'd governed to determine how he'd acted. The leading human rights activist in that area supported the nomination. Eventually, bookmakers in Australia made him a 3-to-1 favorite to win the Nobel Peace Prize.

One of the most respected Indonesian professors was quoted as saying that the nomination could have a "snowball effect," motivating other provincial governors to promote peaceful solutions to complex political problems, so that "governors might become more active in bringing back peace to their regions, and later all regents and mayors will do the same thing."

He didn't win, but this does show that trips taken by members of Congress can make a difference in the way we are perceived in the world. I'm not saying foreign travel isn't abused on occasion—that goes back a long way—but when Americans wonder what Congress actually accomplishes, these are the kind of things I wish they knew about. As another example, I visited Saudi Arabia three weeks after September 11. This was the first of three trips I would make there. I was traveling with a close personal friend of my family, Daniel Abraham, the chairman of the Center for Middle East Peace and Economic Cooperation, which had paid for this trip. So I wasn't traveling on taxpayer dollars.

Three weeks after 9/11 it was vitally important that the leaders of that region appreciate that in a time of crisis, all Americans, Democrats as well as Republicans, were united behind our leaders.

Before I leave on a trip I always speak to the relevant people at the State Department to be briefed. I ask what message I might deliver or what issues they would like me to talk about. Basically, how can I be most helpful? That's in addition to my own objectives, whatever they might be. Some of the time I'll deliver the message, other times I won't—but I always ask. Before going on one of these trips, whether it's an official trip as a member of Congress or on a trip paid for by a private not-for-profit institution, I try to meet with the ambassador to the United States from the country I'm going to visit to learn about that other government's perspective and its objectives regarding its bilateral relationship with America. Most of the time that ambassador has already reached a conclusion about me: Am I thoughtful? Is it worthwhile for government officials in that country to spend time meeting with me? Do I play a relevant role in the Congress? Can I be an acceptable messenger? Often, not always, but often, I meet with the ranking officials of countries I visit. And when I get home I communicate with our State Department either in person or by letter, I speak with other government officials, and I report back to my constituents.

Before I visited Saudi Arabia, it was already known that most of the terrorists who attacked us came from Saudi Arabia and that we wanted the Saudis to allow the FBI to come over there and investigate. The Saudi government was very reluctant to allow that.

When you arrive in Riyadh, you're told whether you will be granted a meeting with the king or the crown prince, but not when. They don't give the king's schedule. Usually you sit in your room by the phone waiting to be summoned. The palace gives you forty-five minutes' notice.

Finally I was invited to come to the palace to meet the king. The palace is the most grandiose building imaginable, certainly the most magnificent government building I'd ever been in. It looked as if it had been built many years ago. As I walked through the long corridors I said to my escort, "If you were to build something like this today it would cost hundreds of millions of dollars. When was this built?"

He said, "Nineteen ninety-nine."

At that point King Fahd was still alive, although he'd suffered a severe stroke and was not functioning well. He was sitting on his throne. Out of respect, diplomatic protocol demanded that I meet with him before meeting with other Saudi government officials. There was no conversation, it was simply a courtesy call that lasted no more than ten minutes. Then I was taken to meet Crown Prince Abdullah, who had actually been running Saudi Arabia since his half-brother's stroke in 1995.

The crown prince, who became king in 2005, is a practical, rational, intelligent man. He speaks perfect English. He prides himself on being a man of the people. Once, we talked about the educational system in Saudi Arabia, which he believed needed to be reformed to incorporate a more modern curriculum and better prepare Saudi students for the twenty-first century. In that part of the world such a vision is unusual. But during our meeting I explained the State Department's position about allowing FBI agents to conduct an investigation. Eventually the Saudis did allow that to happen. Who knows if this meeting had anything to do with that?

We also spoke about the degree to which Saudi Arabia was continuing to finance institutions that trained terrorists abroad. I believe the head fund-raiser for the Palestinian terrorist organization Hamas was about to come to Saudi Arabia to raise money. We spoke about that. Abdullah finally prohibited this man from coming to the kingdom to raise money, although one of Abdullah's half-brothers enabled him to do so. Families are very complicated in Saudi Arabia. But because Abdullah was against it, the Hamas agent raised only a small percentage of what he otherwise would have gotten. Is that a victory or a failure?

But perhaps most important, Abraham and I discussed with Abdullah the possibility of direct engagement between Saudi Arabia and Israel. Abdullah, knowing that we were going directly to Israel, outlined a Middle East peace proposal for Abraham and me to present to Prime Minister Sharon.

The one subject on which now King Abdullah and I disagreed completely was Israel. He is a well-read man with an understanding of history—except when it comes to Israel. It's astonishing. When we talked about Israel he was irrational. He began by telling me the story of Israel's beginnings in 1948, when the Israelis invaded the Arab countries.

Incredible, but yes, the king earnestly believes the Israelis affirmatively attacked several Arab countries in 1948.

The fact that the king and I disagreed was not at all unusual. In the parts of the world I visit, there are often times when I'm in complete disagreement with my hosts. The interior minister of Saudi Arabia, for example, in my view was anti-American and anti-Semitic and said some things that were totally outrageous. Proper protocol inhibits me from telling a top government official that he is hysterical and insane, but I certainly do refute the statements as sternly as possible—while trying not to be disrespectful. I never sit anywhere and concur with statements I find repulsive. I don't know how many Jewish people Abdullah might meet in a year. Five? Ten? Certainly not too many. So to the extent he's talking about Israel, I want to give him the best counterpoint.

Admittedly, at times it has been difficult to hold my temper. In Kuwait, for example, I almost got into a fistfight with the chairman of their International Relations Committee. And he isn't even a Republican. Another member of Congress and I were meeting with representatives of their Parliament and the subject of Yasser Arafat came up. Arafat had supported Iraq's invasion of Kuwait in the early 1990s. As a result of that decision, Kuwait had expelled hundreds of thousands of Palestinians who had been working in the country. So as I sat there listening to this Kuwaiti official criticizing Israel and praising Arafat, I questioned him about his support for Arafat—considering what he had done to Kuwait. I asked him, "When was the last time Israel supported an invasion of Kuwait? When did Israel kidnap nine hundred Kuwaiti citizens and you never saw them again?" We got into an argument, we both raised our voices, and it started getting really hot. Other people literally had to separate us. I remember thinking, It's a pretty good sign that a diplomatic meeting isn't going well when you start wondering, Can I take this guy? And then I thought, Well, it probably wouldn't look so bad at home if I took a swing at a Kuwaiti minister. I mean, it could be worse. I was defending the honor of America and Israel and I got into a fistfight. So I would suggest that this is an example of a meeting that did not end well.

But about a year later I was back in Kuwait and we had scheduled another meeting. As soon as I walked into the room he stood up and said, "Don't worry, we're not coming to blows this time." I don't want to say we became friends—that would be an exaggeration—but since then he has always been careful about what he says around me.

Listen, I don't hold back. In Egypt I told President Mubarak, whom I respect, the same thing I told the Saudis. He couldn't have it two ways: If he wanted to be a true partner in the war against terrorism and was committed to peaceful coexistence with Israel, he had to destroy the forces of terror, disassociate from people who wanted to destroy Israel, and work to promote peace.

On these trips I try not to limit my contacts to government officials. I want to find out what regular people are thinking, and often that is very different from the official message I get. Just as I do in my own district, I always learn a lot from cabdrivers. I'll ask what they think about America or George Bush or Iraq, and in some kind of broken English they'll tell me. When I was in Ramallah on the West Bank in 2000, I had a free hour between meetings and thought it was important to learn about public opinion and attitudes held by Palestinians about America. So I went into a small café—a little shop with three men sitting sipping black coffee. I sat at the counter and ordered something small, and then struck up a conversation with the owner behind the counter. The other men joined in. They were friendly and had strong opinions and wanted to express them. Did they know I was a congressman? No. But they knew I was an American and they told me what they wanted Americans to know. I learned more talking to those four men than I could have learned from reading twelve books.

I did the same thing in Tel Aviv during the second intifada. I finished my meetings and I took a little walk. I stopped in a bar and ordered a beer. When I went to pay for it, the bartender wouldn't accept my money. I insisted, but he told me, "We haven't seen an American in here in nine months. I'm just glad to see an American." That made a big impact on me. It told me how isolated the Israelis were feeling at that moment.

As opposed to being junkets, or vacations, these trips are exhausting. I try to cram as many meetings as possible into the shortest time. Often the day begins at eight A.M. local time and lasts late into the

night. And these are intense meetings with intense people. The first trip
I took as a member of Congress was to France, as part of a group led
by the committee chairman, New York Republican Ben Gilman. Ben
was in his mid-seventies at that time, but he kept an exhausting schedule. It was very exciting for me, my first trip. I didn't know exactly
what to expect. We went to the presidential palace to meet with French
president Jacques Chirac. This was the first time I'd been exposed to a
world leader in this kind of setting. Ben was sitting right next to Chirac
on a small sofa—and as Chirac spoke to us, Ben just fell asleep. I mean
he was out cold. And he started snoring.

Chirac ignored him completely and just kept talking. And I realized
that Chirac had probably been on enough of these trips to know how
tough they are. We all have to deal with jet lag and plain exhaustion,
and over time each person develops his or her own strategies. Eliot Engel remembers how he dealt with that problem during a trip to the capital of North Korea, Pyongyang:

> Every meeting we had with high-ranking North Korean govern-
> ment officials would begin with a lecture from them about Bush
> and America and why we didn't have good relations with them.
> They would just drone on and on, talk and talk, and we were on
> the other side of the world and we were jet-lagged and it was hot
> and I found myself sitting there listening to these people and falling
> asleep. I kept thinking, "Stay awake, stay awake, stay awake," and
> trying to concentrate. I realized that in order to stay awake I had to
> do something, so I took off my shoes. I was wearing black loafers
> so I could slide in and out of them. I would take off one shoe, then
> the other, and then put them back on. It was working well. I was
> able to stay awake.
>
> I was sitting next to Texas Democrat Silvestre Reyes, who no-
> ticed what I was doing. I kicked off my shoes for probably the fifth
> time and then I went to put them back on—and they were gone. I
> started feeling around with my feet but they weren't there. I didn't
> dare look down, I didn't want to risk creating an incident, so I was
> trying to figure out what to do.
>
> I sort of looked over to the side and there were my shoes—
> where he'd kicked them. I wanted to laugh, but I couldn't. And
> eventually he pushed them back in my direction. The whole thing
> had taken maybe ten minutes, but it had kept me awake.

Some people think congressional travel is full of perks. I admit there are some, but they can also backfire. To assist government officials in foreign countries, there are often official passport lines and separate waiting facilities. Once when I was coming home from Turkey, for security reasons I was escorted around the regular line in the waiting room and boarded the plane separately. An American woman in the waiting room was apparently sizing up everyone, making sure they went through Turkish security. And when she got on the plane she saw me for the first time—and knew I hadn't gone through the normal security procedures. As far as she was concerned, this was a security breach, and something terrible could happen. I happened to be sitting right in front of her. She complained to the flight attendants, who tried to reassure her.

My son was soon to have his bar mitzvah, so when I sat down I opened the section of the Torah I was to read to practice for my son's service. Seeing me reading a prayer book in some strange language, this woman decided it had to be a Koran and really got upset.

That was it for her: She screamed for the flight attendants and told them that I was reciting the prayer Muslims say before doing terrible things. She was terribly upset, shouting at them that they were allowing this to happen. Finally I turned around and introduced myself. Her name was Betty. She wanted to know precisely how I got on the plane without going through security. She knew I hadn't gone through security, she told me, because she'd watched very carefully.

I explained that I was a congressman traveling on a diplomatic passport. I gave her all the details. And when I finished, her husband looked at her, shook his head in disbelief, and told her, "Way to go, Betty!"

When I told the story to my wife, Laurie, her response was right to the point. That wouldn't have happened if I had gone through security like everybody else!

11

Taking Care of Your People

All politics is local.

—Tip O'Neill

One of Queens Democrat Gary Ackerman's constituents had a serious problem. Apparently he was dead and didn't know it. After having surgery, this man was told he needed additional surgery. But when he applied to Medicaid to get a clearance for this second operation, he received a letter explaining that he couldn't have the operation because he was already dead.

This man did not have a great sense of humor and was quite upset about being dead. He tried to explain to a Medicaid representative that he wasn't dead, but they refused to take his word for it. So he called his congressman's office. As Gary Ackerman explains it:

> This man was getting desperate. He needed the surgery, and these people refused to take his word for the fact that he was alive. The caseworker in my office went over to see him and assured him

that we would help him get the approval he needed. So we wrote a letter to the proper office and they wrote back, and we wrote back and they wrote back, continuing to insist that this man was dead. The letters were beginning to get a little tougher. "Let me assure you, Congressman," they wrote, "a qualified member of our trained staff has carefully reviewed this file and concluded Mr.—— is dead. Thank you for your interest . . ."

I wrote back that a completely unqualified, untrained member of my staff had visited Mr. ——. In addition, I'd spoken to him on the phone. "I don't know anything about your business," I wrote, "but I can assure you that he has confirmed to me personally that he is not dead."

Then they started getting nasty. "He's dead. Our records prove it."

Finally I called a radio station and went on the air to talk about this. I wondered, "If Mr. —— is dead, why do they keep writing him letters?"

As we finally discovered, when he was discharged from the hospital after his first operation, a hospital clerk had abbreviated "date of discharge" on the form as DoD. A clerk at Medicaid interpreted that to mean "date of death." Somebody had checked off the wrong box, legally killing this man. But we finally managed to get it straightened out for him and get him his approval.

I'd have to be living in George W. Bush's universe not to know that a majority of Americans believe Congress is doing a poor job.

Believe me, I understand the reasons that Congress is rated so poorly. I hear the criticism every day. I've read the stories about individual corruption, about the use of your tax dollars to build bridges that go nowhere and conduct research into cow flatulence, about lobbyists who buy legislation for clients. And I know that Americans tend to judge Congress on the basis of the major legislation that it passes, and on those big issues, for six years, the Republicans simply rubber-stamped the unpopular Bush agenda. It's going to take the Democrats a while to unravel the Republican knots that have tied up Congress so severely. Being a critic of Congress is easy, and it's as American as booing the umpire.

But there is another area in which members of the House have been very active, and to me, at least, it's every bit as important as passing major legislation—in specific cases, much more important. And that's looking out for the little guy. The primary job of a member of Congress is to serve his constituents. My district office in Florida is the one place that my constituents can walk in off the street, talk to government representatives about their problems, and actually get some results. In the House I'm one of 435 members, and my vote generally isn't going to make the difference between a bill's passage and failure; in my district I'm the only one, and my work can make all the difference in the world.

New York's former Republican senator Al D'Amato survived three terms despite that state's overwhelming Democratic majority because of his exceptional constituent service. His ability to get problems solved for constituents earned him the nickname "Senator Pothole." If a member wants to be reelected, almost nothing is more important than constituent services. Many of the problems my office deals with on a daily basis may not seem glamorous to the media, but they are vitally important to the people whose lives they affect. Certainly people cast their votes based on the big issues—how I voted on the war in Iraq, abortion, or the tax cut—but they also vote based on whether I was able to stop the postal service from building a depot in the neighborhood, cut through the bureaucracy at the VA to make sure a vet got the necessary care, or get the new interchange built that cut their commuting time by twenty-five minutes a day. They vote based on what their congressman did to help them when they needed help.

My constituent Irv Rosenfeld, for example, is one of only a handful of people in America still receiving medical marijuana by prescription from the federal government. He has a rare bone disease that results in tumors forming at the ends of his longer bones, a painful condition alleviated by marijuana. There has been a tremendous amount of controversy about using marijuana as a pain reliever, and there are government experts who will insist it does no good—except that it enables stockbroker Irv Rosenfeld to go to work every day and lead a productive life—without hurting anyone else. He began receiving marijuana from the government in 1978, and when the program was canceled during the Reagan administration in 1982, he was grandfathered, legally permitted to continue using it. Apparently it is grown on a government-owned farm in Mississippi. I was not Irv Rosenfeld's representative when he was originally enrolled in the program, but he knows that my office is there to help him resolve any problems, and he comes up to Washington on occasion to testify at hearings about legalizing marijuana strictly for medical purposes.

Constituent services are the issues that affect people's lives on a daily basis. This is the nuts and bolts of the job. And this is where a member of Congress is almost completely dependent on his staff. Many of the things done in my name by my staff I won't even know about; this is the normal type of service we try to deliver every day. But my staff better get it right, because I'll get the credit for it when things go right—as well as the blame if they don't. That's fine, that's the way it's supposed to work. I'm fortunate to have a truly professional and genuinely caring staff to handle these situations.

In addition to an office in the Capitol, every member of Congress has at least one and often two or more satellite offices in their district. I have two offices in my district, staffed by seven paid employees and several interns. These are the people who answer the telephones every day and work with constituents to solve their problems. My district director, Wendi Lipsich, is problem solver in chief. She knows my district as well—and sometimes better—than I do. Probably the majority of phone calls received by my office every day come from senior citizens seeking assistance. Often these calls come from people who are struggling. They haven't received their monthly Social Security payment, they're having difficulty being reimbursed by an insurance company, they need to be placed in an appropriate assisted living facility, or their mail isn't being delivered. There are more than 150 different federal agencies delivering services to individuals, ranging from benefits available to former miners suffering from black lung disease, to loans to start a small business. A primary function of the district office is to make sure constituents know what assistance is available and then help them navigate through the bureaucratic maze. As Wendi explains it, "What we try to do is direct people to those places where they might be able to get some help right away. For example, there are a few places that will help pay part of their electricity bill and telephone or provide food, but there isn't very much. Sometimes they are confused about their rights under the prescription drug plan, for example, and we'll be able to help them with that."

These are the everyday issues. But we'll also get calls from constituents with very special problems. One of my constituents desperately needed a kidney, and a caseworker in the office contacted various hospitals and donor lists and was actually able to get this woman a kidney. Once, for example, there was an issue with a silverback gorilla who needed a good home and we were able to help arrange a transfer to a well-regarded zoo.

Certainly we get a lot of requests that we can't fulfill. While we can, and will, arrange a tour of the Capitol and help a constituent get a passport, a visa, or a flag that has flown over the Capitol, we can't arrange tickets to Oprah or, as one represersive was asked during the Clinton administration, arrange for Hillary Clinton to read a story to a constituent's six-year-old child.

Constituent service is the one place where representatives really do get involved in family matters. Unfortunately, we're not always successful. A couple in my district had applied to adopt the twin half-sisters of a Romanian child they had adopted eight years earlier. After these people had visited the twins and suffered through a multiyear legal effort in Romanian courts, the Romanian government issued a moratorium on foreign adoptions and refused to allow the couple to bring the twins to America and reunite the sisters. The couple came to me because I was their congressman, and as a member of the Foreign Affairs Committee and the Europe Subcommittee, I already had some knowledge about the adoption situation in Romania.

It truly was heartbreaking. You can spend your career in the House debating billion-dollar legislation and the Iraq War and a prescription drug benefit and numerous important issues, but when you sit with a couple who want to take young children out of a sterile and cold orphanage in Romania and give them a warm, vibrant, loving home, it's almost impossible not to become personally involved. This was one of those instances when I had a hands-on opportunity to change lives. And it wasn't just this couple. More than a thousand American and Western

European families had obtained legal adoption orders for Romanian children before the moratorium went into effect. All of those beautiful children were helpless and in limbo.

I tried. I met with the Romanian ambassador to the United States to discuss the case. Eventually I joined New Jersey Republican Chris Smith and issued a resolution urging the Romanian government to allow those families who had properly filed paperwork prior to the ban to complete the adoption process. The State Department also issued an official request. Finally, during the 2006 December recess I flew to Bucharest and met with both President Traian Băsescu and Prime Minister Călin Popescu Tăriceanu to discuss the adoptions and other bilateral issues. I sat with them and explained the benefits to the children as well as to the relationship between our countries. It's a very complicated issue, both men explained. The prime minister explained that the Romanians were simply trying to adhere to the requirements of the European Union, which Romania hoped to join. Basically, no child would be permitted to be adopted by foreign families if they could find an adoptive home in Romania.

I was completely frustrated. I later traveled to Brussels to meet with adoption officials of the European Union, then worked with members of the European Parliament to help facilitate passage of a resolution encouraging the Romanian government to go forward with the adoptions. I wrote numerous letters and we made many phone calls. I even enlisted the assistance of a variety of European officials, including prime ministers, ambassadors, and heads of national parliaments.

And in this case, I failed. The intransigence of the Romanian government has prevented any of these adoptions from going forward.

American children are taught that this is a country in which one person can make a difference, that each individual has power. That's the American way. We're taught that, but the reality can be a bit more complex. One way an individual can make a meaningful impact is through his or her member of Congress. For example, my office received a letter in 1998 from a constituent named Lewis Myers of West Boca Raton asking that I try to help thirteen Iranian Jews who had been arrested in Tehran on the eve of Passover and charged with spying for Israel. That is a grave and ominous charge. Within the previous two decades the Iranians had executed seventeen Jewish people for espionage. "If enough Jews raise their voices," Lewis Myers wrote, "anything can happen."

I knew very little about the situation before I received this letter. But once I started looking into it I was more shocked than angry. And I decided to try to do something about it. Among the few real powers an individual member has is the ability to bring attention to a problem or situation. As I explained to a reporter while trying to get as much publicity for this issue as possible, "The most important thing that we can do for Iranian Jews that are being held captive is that they not become forgotten. Because if they are forgotten, they're as good as dead."

I sent a Dear Colleague letter to those members I believed would be sympathetic, urging Secretary of State Albright "to condemn in the strongest terms the recent actions of the Islamic Republic of Iran." Fifty-three members signed on to the letter, enough to provide some ammunition for Secretary Albright. Eventually some of our European allies and human rights organizations also focused the spotlight of public scrutiny on Iran, making it difficult for that country to conduct its business secretly. I'm not claiming that my letter initiated the entire process, that's doubtful, but it certainly drew substantial attention to this travesty. I followed up through discussions with high-ranking German and French diplomats to gain their assistance, as well as with leaders of the American Jewish community. Dozens of prominent people and organizations became engaged.

In 2000 the Iranians staged a show trial, convicted ten of the thirteen men, and gave them prison sentences ranging from four to thirteen years. Eventually an Iranian appeals court overturned most of the verdicts and reduced all the sentences by a third to a half. Gradually, because world attention was focused on Iranian treatment of its Jewish citizens, the remaining imprisoned Jews were released. No one will ever know for certain, but I do believe that without Lewis Myers's letter, the outcome could have been very different.

These aren't just bread-and-butter issues. In my district they're more often matzo issues. Eighty-four-year-old Abe Asofsky was another man who wasn't going to take it anymore, which began the great matzo investigation. My office received a letter from Abe just before Passover in 1997 wondering why the same twelve-pound box of matzo cost $12.95 in South Florida but only $4.95 in Manhattan. It seemed like a fair question to me, so we conducted a preliminary investigation with supermarkets, food suppliers, and distributors and concluded that there appeared to be some unusual financial arrangements in our region regarding the distribution of matzo. As a result, we contacted the state attorney general's office and asked him to investigate the possibility of price gouging. It may not seem like a very important issue, but when you're living on a fixed income and need to buy several boxes of matzos for Passover and the stores have raised the prices again, it's a big deal. The attorney general's office eventually investigated nine supermarket chains for price fixing—but did not find enough evidence to support the charges.

So one person can indeed make a difference. But in addition to serving as a voice for individuals, members of Congress must also act as a voice for all the neighborhoods in their district, especially on quality-of-life issues. Again, these are the things that matter in people's lives—and the issues that people remember when they go to the polls.

While the obvious objective of performing constituent services is to get things done for people who need them done, it's not a substitute for actually meeting with the voters. My office receives countless letters and telephone calls and e-mails in which people express their opinions, but there really is no better way of finding out how people feel about various issues—and about the job I'm doing—than listening to them. The voters in my district watch the news and diligently read the newspapers. They know what's going on. They also know that most of my time is spent in Washington—they sent me there to make certain their interests are represented. But they also want to see me. They want me to stand in front of them, sometimes to explain or defend a vote, most often just to answer questions. I like doing these town-hall-style meetings because I get important feedback.

I do as many of them as possible. In one day, for example, I may appear at all three Century Village condominium complexes in my district. At many of these meetings there'll be as many as four hundred people, and the local media will be there and help me get out my message. Like most politicians I have one rule about the places I'll speak—anyplace that will have me. Synagogues, high schools, elementary schools, political clubs, condos, Rotary Clubs, Hadassah, golf clubs, Chamber of Commerce meetings, Planned Parenthood meetings, grand openings of libraries or parks, two people standing on a corner. When I was first elected to the state senate, for example, my district included both urban and agricultural areas. Most of the agricultural leaders had supported my opponent. With the exception of running over a dog, I hadn't made much of an impression in these areas, so I had few strong relationships in about a third of the district. Maybe I knew a dozen people well. And in a totally gracious gesture, the leaders of Clewiston, Florida, invited me to come out for a welcoming picnic. It was a kind of "Meet the New State Senator" barbecue.

I was a bit late getting there—I could never figure out how long it took me to get out to the Glades region. It was just a completely different world from suburban Palm Beach County. It was a friendly, welcoming world, but different from what I had experienced. At that time I wasn't fully observing Jewish dietary laws, but I didn't eat pork. As I drove up to this picnic, the first thing I saw was the biggest pig, hog, whatever you call it, I'd ever seen, rotating over a fire on a huge stick with a pineapple stuck in its mouth.

I found someone I presumed to be in charge of this event and whispered, "Look, that pig is lovely, but I'm really sorry, I can't eat that." And just as I finished explaining that, someone else announced, "Let's all give a nice welcome to our new state senator, Robert Wexler, and invite him to come on up here and have the first bite. Come on up here, Robert."

I was new at the business of being a politician. I didn't know how to handle this situation. "Listen," I said quietly. "Thank you so, so much for having me here. The community is being so gracious and I'm delighted to cut it, but I don't eat pork." Everybody got silent. They mistakenly thought they had offended me, and I was feeling bad because they felt uncomfortable. "No, honestly, it's fine," I repeated. "Just give me a piece of that corn on the cob and I'm as happy as I can be. In fact, give me two pieces."

12

Anthrax and Hurricanes:
When Disaster Hits Home

The buck stops here.

—Harry Truman

The time when any elected representative earns his salary is during a crisis. When lives are at stake, when property is destroyed, when power and telephone lines are down, when streets are blocked, people expect their government to provide assistance. This is when you must prove to voters that they made the right choice in voting for you. The legendary example of this was a February 1969 storm that dumped fifteen inches of snow on New York City. The inability of the then popular mayor John Lindsey to get the streets of Queens cleared for weeks afterward essentially ended his political career.

Long before Katrina exposed forever the ineptitude of the Bush administration, politicians found themselves racing to local areas damaged by man-made or natural causes. When your constituents are suffering, it's your job to be there to help in any way you can. Two months after

Hurricane Katrina had devastated the Gulf Coast, Florida was hit by Hurricane Wilma. People were already enraged about the government's lack of preparation and disastrous response to Katrina, so the media was watching carefully to see how we responded to this hurricane.

Before the hurricane made landfall, the entire Florida congressional delegation met in Washington to lay out contingency plans. This was as nonpartisan as politics will ever get. A year earlier Florida had been hit by three hurricanes, so we had considerable experience to draw upon. At that meeting we laid out a basic response plan.

The first thing I did after Wilma had swept through South Florida was contact as many of the community leaders as possible to determine the amount of damage in their areas and find out exactly what they needed. Then my office contacted the organizations that provided social services to find out what they needed. I spoke to many people I'd known for years. These are survivors, these are people who had lived through the Depression and the Holocaust and World War II. It was truly amazing: Many of them admitted that this was a difficult situation and would cost them a lot of money, but almost without exception they said they would manage. But I also spoke to elderly people who told me they were all alone and scared, they had no electricity, their medicine had been ruined, and they needed assistance. As much as possible we coordinated with local officials. My friend County Commissioner Burt Aaronson was terrific; he was sort of the local quarterback in terms of getting supplies to people who needed them. My responsibility was to manage all the issues that needed to be dealt with at the federal level. What was needed most, we discovered, were tarps. Thousands of people had lost some or all of their roofs and needed some means of protecting their homes. And they needed it immediately.

The House was in session when Wilma hit, so I was in Washington. At six A.M. the morning after the hurricane, I flew as far south as I could go. Getting there mattered. The South Florida airports were closed, so I landed in Orlando. I rented a car and started driving south, having no idea what I might encounter on the turnpike. There was a great deal of traffic going north, but the road south was relatively clear. It took me about four hours to get to my district. I drove past the condominiums, through neighborhoods, through towns. It was just terrible. Homes and buildings had been destroyed or badly damaged, roofs had collapsed, landscaping was completely wiped out, huge metal utility poles were bent over and cracked, power lines were down, low-lying areas were flooded. It was impossible to estimate how many people had lost their homes, but it was obvious that several retirement communities had been hit hard. Tens of thousands of people had lost their electricity. I'd lived in this area for almost forty years and I'd never seen anything like it.

The storm had hit Florida on a Monday. Almost all other business in my office stopped as we focused all our resources on getting help to South Florida. I got there Tuesday morning. Wednesday night I returned to Washington and Thursday morning flew back to Florida on Air Force One with President Bush. I have to admit that the president was actively engaged on the flight down, inquiring about the conditions and the needs of the community. He even asked me about my family. "My mother did not have power," I told him.

That afternoon all the local and national officials met at the Hurricane Center in Miami. Governor Jeb Bush, who ran the meeting, was well prepared and meticulous in his presentations. Eventually he went around the room asking each of us what we needed. I said, "The only thing you don't seem to have are tarps for people to cover their roofs."

"You're right," Governor Bush said. "What are your estimates of what we need?"

I had spoken with several local officials and conveyed our consensus: "We need at least twenty-five thousand tarps," I said.

President Bush was sitting next to FEMA director R. David Paulison. When I said that, it was like a lightbulb went off in the president's head. He turned to Paulison and asked, "Where are the tarps?"

The FEMA director's response clearly was not what the president wanted to hear. It was obvious the president understood this problem: If somebody is missing a roof, he needs a tarp. Pointing to me, he said, "The man needs his tarps. We got to find twenty-five thousand tarps."

Paulison tried to explain to George Bush why those tarps were not readily available, but the president didn't want excuses. It was a heated exchange. In contrast to Katrina, President Bush was determined that the government's response to this storm would be rapid and successful. Two days later, twenty-five thousand tarps were delivered to the South Florida Fairgrounds. Score one for the president. In fact, my mother's condominium was among the earliest to have its power restored. So score two for the president.

The following morning I was at the South County Civic Center helping volunteers hand out buckets of ice and fresh water to people who'd lost their electricity. This was the visible part, reassuring people that their representatives were doing everything possible to get them the help they needed—even little things like buckets of ice. The line of cars waiting for ice and water was probably three miles long, and included several luxury cars. These were very affluent people and they were willing to wait in line for hours for a bucket of ice. As I walked down the line I saw someone I knew vaguely, sitting in his Rolls-Royce. I was surprised. I couldn't believe that he needed the supplies we were handing out. I was curious. "What are you doing here?" I asked. "This is for people who really need it. Not you."

He looked at me and admitted shyly, "My wife wanted me out of the house. I've got nowhere else to go." That was the first laugh I'd had in at least four days.

It hadn't occurred to me that gas stations that lost their electricity couldn't pump gas. It's obvious when you think about it, but no one had thought about it—until we were in the middle of a gasoline shortage. There wasn't much we could do to solve that immediate problem, but we wanted our constituents to know we were as upset as they were. Miami Republican Mario Diaz-Balart and I wrote a stinging letter to the CEOs of all the major oil companies, telling them, "We find it inexcusable and irresponsible that gas stations in South Florida were not equipped with electric generators to deal with power outages. The failure to adequately prepare for such an emergency . . . indicates a serious disregard for corporate responsibility . . ."

Our objective was to make certain that the oil companies would be prepared to provide an absolutely essential service the next time a hurricane hit. And as a result of the efforts of many people, gas stations in Florida are now equipped to pump gas even during power outages.

Sometimes there are only a limited number of things you can accomplish. You can only push and pull and beg and threaten and cajole so much. After the initial problems caused by the storm had been solved, the roads had been cleared, the water had receded, and the electricity was back on, we started to deal with longer-term problems. For example, more than sixty-two thousand housing units were damaged in Palm Beach County alone, but before residents could receive federal assistance, the property had to be inspected by one of only three hundred FEMA inspectors. That meant that some people would be waiting months before they could begin repairing their homes. So I proposed that FEMA permit local inspectors to assist with the work. And naturally, in typical bureaucratic fashion, maybe because it made so much sense, they refused to consider this proposal.

I also worked with then state senator and later congressman Ron Klein and Commissioner Aaronson to push FEMA to provide trailers for people who had lost their homes. We asked for sixty-four hundred trailers—and in response they offered us a hundred. We put as much pressure on FEMA as possible. And let our constituents know we were working on it. "Working on it" really was the key phrase. The result wasn't perfect. People suffered great loss, lives were changed and disrupted, but we made tangible improvements to make the situation more tolerable. Perhaps we weren't able to provide as much assistance as we would have liked, but at least we alleviated that dreadful feeling of being in a terrible situation all alone.

I wasn't a Robert-come-lately to this battle with FEMA. My constituents knew I'd been a critic of this organization and its management long before Katrina made FEMA and its then director Michael "Heck of a Job" Brown infamous. Long before FEMA's incompetence led to such heartbreak, I had publicly called on President Bush to fire Michael Brown for his ineptitude. That was clearly a harbinger of what was to come.

This is the incredible story of the ten-million-dollar bed. In early September 2004, Hurricane Frances swept through Florida—and caused very little damage. Its highest sustained winds were only 63 miles per hour; it was really a heavy rainstorm. But it hit Florida only weeks before the presidential election. A memo from a consultant to FEMA warned that anything less than a rapid response could hurt Bush and other Republicans in the election. So FEMA began handing out money to just about anybody who asked for it. The *South Florida Sun-Sentinel* discovered that FEMA paid for new wardrobes, cars, lawn mowers, and even three funerals without requiring sufficient evidence of actual loss—or death. According to a report, FEMA distributed ten million dollars to replace household items, even though the only item specifically reported damaged was a bed. The total alleged fraud was more than thirty million dollars. Several months later, at a hearing, Maine Republican senator Susan Collins pointed out that Brown "had approved massive payments to replace thousands of televisions, air conditioners, beds, and other furniture, as well as a number of cars, without receipts, or proof of ownership or damage, and based solely on verbal statements by the residents, sometimes made in fleeting encounters at fast-food restaurants."

Your tax dollars at work. It was a disgrace. As I wrote to the president eight months *before* Hurricane Katrina, suggesting that he fire Brown, "I am sure you agree that such a gross waste of taxpayer monies cannot be taken lightly."

Apparently he didn't agree with me. A White House spokesman responded, "The president has full faith in the outstanding job that Under Secretary Mike Brown and FEMA are doing in providing assistance to hurricane victims." And, apparently, buying goodwill for the election.

Eventually about twenty Miami-Dade residents were indicted for making fraudulent claims. Brown later boasted that FEMA's work in Florida was "one of our best response efforts." And as a result, he remained in charge of FEMA when Katrina devastated the Gulf Coast.

Certainly our ability to respond to a completely unexpected tragedy in my district was tested in the weeks following 9/11. I had been in

Washington the morning of the attack, getting ready to drive my mother to the airport for a flight back to Florida, when Jonathan Katz, my staff legislative director, responsible for foreign affairs, called within seconds of the first plane hitting the World Trade Center. "It's got to be al-Qaeda," he said, making an educated guess.

That didn't surprise either of us. Because of my concentration on the Middle East, we'd been keeping track of several terrorist organizations. In fact, more than a year earlier, during a Foreign Affairs Committee hearing on global terrorism, I'd warned, "We must be particularly concerned about increased terrorist activities originating from South Asia, particularly Afghanistan and Pakistan . . . Over the past several years, Afghanistan has become the training ground and base of operations for terrorists all over the world. According to the annual State Department Report on Terrorism, the Taliban . . . has given permission to and provided logistical support for non-Afghan terrorist organizations . . ."

So we knew about al-Qaeda—because the State Department and others had been warning us about them. But in those hectic first days of the fight against terrorism, one thing I did not expect was that my district would become directly involved in this national crisis. Within days it was revealed that nine of the hijackers had lived in Delray Beach—they had lived in my district. "Nothing in this operation was by chance," I told reporters. "So why did they choose to live in South Florida? Why did they choose to train in South Florida?" And what I didn't say, but wondered, Were there more people like them still in the area? Were there people living there who had provided the hijackers with logistical support, with a place to live, with anything at all? My constituents were scared—and justifiably so. My job was to determine what particular risk, if any, existed as a result of the hijackers' proximity to my district.

My objective was to provide as much information to my constituents about this as quickly as possible, hopefully to allay some of their fears. I contacted the FBI and other divisions within the Justice Department, and it became apparent that the primary reason the hijackers had located in South Florida was to attend one of the many flight schools there serving primarily foreigners.

While that investigation was still progressing, what was originally believed to be the second terrorist attack on America took place, when letters containing deadly anthrax spores were mailed to media outlets and Democratic politicians. And once again, tragically, my district was a focus. One of the recipients was American Media, Inc., publisher of the *National Enquirer,* whose office was in the heart of my district, in Boca Raton. Terrorism had come to South Florida and it proved deadly. An employee of American Media, photo editor Bob Stevens, opened an envelope containing anthrax and died a few days later. Four other people outside of Florida, including two postal employees, were also killed.

The AMI building was evacuated immediately. When cleanup crews finally went back in a year later, half-eaten sandwiches still lay on work tables. CEO David Pecker had walked out leaving his glasses and his car keys on his desk. Once again in this situation, my job was to be the conduit between my district and the federal government. I had to provide as much information as possible to my district and make sure that the federal government provided assistance and activated relief efforts both in the public safety and health arenas. This wasn't a local matter; it wasn't something the Boca Raton police department could handle. This was national security, and only a few agencies had developed the expertise to deal with anthrax.

I had been aware the *Enquirer* was printed in my district, but not precisely where. It turned out the American Media building was less than two miles from my district office. We had to avoid a sense of panic breaking out in the community. People who suspected they might have had contact with anthrax, or were just plain worried, desperately wanted to get Cipro, the only effective treatment for anthrax exposure. The EPA and the Palm Beach County Health Department were in charge, and I was in constant contact with the head of the local agency, Dr. Jean Marie Malecki, to find out what we could do to help. As is the case so often in these types of emergencies, the public health professionals are the unsung heroes as they calmly go about saving lives in the midst of near pandemonium.

We took all the obvious steps, essentially making certain that supplies were available and, maybe more important, doing our best to reassure everyone that as much as could be done to ensure public safety was being done.

It did occur to me that because of my strong support for Israel, and the fact that nine of the terrorists had lived in the district, my district office might well be a target. I didn't want to be paranoid, but I also did not want to be complacent and fail to take reasonable precautions. And almost immediately a Boca Raton postal worker discovered an envelope coated with powder in the second floor mailroom of the commercial building in which my district office is located. The building was evacuated immediately and stayed shut for two days until tests proved that the material covering the envelope was completely harmless.

But that was enough to shake up the whole staff. We'd had numerous death threats and bizarre communications through the years, and my staff had been amazingly steady, but this was different. This was more than a threatening letter or a crazed voice yelling on a telephone. This was real and potentially deadly. With the assistance of the FBI we immediately instituted some strong security measures, particularly regarding the way all mail should be opened. Wendi Lipsich took personal responsibility for opening all of it. She had to lock herself in a contained area, actually a small room, wearing gloves and a face mask that covered her mouth and nose. The first thing she did was inspect the envelope; she was warned not to open any envelopes without a return address or that had an unusual amount of postage or in any way looked suspicious. And when she opened the mail, a coworker had to be in a room next door, instantly reachable by intercom in case anything happened. Wendi is married and the mother of two adorable young children. The fact that she had to endure such an ordeal is infuriating. The fact that so many years after 9/11 Osama bin Laden is still on the loose is even more infuriating.

Those procedures were followed for quite some time, and certain security measures are still in effect, but like everyone else in the country, eventually we got back to as close to normal as possible. Not normal, just as close as we could with the new security in place.

I was involved in the anthrax episode in a hundred small ways, from helping determine the fate of the building—it was left standing and the federal government paid to have it decontaminated—to taking steps to make sure we had supplies on hand in case there was another attack. We worried constantly about that building being hit by a hurricane before it was cleaned. And thank God that never happened.

13

He Betrayed His Wife, Not the Country: The Impeachment of Bill Clinton

Politics is civil war carried on by other means.

—Alisdair C. MacIntyre

The only thing predictable about politics is that nothing is predictable. When I first decided to run for elective office I had no idea where it would take me. No politician does. But one place I never could have imagined being was in the back of my clothes closet, late at night, talking on the telephone to the president of the United States.

David Bonior warned me about requesting a seat on the Judiciary Committee. Many of the hottest issues that have so bitterly divided this country are the province of Judiciary—and they divide the committee in much the same way. I don't know how it was throughout history, but we've come to define politicians based on their positions on a few key issues: Liberal Democrats believe this about abortion, gun control, the death penalty, and individual privacy. Conservative Republicans believe that about school prayer, affirmative action, the Patriot Act, and voting rights. These are all the issues that cause the most passionate arguments, the issues that most of the shouting is about on the Sunday morning talk shows. These issues can be dangerous to careers because people will vote based on a candidate's stand on these few key issues. Few candidates ever lose an election because a road didn't get built or a grant didn't get renewed or taxes weren't cut enough, but constituents will punish an incumbent for voting against their core beliefs. That's why many representatives and senators avoid the Judiciary Committee.

For me, for a liberal, it was the center of the action. It's the place where decisions are made that move the country. To me, at least, nothing symbolized the magnitude of the change that took place in this country after the 2006 election more than watching John Conyers (D-MI) replace James Sensenbrenner (R-WI) as chairman of the House Judiciary Committee. Conyers was the first African-American chairman of the committee. His life experience was completely different from that of the affluent man he replaced. I remember thinking as I watched Conyers move over one seat and pick up the chairman's gavel what a huge distance he'd just traveled. Finally somebody was going to be watching out for the people who need it most.

Believe me, recent American history would have been very different if Conyers had wielded the gavel earlier. One thing I know for certain, the country wouldn't have suffered through the disturbing political witch hunt known as the Clinton impeachment.

Most members of Congress maintain a low profile during their first term. It's not quite an initiation period, but you learn to let the more experienced people stand in front. The impeachment battle took place during my first term, and it put me in a position I had never anticipated or sought. Anticipated? I remember trying to keep a straight face when David Bonior warned me that the Republicans would try to impeach President Clinton. I thought he was crazy. That wouldn't bother me, I told him, but I really didn't take the possibility seriously. Impeachment was constitutionally limited to "treason, bribery, or other high crimes and misdemeanors." It had to do with affairs of state and serious crimes. Impeachment was never intended to be used as punishment for private actions that had no bearing on the official duties of that office.

What I didn't know at that time, what I couldn't possibly have appreciated, was the depth of the hatred the right wing had for Bill Clinton. A lot of people have wondered where that came from; politically, President Clinton was much more of a moderate than a liberal. But he was the first president who had come of age during the Vietnam War, and he had been active in the antiwar movement; that certainly might have had something to do with it. He'd beaten the Republican incumbent, George H. W. Bush, who was seen as carrying forward the Ronald Reagan legacy. That certainly engendered some anger. And his wife, Hillary, was a strong, independent woman; there had never been a First Lady like her—she actually had her own career! Certainly many conservatives despised her, too.

But most likely they hated Bill Clinton because they just couldn't beat him. He'd finally found the formula to break the Republican lock on the White House. So how could they get even? They would cheat and break rules and throw the country into disarray because they couldn't win on Election Day.

For all these reasons, the Republicans began going after Clinton his first day in office and never stopped. In his first term they conducted thirty-seven different investigations meant to destroy him politically. They investigated everything from the fact that he replaced the staff of the White House travel office with his own political appointees to the Whitewater land deal on which he had actually lost money. Many of these investigations were conducted by the Judiciary Committee, and there wasn't much the Democratic minority could do to stop them. But not a single one of these investigations resulted in the slightest evidence of wrongdoing. So after spending millions of taxpayer dollars, after spreading all kinds of despicable stories, the Republicans were incredibly frustrated; they just couldn't get the guy.

The one important thing these investigations did accomplish was to encourage support for Republican fund-raising efforts. In politics, passion translates into money. By continually promising Republican donors that they would eventually get rid of this "immoral" man—and his terrible wife—the Republicans were able to motivate their base as well as build a substantial war chest.

To satisfy conservative demands for an investigation into the supposedly illegal land deal, in August 1994 a three-judge panel appointed a special prosecutor, Kenneth Starr. Starr had been handpicked to replace Robert Fiske, who was not zealous enough in pursuing Clinton—prompting five former presidents of the American Bar Association to write a letter complaining that "political considerations" had influenced Starr's selection. They were absolutely right: Starr spent tens of millions of dollars and uncovered exactly nothing. It was clear to every sane person that the Whitewater investigation was nothing more than a partisan attack masquerading as an investigation. Starr was desperately trying to come up with anything that could cause trouble for Clinton. In addition to the land deal, Starr spent three years and millions more dollars investigating preposterous claims that President Clinton and Hillary had somehow been involved in the death of their friend and White House aide Vince Foster, who had committed suicide.

Conservative dreams came true when a woman named Paula Jones, who had worked for Clinton when he was governor of Arkansas, sued him for sexual harassment. There had been rumors floating around for a long time about Clinton's sexual infidelity, even a supposed rape. It appeared that Paula Jones's lawsuit was being indirectly supported by wealthy right-wing publisher Richard Mellon Scaife for cynical political reasons, but that didn't matter. It gave the Republicans another issue on which to attack Clinton, and they exploited it. The Republican-dominated Supreme Court decided that the president had to respond to a civil lawsuit while he was in office, explaining that no one is above the law. The fact that he was busy being president of the United States, and this civil lawsuit probably could wait until he had concluded his term, apparently didn't occur to the Court.

Let me remind you what this was all about: During the Paula Jones investigation, her lawyers supposedly suggested that Starr look into rumors that a White House intern named Monica Lewinsky was having an affair with Clinton. Clinton denied it and Monica Lewinsky denied it, but an older friend of Lewinsky's had secretly been taping her conversations with the intern, which certainly made it sound as if there was some kind of relationship. Attorney General Janet Reno permitted

Starr to expand his investigation to include this aspect of Clinton's conduct. I have great respect for Janet Reno and think she was a superb public servant; however, this proved to be a gargantuan mistake.

While being deposed under oath in the Jones sexual harassment lawsuit in January 1998, Clinton swore that he had not had sexual relations with Lewinsky as defined by the statute the court was applying. What had been an investigation into a land deal now focused on Clinton's sexual behavior. The general public hadn't really been all that interested in complicated land deals, but sex? Starr's investigation had struck pay dirt. The Republicans seemed delightedly shocked. And eventually, based on the tape recordings and a certain blue dress, Clinton admitted he had had "improper relations" with Monica Lewinsky. Starr believed he had finally been able to pin something on Clinton—perjury. Lying under oath. Over and over the Republicans said as loudly as possible, It's not about the sex, it's about the lying. It's not about the sex, it's about the rule of law.

It was a vendetta. It was about gaining a political advantage no matter what the cost to the nation.

Initially I watched the Republicans' seemingly relentless attacks on Clinton with a sense of detached disbelief. I was a freshman member of the House, so new that most members had no idea who I was. When I was elected to Congress I hadn't expected to be in the middle of one of the most serious constitutional crises in our history. Only one president, Andrew Johnson, had ever been impeached. Richard Nixon had resigned before the full House could bring proceedings against him. The notion that impeachment would be used to achieve a political goal was something few people considered probable in modern times.

Almost a decade earlier, in November 1990, I had become one of the very earliest supporters of Bill Clinton. This was just after I was elected to the Florida Senate. I'd seen him on television, I'd seen him speaking at the Democratic Convention, and I was convinced he was smart, charismatic, and electable. I was sick of losing presidential elections and believed the Democrats needed a southerner to head the ticket. Clinton was then chairman of the Democratic Leadership Conference.

I wrote him a letter, somewhat naively, and said, "Please run for the presidency, and if you do I'd love to support you."

I got a form letter back; it said something like "Thank you very much for your letter of support and your kind words of encouragement. When we decide what we're going to do we'll be in touch with you."

By the time Republicans began talking seriously about impeachment, I had met Clinton a few times. During his run for the 1992 Democratic nomination I'd arranged meetings for him with South Florida community leaders. I'd even set up a major event at a synagogue in Delray Beach. After my election to Congress, I'd been to the White House when he was searching for votes to support a trade bill. And while I didn't agree with him on every issue, generally I thought he was an excellent president. I just couldn't believe the country would allow the Republicans to get away with impeaching him over his relationship with Monica Lewinsky. The whole thing seemed insane, and I kept waiting for one Republican leader to regain his sanity.

Just as Bonior had warned, as a member of the Judiciary Committee I became personally and deeply involved. Of all the tasks assigned to the House by the Constitution, impeachment is probably the one that occurs least frequently. When the Republicans started down this path, very few people even knew the proper way to proceed. Essentially what happens is that after charges are made against the president, the Judiciary Committee considers the evidence, and if the committee votes or reports out a resolution of impeachment, the whole House votes on it. In that sense it's similar to other legislation. But after that, everything changes. It then goes to the Senate, where a trial is held, with members of the House acting as prosecutors to present the case. The whole Senate then votes for or against removing the subject from office. The parliamentary procedure is obviously more complicated than this, but generally this is the way it happens.

The key legal event for which we were all waiting was the submission of Ken Starr's report to the committee. Every day there was another rumor about what he had uncovered, what his report would contain. It was generally accepted that Starr would present evidence that Clinton had committed perjury by lying under oath about his relationship with Lewinsky and, possibly more damning, had then obstructed justice by convincing other people to lie to investigators. Obstruction of justice is a serious charge. The probability that the special prosecutor could prove that against Richard Nixon was what had caused him to resign. If Starr could prove that Clinton had done that, that he had convinced other people to lie or not fully cooperate with the investigation, the president would have a tough fight to stay in office.

This was a tremendously complicated issue for me. Obviously I couldn't defend the president's behavior. His behavior was impossible to condone. But I didn't believe the Founding Fathers had intended a president to be removed from office for his personal conduct. My natural inclination was to defend the presidency, but not the president's behavior. I remember sitting in a restaurant with Eric Johnson and several other members of my staff for hours trying to sort it all out. Laurie and I spent a lot of time talking about it. Our oldest daughter, Rachel, was nine years old, and Laurie said simply, "Until you can explain this to Rachel in a way that you're comfortable with, you ought to think twice about defending him." She warned me that this could end up being my defining moment in politics. And then she asked me, "Is this why you got into politics? To defend this kind of behavior?"

She was right. If I couldn't explain this behavior to my own daughter, maybe the best thing to do was distance myself from the issue. Keep my mouth shut. Vote when it was necessary to cast a vote but not align myself with him. There really was little for me to gain by publicly supporting him. And if I did defend him there was a real chance people would mistakenly believe that I was approving his behavior.

This was another one of those issues about which I wasn't certain how my constituents felt. They had strongly supported Bill Clinton in both the 1992 and 1996 elections, but these were older, very moral people. The Republicans wanted to force every elected Democrat to make a choice: either criticize the president or be seen to be defending his behavior. I just didn't think I could stand on the sidelines as a president I admired was being destroyed for political purposes. So when I was asked about it by the media, I defended him. I never defended his actions;

instead I tried to state the facts as I saw them. This was a political witch hunt. Nothing more. And certainly nothing Clinton did rose to the level of an impeachable crime. I said it often, and I said it loudly.

I remember the first time the president called me at home. It would be an understatement to say that I was surprised. I mean, the president of the United States calling a first-term congressman to talk strategy? Despite my support for his campaign, we weren't exactly friends. Apparently he had seen me on television speaking passionately against impeachment. But when I began to think about why he was calling me, it made sense. He was trapped in the White House and there was almost no one he could speak with who couldn't eventually be subpoenaed. As a member of the Judiciary Committee, I was not going to be questioned about conversations with the president. So he could talk to me—as well as other members of Congress.

These White House calls came late at night, almost midnight. At our house, like most people, when the phone rings late at night our first thought is that something is wrong. So I was at least partially relieved to know it was the White House. Laurie was not impressed. Our bedroom was right next to the room of our younger daughter, Hannah. Laurie was adamant that I not wake up our kids. So when he called, I either went into the bathroom and closed the door or sat inside a closet where the clothes muffled my voice. I'd speak as softly as possible, but with my voice that's not close to a whisper. I would envision him sitting alone in the White House; I didn't think he envisioned me sitting in the back of a closet.

One night the White House called about seven o'clock. Laurie picked up the phone and the operator told her, "The president is calling for Congressman Wexler." Laurie and I have known each other since we were teenagers, so she isn't impressed by my job. When I took the oath she was given a spouse pin, which carries with it certain privileges. She put it down somewhere and hasn't seen it since. She has always managed to keep our lives in perspective. The president was calling me? Great, but we were in the whirlwind of homework and baths and dishes. She responded politely, "He's doing the dishes. He'll have to call you back." And she hung up the phone.

I returned the call later that evening, but I didn't get through to the president.

The operator must have told Clinton why I was not available, because when he called again the next day he began by asking, "You done with the dishes yet?"

Our conversations sometimes lasted for quite a while and often covered a lot of different areas. It would be inaccurate to describe them as back-and-forth dialogue. He did most of the talking; I mostly listened. Sometimes he would talk about what he'd accomplished during the day. Once he started talking about a Fruit of the Loom plant closing in the South, which led into a discussion about unemployment in America and the need for job training and how he intended to address that issue. When we did discuss the impeachment situation he was completely dispassionate about it. He would talk about it in the third person and we would discuss strategy as if it involved someone else. If some Republican was trying a legal tactic, he would dissect it, explaining why he thought it was not a persuasive argument. He never asked me to do anything specific or spoke about Democratic strategy. I think it was simply that he felt isolated and needed people to talk to, and I was one of them.

It was surprising to me that he was able to keep it on this level without ever losing his temper. The few times I spoke with him, I'd end up even more disturbed about what the Republicans were doing than I'd been before the conversation. I wasn't a close friend of Bill Clinton's, but I hated what they were doing to him and what they were doing to our country.

I certainly wasn't blasé about these conversations. I can't imagine anyone not used to speaking with the president not being somewhat overwhelmed by the reality that they are talking to the president of the United States on the phone. The fact that I was a member of Congress did not make it any less exciting; I retained my childhood awe of the office of the president. I still have it. In some ways it was more exhilarating than being in a meeting with him, because in that situation there are always other people around. One afternoon I was driving home from the Capitol when the White House called on my cell phone. I was sitting at a red light looking at the people in the car next to me as I was talking to the president, thinking, I want to roll down the window and scream, "I'm talking to Bill Clinton. What are you doing?"

The most important tool any politician has is the telephone. I spend hours each day on the phone, doing everything from discussing policy to fund-raising. Truthfully, I'm on the phone a lot when I'm driving—that extra hour a day is extremely valuable. When I was trying to decide whom to support for the 2008 Democratic nomination, for example, I was told by a supporter of Barack Obama that he really wanted to speak to me. Most of the other South Florida Democratic members had announced their support for Hillary Clinton, but apparently the Obama people had decided to try to get my support. They knew I could be helpful, particularly in the South Florida Jewish community. Eventually Eric gave Obama's team my cell phone number with the understanding that at some point he would call. We didn't arrange a specific time.

Late one afternoon I was driving home in bad weather and saw a woman standing next to her car on the side of the road. It was obvious she was having difficulty, because the hood of her car was raised. I stopped to see if I could help her. The battery was dead, she said, could I give her a jump? She had the cables we needed. My problem was that I was driving Laurie's car; I was trying to figure out how to open the hood when Barack Obama called. This was at the height of his rock star introduction to national politics.

So while I was trying all kinds of different things to get my hood open, Barack Obama and I were discussing those issues that were important to South Florida. I was pulling and pressing every button and lever I could find while talking about Israel and national catastrophic property insurance and flood programs, and I still couldn't get the hood open. I gave him some candid advice, and he had some suggestions about what levers to pull, but nothing worked.

After about fifteen minutes, someone in a pickup truck stopped to help, and this man got his hood open in five seconds. As I got off the phone, the woman who had been standing there watching me fail to get the hood open while talking on my phone said to me, "Boy, that was an intense conversation. It sounded like you were talking to the president of the United States."

"Well, maybe," I said cryptically. Ordinarily I would never have gone further, but she seemed like a nice woman and I felt like a total failure, so I added, "I was talking to Barack Obama."

Her jaw just dropped open. "Really?" She was clearly impressed.

I smiled. "Yeah." And then added, "But he didn't know how to get the hood open either."

The way that woman felt, that's how I felt every time President Clinton called.

I became more actively involved in defending the president when the Starr Report was issued. We'd been waiting for that. Prosecutors already had the "smoking dress," but nobody knew if Starr was going to be able to make a case against Clinton for obstruction of justice.

In September 1998 I was flying to Orlando with the president on *Air Force One,* where he was going to campaign for Democratic gubernatorial candidate Buddy McKay. During the flight the president came to the back of the plane and said that the Starr Report did not contain any substantial evidence of obstruction of justice. I don't even remember who else was there; and, truthfully, I wasn't sure if he meant that the report contained no evidence or was speculating that the report could not show obstruction of justice because there had been no obstruction of justice.

For the first time I felt confident enough to tell him what I believed he needed to do. Or more accurately, what Laurie believed he needed to do. I told him he needed to apologize to the American people and explain what he'd done in a way that enabled every parent to sit down with their child, whether that child was eight or fifteen, and talk to them about what had happened. And until parents could explain all this to their children in some comfortable way, he was going to have a serious problem moving beyond it. This is a fair country, I told him, and I believed that if he was honest with the American people, he would find out that this country has a huge capacity to forgive.

Obviously I didn't mean he should explain it in graphic detail, but rather explain the lesson to be learned, the values that were involved, and the morality of it. I suggested he think about it as if he were writing a children's book about the subject. If you can imagine that.

He spoke in Orlando the next day. "I let you down," he said. "I let my family down. And I let this country down. But I'm trying to make it right. And I'm determined never to let anything like that happen again . . ." He told the story of meeting a young boy that morning, who told him that he wanted to grow up to be president. Then he added, "I thought, I want to be able to conduct my life and my presidency so that all parents of the country could feel good if their children were able to say that again."

No one who was in Congress the day the Starr Report was issued will ever forget it. We knew we were reading a document that would greatly affect the history of this country. The members of the Judiciary Committee got copies of the report about half an hour before it was generally distributed. As soon as we got it, the key members of my staff gathered in my office. We were speed-reading it, trying to find the core claims that would form the articles of impeachment. We were wondering whether Starr would present real evidence that the president's friend Vernon Jordan had tried to coerce Monica Lewinsky's testimony by offering her a job, or that the president had tried to influence the testimony of his secretary, Betty Currie—he didn't. We thought there might be material about the so-called Travelgate or Whitewater scandals. We were racing through it, you could hear pages turning, and then people began saying, somewhat incredulously, "There's nothing new in here." Or "This is total baloney." The crux of the entire report was that Clinton had lied under oath about having sex with Monica Lewinsky. The Republicans were going to impeach the president because he'd had an affair and lied about it.

After going through it, I felt a lot better about the situation. A little while later I put the report in my bag and walked out to the parking lot to go home. My car was parked at the far side of an area known as the triangle. As I began walking across the triangle, I saw all of the national media gathered in front of the Capitol—every television station and countless newspapers. It was a media frenzy. I noticed that several Republicans critical of the president were lined up ready to hang him.

This was the red meat they'd been waiting years for. The only Democrat around was Californian Zoe Lofgren, who was also on Judiciary. "Where is everybody?" she asked me. I shook my head.

I had appeared on television numerous times in the past few months on a variety of issues, but primarily to discuss the Republicans' impeachment campaign. But none of this group of reporters recognized me. "Are you a Democrat?" one of them asked.

I suspect it was a guess. But they were desperate for a Democrat, any Democrat, to respond to the report. They shoved several microphones in front of me and asked what I thought. My outrage just bubbled to the surface. I said the president had betrayed his wife, but he hadn't betrayed the country. And as I said that, I realized that it was exactly what I'd been trying to say for a long time.

That news clip was used on several of the national news programs that night. After I'd said those words, I began wondering if I'd said the right thing. What I meant was that the charges in this report didn't come close to meeting the constitutional standard for impeachment. But I worried that President Clinton, if he saw this interview, would be offended by it. I used the word *betray*. I thought maybe his reaction would be, Who the hell is this guy to be commenting about me and my wife and our marriage?

The next day I began receiving invitations from every show on television—except *The Simpsons*—to appear opposite some Republican to debate the impeachment.

A careful reading of the entire 453-page report over the weekend only strengthened my belief that the Republicans really weren't going to go forward with it. The people who knew Congress the best, the smart money, kept saying that eventually wiser heads were going to prevail. The chairman of the Judiciary Committee, the late Henry Hyde, was considered the wisest head, and those same smart people continued to predict that Henry was simply too reasonable to drive the Republican train over the cliff. He would apply the brakes before it went too far. There were different rumors every day—this person was meeting with that person to work out a deal. For a time it looked like there would be a compromise: The president would agree to be censured and would voluntarily give up his pension. That way the Republicans would get their pound of moral flesh but the business of Congress could go on.

I tried to look at it pragmatically: What did the Republicans have to gain or lose? Public opinion polls were strongly against impeachment—unlike the later polls regarding the impeachment of Dick Cheney—and after the release of the report the numbers dipped a bit but the feeling in the nation did not change. President Clinton did an awful thing, but it was not grounds to remove him from office. Under President Clinton the nation was in the middle of the longest period of sustained economic growth in history. That was the issue that affected day-to-day life in America, not the fact that the president had had an affair. So it seemed logical that the Republicans' best strategy was to go after the president strongly enough to satisfy their base, but stop before an impeachment ripped apart the country.

I realized that wasn't going to happen, that these people were serious about impeaching the president, a few days later. While the report was made public, seventeen boxes of supplementary material and more than two thousand pages of appendixes were kept locked in rooms in the Ford House Office Building and were available only to House members. This was all the evidence Starr had collected. There were separate rooms for the Democratic and Republican members to look at the material, but they were off the same hallway. Reading the details made me very uncomfortable. We were like Peeping Toms, voyeurs. We were reading material that should have been none of our business, neither individually or collectively. I couldn't imagine a supposedly respectable attorney like Kenneth Starr spending more than a year of his life digging into the details of a sexual relationship like a desperate reporter for a tabloid newspaper. I was leaving the Democratic evidence room one afternoon at the same time Florida representative Charles Canady was leaving the Republican room. We knew each other a bit. But as we walked down the hall he said in disgust, "He's just a pervert. He's just perverted."

I believe I responded, "As far as I'm concerned, the only perverts here are us. We're the people looking at this stuff." To me, the fact that members of the United States Congress were wasting our time examining this evidence was the true perversion. And for somebody to make that proclamation about a private, consensual affair, in that judgmental tone of complete disgust, actually frightened me. But when I heard him say that, I realized that they were not going to stop. These people believed they were on a moral crusade, and in their fit of righteousness they were going to do an unthinkable thing and no one was going to be able to stop them.

The people who would decide the fate of the president were the twenty-one Republican members of the Judiciary Committee. There was nothing the sixteen Democratic members of the committee could do to even slow them down. But what we could do was try to sway public opinion. As members of the committee, we had credibility with the media. We were behind the closed doors, we knew what was going on, and so we became the Constitution's first line of defense. As I told *The Washington Post* after reading the entire report, "It's clear from the report that Clinton didn't tell the truth . . . I think what's in the report regarding the president's behavior is repugnant, repugnant to everything I believe in as a husband and a father. But it doesn't add up to what Thomas Jefferson and James Madison and George Mason called high crimes and misdemeanors."

I hadn't been in Congress long enough to appreciate the level of partisan bitterness that divided the House. Any residue of bipartisanship that might have remained dissipated in early September when the online magazine *Salon.com* revealed that Henry Hyde had had his own affair thirty years earlier. Hyde wrote it off as "a youthful indiscretion"—although he was in his forties at the time the affair took place. (To this day there are many people in Congress grateful to Henry for expanding the statute of limitations on youthful indiscretions into one's forties.) Hyde offered to resign as chairman, but the Republicans rejected his offer. House Majority Whip Tom DeLay claimed without the slightest evidence that the information about Hyde's affair had been leaked by "the president's attack dogs," which was denied by a White House official, who blamed it on the "Salem witch trials atmosphere." Eventually the source of the leak, the man whose wife had been involved with Hyde, who had absolutely no connection to the White House, explained that he had begun calling media outlets about the story a couple of months earlier.

Now the sex lives of every member of Congress had become fair game. White House special counsel to the president Lanny Davis described the atmosphere in the House as "close to McCarthyism." Some of the people screaming the loudest for impeachment had their own marital problems. On CNN Bill Press described the thrice-married Bob Barr's marital history as "a sometimes arrangement between one man and three women." Newt Gingrich admitted later that while all this was going on he was in the middle of his own affair. When Gingrich resigned as Speaker in 1998, Bob Livingston was chosen to replace him—until *Hustler* magazine publisher Larry Flynt alleged that Livingston was having an affair, which caused him to resign. The unmistakeable stench of hypocrisy was becoming unbearable.

The committee was in partisan shambles. I have no doubt that many of the Republican members disliked me intensely. I don't delude myself. I was loud and outspoken, I was on every channel, and I had the facts on my side. Of course they disliked me. There were Republicans on the committee whom I liked and with whom I'd had gotten along well, people like Steve Chabot and Lindsey Graham, and I never doubted that they really believed there was a constitutional infringement. I think Bob Barr genuinely believed that what they were doing was right. I vehemently disagreed with them, but I respected their integrity. I actually thought Lindsey Graham summed up his position very well when he said, "I don't know if we're dealing with Watergate or Peyton Place. I don't know which one it is here, and that's what we have to figure out. If it's Peyton Place, it's not enough. If it's Watergate, that's impeachable."

Lindsey Graham eventually voted for impeachment.

A lesson Democrats have had difficulty learning is how to hit back. The bottom line in any campaign is that when you're being punched, when you're taking a hit, you can't assume that people will be able to differentiate the truth from the lies. You have to assume that people are going to believe the lies. So you have to throw the first punch or be ready with a counterpunch.

But in this situation, President Clinton was silent, so others had to do it for him. I wasn't the only Democrat out there. John Conyers called this a "Republican coup d'état," explaining, "Impeachment was designed to rid this nation of traitors and tyrants, not attempts to cover up an extramarital affair," and Barney Frank, when asked if the president should give Ken Starr a blood or saliva sample, responded, "I'm inclined to think there are times when the president might have volunteered to give Mr. Starr a saliva sample." But certainly I was one of the most aggressive critics of impeachment. There were some members who thought I was grandstanding. I was young and brash, I hadn't paid my dues, and there were some Democrats who became patronizing toward me. I didn't care; I was doing what I thought was right.

I recall one night in particular when I was walking in a hallway that connects the House to the Senate. It was another late night of voting and I was exhausted. Suddenly I heard this booming voice echoing in the hallway, "Wexler!" I turned around and it was Senator Ted Kennedy. I had never met him, and had no reason to believe that he knew who I was. He was by himself and was quite an imposing figure. I'd admired Ted Kennedy for a long time. He put a hand on my shoulder and said, "My wife, Vicki, thinks you're doing a terrific job." Then he added, "It's important to support your president."

I desperately wanted to say, "Like you did with Jimmy Carter." But I didn't, because I genuinely appreciated the compliment. Besides, I'd voted for Ted Kennedy in the primary against Jimmy Carter.

"Just keep doing what you're doing," he said, and then walked off. Believe me, as I walked back to my office there was a bounce in my step.

I became a regular on national television. I can't even begin to estimate the number of national and local television shows and print interviews I did. This had to be done. The Republicans have mastered the art of the destructive sound bite. We had to call them on their avalanche of misstatements and half-truths.

It wasn't as if spending time doing that distracted me from other important business in the House. There was no other business. The producers of network and cable shows liked having me on because I was blunt and spoke in sound bites.

I believe it was NBC's Lisa Meyers to whom I explained, "The whole thing is ridiculous and the American people understand it's ridiculous. The Republican leadership has made a mockery of the Constitution. The people in my district care about the economy, they care about trade, they care about a thousand different things. The last thing on their list is impeachment." In an interview with *The Palm Beach Post*, I mentioned that I'd just returned from a trip to Europe, "and they were laughing at us as a nation. They don't understand how allegations of a sexual encounter could lead to the possible resignation of the president." In a debate with Pat Buchanan, I asked him, If he believed Clinton should be impeached for misleading the American public, why did he not support impeaching Ronald Reagan for misleading the American public about covert military operations in Central America? On *Late Edition*, I told Wolf Blitzer, "Clinton . . . lied to us about an extramarital affair. That speaks for itself, but it's not a high crime." On *Fox News Sunday*, Bob Barr charged, "It's not a private matter when you go into court and lie," to which I responded, "That's a serious matter and it's wrong if he did it. But it's not impeachable. You don't take the president down over this." I appeared on so many TV and radio shows that *Los Angeles Times* reporter Ron Brownstein wrote that I had become "the human advertisement for the mute button."

The Republicans despised me. A decade later a Republican lobbyist whom I'd known for many years suggested to a client that he contribute to my campaign. The client was astonished. "Are you kidding?" he said. "Wexler's an asshole."

The lobbyist smiled. "No, he really isn't. He just plays one on TV."

The Republicans were also loud, and stayed on message, although sometimes they couldn't stop themselves. For example, I was on a show with representative J. D. Hayworth (R-AZ), who called the president "a scumbag," a phrase initially used by Dan Burton, the chairman of the Government Reform Committee, who boasted he was "out to get"

Clinton before he referred to him as a scumbag. Only a couple of months earlier I would have been thrilled to have been invited to appear on C-SPAN, but suddenly I was turning down *Larry King Live* because I would rather attend my son's kindergarten open house. Only once was I nervous, and that was when I found myself sitting across from Tim Russert on *Meet the Press*. My stomach was churning, because that's the one show on which you really don't want to make a major gaffe or appear ill-prepared or not be aggressive enough or too aggressive.

The reaction to all this exposure was mixed. Every time I appeared on TV, the telephones in my office would start ringing. Every day we'd receive piles of letters. Although the majority were supportive, I also received several threatening letters and calls.

That happens. It's an unfortunate part of the job. But during the impeachment proceedings the threats came often and we took some of them very seriously. Often the calls or letters were anti-Semitic. Callers would tell staffers, "If that Jew bastard doesn't shut up we're going to take care of him." Another letter said that I would be killed and President Clinton targeted, and "Only a loudmouth Jew like you would support Clinton." As members of Congress are instructed to do, we turned some of the seemingly more serious letters over to the FBI and the Secret Service. For the first time, I actually had Secret Service protection. I remember doing a local show in West Palm Beach and counting ten officers from the Palm Beach County Sheriff's Office in addition to Secret Service in the studio. One letter mentioned Laurie and our children by name and included other personal details, so clearly this was somebody who had done some background checking. We also began receiving calls at home. Somehow people had gotten our private number. One person called several times and really scared our children. Eventually the Capitol Police Department assigned some police cruisers to just sit outside our home. There's not much you can do about these threats; as much as possible I just tried to ignore them.

My task at that time was to know what was going on and be ready to respond quickly. I remember going to work every morning wondering what craziness was going to take place that day. There was a lot going on in the House. It was an extraordinary show: hearings, votes, accusations, incredible anger and bitterness. The Democratic caucus would meet regularly to discuss the latest events and strategy. Democrats on the committee were continually having meetings. We were inviting lawyers and parliamentary experts into our offices or other members' offices to learn as much as possible about what was possible. There was something going on all day, every day. But as it gradually became apparent, it was all a show. The thing that seemed to matter most was public opinion. There was a group of hard-core conservatives who wanted Clinton impeached and perhaps were willing to sacrifice their own political careers to do that, but there were many more Republicans, and some Democrats, out there listening to the winds. Bill Clinton was going to be tried in the Senate, but the real trial was in the court of public opinion.

The courtroom was the Judiciary Committee. We began hearings to consider the scope of the investigation in October 1998. We all knew what the outcome was going to be, but this was our best opportunity to lobby the American public. Each of us had an opportunity to make an opening statement. "Many of our colleagues have referred to our role here today as the most important work a member of Congress can perform. I sincerely hope not," I began. "This may be the most attention this committee will ever receive. This may be the biggest news story in which we will ever play a part. But God help the nation if this is the most important work we will ever do in Congress . . ." As I pleaded with the committee, but really the jury, to "end this nonsense," my Democratic colleagues gave me a nice round of applause, which Chairman Hyde gaveled into silence.

I'm rarely nervous when speaking in the House, and on the day those hearings opened I was very comfortable. In sports terminology, I'd spent several years in the metaphorical minor leagues, the state senate, in which hearings are rarely televised and the only people who hear you speak are sitting in the room. Believe me, as far as actually affecting lives, much of what we did in Tallahassee was more important than these hearings, so the fact that millions of people were watching really didn't affect me. Making a speech or questioning a witness was something I was comfortable doing. And when you get to your office after a day like this, it's sort of like coming back to the locker room. Everybody on your staff is telling you how well you did, and there's a pile of congratulatory messages. I was lucky to be married to Laurie—her message was usually what time I was supposed to pick up which child from hip-hop dancing, piano lessons, or basketball practice.

At the end of the initial hearings the Judiciary Committee voted that grounds existed to go forward with an inquiry of impeachment.

The first verdict to be rendered was going to be the election of 1998. More than anything, this was a referendum on the Clinton impeachment. As the elections approached, the Republicans were confident that Clinton would be an anchor dragging down the entire Democratic Party. In fact, in the weeks just before the election, Newt Gingrich approved a series of ads attacking Democrats for their support of the president. Historically, the president's party loses congressional seats in midterm elections, and Gingrich believed he could solidify the Republican House majority by running against immorality. Probably the entire election could be summed up in the story of Republican Mike Pappas from New Jersey, who was running against a Princeton University physicist nobody had ever even heard of, Rush Holt. Pappas was so cocky that he stood up on the floor of the House and sang the ditty "Twinkle twinkle Kenneth Starr, now we see how brave you are . . ." I didn't see him do it. It was probably done in one of the morning opportunities to tape a speech on the floor. But Rush Holt responded by essentially basing his entire campaign on that song: "He's against what really matters . . . Congressman Mike Pappas. Out of tune. Out of touch." What a fantastic commercial!

A week before the election, political experts were speculating about whether we would lose as many as five Senate seats and two dozen House seats. Instead, for the first time since 1934, the incumbent president's party gained seats, winning five House seats—including Rush Holt's victory over Pappas by five thousand votes—and breaking even in the Senate. Even in the conservative South we unexpectedly won several close races. The American people made it clear that they did not support this impeachment. I remember thinking the morning after the election that this really had to be the beginning of the end of it; pushing impeachment was putting Republican political careers in jeopardy.

But they couldn't stop themselves. This train was out of control. We began the actual impeachment hearings two weeks after the election. In my statement before I began questioning Ken Starr I said:

> [T]he House of Representatives [is] uniquely qualified to deliberate on the removal of an elected president because we . . . take into account the views of the president's ultimate jury: the people of the United States of America.
>
> And make no mistake about it: The jury rendered its judgment loud and clear on November third, and this committee did not listen. This committee is ignoring the will of the American people, and instead following the lead of this so-called independent counsel who has conducted a politically inspired witch hunt in search of a crime to justify five years and forty million dollars in taxpayers' money. The American people do not approve, Mr. Starr. They know unfairness when they see it. They know injustice when they feel it. They know hypocrisy when they smell it. They know partisan politics when they are victims of it. In their gut they've figured this thing out . . .
>
> The president had an affair. He lied about it. He didn't want anyone to know about it. But he didn't bribe anyone. He didn't obstruct justice. He didn't commit treason. He didn't subvert the government . . .

I then proceeded to ask Ken Starr four questions, which he tried to avoid answering. I think the questions provide all the information anyone needs to know about the type of investigation Ken Starr conducted:

> On January 16, 1998, do you admit or deny that your agents threatened Ms. Lewinsky with twenty-seven years in prison, if she contacted her attorney as she testifed?
>
> Do you admit or deny that your agents threatened to prosecute her mother if Ms. Lewinsky called her attorney as she testifed?
>
> That your agents told Monica Lewinsky that she would be less likely to receive immunity if she contacted her attorney as she testified?

Do you admit or deny that your office threatened Julie Hyatt Steele, a witness in the Kathleen Wiley matter, that they would raise questions about the legality of her adoption of her eight-year-old child, unless she changed her testimony?

Starr huffed and puffed and refused to give direct answers, instead claiming that he and his agents had "conducted ourselves properly and lawfully . . ."

As my allotted five minutes expired, I again asked him to answer at least one of my questions. "Mr. Starr . . . All I asked you was a factual question: Did your agents or did they not threaten Ms. Lewinsky with twenty-seven years in prison? It's either yes or no, not the legality." Although it reads dispassionately, believe me, there was some pretty intense passion in my voice as I asked those questions.

Starr knew that the answers to those questions would accurately describe his actions and undoubtedly embarrass him. So rather than answering a simple question, he responded with the answer we have so often heard during recent investigations: "I do not—I know what Ms. Lewinsky has said. I would have to conduct an interview with my agents to know what the position of the office is."

So I helped him out. I couldn't resist adding, "The answer was yes."

In fact it didn't matter how he answered the questions. The Republican majority in the committee voted 21 to 16 that Clinton had "committed perjury and obstructed justice" and that Congress should proceed "with impeachment with a view toward removing him from office."

Eventually the House voted 228 to 206 to impeach President Clinton. The show moved to the Senate. And in the Senate trial, proving that they had learned absolutely nothing from this whole affair, the Republicans actually wanted to call Monica Lewinsky as a witness. Fortunately, the Democrats prevented that from happening. Eventually, the Senate acquitted the president.

More than many things we do in the House, the impeachment proceedings changed innumerable lives. Among other Republican leaders, Newt Gingrich and Bob Livingston left Congress. It's reasonable to conclude that impeachment cost Al Gore an easy election victory in 2000, as he did not use the tainted but still popular Clinton during the campaign—and as a result, George W. Bush was appointed president of the United States.

And we all know how that has worked out.

14

Let My People Vote:
The Stolen Election of 2000

Although we may never know with complete certainty the identity of the winner of this year's presidential election, the identity
of the loser is perfectly clear. It is the nation's confidence in the
judge as an impartial guardian of the law.

—Supreme Court Justice John Paul Stevens
in his dissent to *Bush v. Gore*

It's rare when a local issue takes on worldwide significance.
But that's what happened in Florida 19 in November and December
2000. More than anything else I do, my job is to fight for the rights of
the people I represent. Doing that put me at the epicenter of one of the
saddest chapters in American political history—the 2000 presidential
election recount and a legal fight that would change the world for the
worse. We have been living with the results of that calamity since that
time. There is no doubt in my mind that the wrong man moved into the
White House in January, 2001. And I believe he knows it. George Bush
knows as well as I do that, on Election Day, thousands more people

went into Florida's election booths intending to vote for Al Gore than for him. Bush lost nationally by half a million votes and most likely lost Florida by several thousand. But the battle that ensued in my district and the disturbing political and legal tactics employed by the Bush campaign—aided by a largely indifferent media, more concerned with the drama of the story than the facts, and an outrageous intervention by a Republican-dominated Supreme Court—led to Bush ultimately taking the oath of office.

Never before has the political adage "all politics is local" been more correct. And fittingly, my involvement began with a phone call from my mother-in-law.

Even before Al Gore announced he was running for the presidency, I believed he would make a wonderful president and I supported him. In fact, in 1998, at the very beginning of the election cycle, I called his office and he quickly returned my call. I remember it well because it was a Friday night, just after the Jewish Shabbat had started. It wasn't that late, but it was after sundown, so ordinarily I would not have answered the phone. But when I saw the caller ID reading *Vice President's Office,* or something like that, I picked it up. Gore was running for the Democratic nomination against Bill Bradley and I thought I had a great idea. I thought he should run as the "prescription drug president."

The message I wanted to give him was that I didn't know about the rest of the country, but the outrageous cost of prescription drugs and the lack of Medicare coverage was the most pressing issue in Florida, and he would be missing a huge opportunity if he didn't present himself as a pioneer in proposing Medicare prescription drug coverage.

Our conversation lasted perhaps fifteen minutes. Mostly the vice president just listened. I gave him some very specific suggestions. He gave me very little feedback, and certainly no positive feedback. In fact, when we hung up I felt kind of foolish. I was especially excited about talking to him because I thought I was giving him an idea that would have been fabulous for him personally, great for his campaign, and terrific for my constituency. But when I got off the phone I told Laurie, "I just made a big fool of myself." From his lack of enthusiasm, from the lack of any kind of meaningful response, it was obvious to me that the vice president thought it was a goofy idea, or that it wasn't relevant, or he wondered how I could take up his time and be so excited over something that affected just one state or a small group of states.

The problem was that I didn't read him well at all. By comparison, if I'd had the same conversation with President Clinton, he would have made me feel like I was the smartest guy on earth. What an amazing idea, he would have said. I'm going to look into it! I'll definitely consider it! Thank you so much, Robert. I would have gotten off the phone thinking, My goodness, I'm so glad I called. I've just changed the world.

I didn't hear another word from Vice President Gore for at least six months. Then one day his office called to tell me he was going to Florida to announce a prescription drug plan and wondered if I would like to join him when he did.

I'm certainly not suggesting that Al Gore became interested in a Medicare prescription drug plan because I happened to mention it to him. But he had listened enough to know this was an issue of real importance to me and remembered to include me when he made his announcement. So I developed an enormous amount of respect for him—not because he listened to me, but because he listened.

I campaigned with Vice President Gore on several occasions. I thought the world of Al Gore and was convinced he was poised to be an extraordinary president. The remarkable role he has played as a private citizen championing the issue of global warming proves as much. As much as I admired and respected Bill Clinton's intelligence and charisma, Al Gore had an intensity about important issues unlike anyone I'd ever known. I was also very fond of his vice-presidential running mate, Joe Lieberman, who'd offered such brotherly advice when I arrived in Washington.

It was obvious almost from the very beginning that Florida was going to play a pivotal role in the election, and Lieberman campaigned there often to try to turn out a large Democratic and Jewish vote. I spent a considerable amount of time with him.

On Election Day I was cautiously optimistic. The polls were promising, if you read them the way you wanted to read them, but after living through several elections, politicians develop a feeling. You may not know the outcome, but you know the signs. My mother-in-law went to vote early in the morning. She was at the polls by seven-thirty. The first thing she did when she got out of the voting booth was call me. Something was wrong with the ballot, she said. It was very confusing. She told me that several people were standing outside the precinct comparing experiences and complaining that they weren't sure which presidential candidate they'd actually voted for. My mother-in-law's voice had a sense of urgency; she was upset. I told her I'd see what was going on.

I went to vote myself. And it was obvious she was absolutely correct. Something was very wrong with the ballot. In fact, I was running for reelection and in certain precincts my name—the whole congressional election—didn't appear on the ballot. Suddenly my office began receiving panicked phone calls from constituents literally crying that they'd mistakenly voted for Pat Buchanan, the right-wing conservative candidate. Then my cell phone began ringing as other people called to tell me about their problems voting. It was a nightmare. But at that point the real extent of the voting irregularities wasn't known. I decided to visit the Palm Beach County supervisor of elections, Theresa LePore. State Senator Ron Klein was already there when I arrived with Eric Johnson and my press secretary, Josh Rogin. Klein was upset about the ballot, too. I immediately had a conversation with Theresa. As I frantically began to question her, she started to cry. I noticed a TV camera across the room and instinctively moved in front of her to block the camera shot.

I was surprised that this controversy occurred at all. Theresa LePore was a Democrat and good at her job. She'd started working in the election office as a teenage file clerk and remained there for almost thirty years, finally being elected supervisor. At that point, we were friends. I'd actually contributed to her campaign with my own campaign funds. Eric had also known her a long time. If there was a problem, I believed she would want to remedy it. She certainly did not set out to intentionally hurt anyone.

Theresa had designed the ballot. It was called a butterfly ballot. In an attempt to make it easier for elderly people to vote, she'd used large type to list the ten presidential candidates, which made it impossible to get all the names on one page. So the ballot was two pages long, and confusing. To register a vote, voters had to punch out a perforated hole that was supposed to be directly opposite their candidate's name. Unfortunately, the hole voters had to punch out for Al Gore was not directly opposite his name. He was the second candidate listed on the left-hand side of the ballot, but to vote for him the proper hole to punch was the third down from the top. Pat Buchanan was the first candidate listed on the right-hand page and the second hole down from the top. So it was quite easy for voters to mistakenly cast their vote for president for Pat Buchanan by punching the second hole in the belief that it was a vote for Al Gore.

By the time I got to the supervisor's office, Theresa was aware of the problem and had already agreed to distribute a memo calling attention to the confusion: "ATTENTION ALL POLL WORKERS," it read in bold capital letters.

> PLEASE REMIND ALL VOTERS COMING IN THAT THEY ARE TO VOTE ONLY FOR ONE (1) PRESIDENTIAL CANDIDATE AND THAT THEY ARE TO PUNCH THE HOLE NEXT TO THE ARROW NEXT TO THE NUMBER NEXT TO THE CANDIDATE THEY WISH TO VOTE FOR. THANK YOU!

Well, that clarified nothing. Next to the arrow next to the number next to the candidate . . . The memo was as confusing as the ballot. We were nervous about it, but we never, ever believed a few votes in my district would determine who would become the next president of the United States.

We sent people to many precincts to try to warn voters about the ballot. Unfortunately, by the afternoon most seniors had already cast their votes. I called Joe Lieberman and told him about the problem. At this point it still seemed as if the butterfly ballot was nothing more than a minor glitch. More than a hundred million people were voting that day; a few thousand votes in Florida shouldn't make too much difference. I was quite agitated by this point, and in an effort to calm me down, Eric Johnson reminded me that in order for this to matter, first, the national election had to be decided by Florida, and the vote in Florida had to be close enough to be decided by a few thousand voters in Palm Beach County who mistakenly voted for Pat Buchanan rather than Al Gore. Chances of all that happening were minuscule. I remember Eric stating firmly, "I bet my life that the election won't come down to this."

Throughout the day the phones in my office never stopped ringing. My constituents were frustrated and angry. I had an uneasy feeling about the whole situation. I called popular local radio talk-show host Randi Rhodes, who has since become syndicated throughout the country, and spent an hour on the air with her to forewarn voters about the problem and urge them to double-check their ballot. "Everybody needs to punch number five for Al Gore. And once you do it, you need to look at it again, and look at it again." Precincts throughout our district were reporting problems. People who had voted earlier in the day were returning to the polls in tears, begging to be allowed to vote again—and correctly. We contacted Joe Lieberman again, and he went on the air with Randi Rhodes to inform people who hadn't yet voted about the peculiarities of the butterfly ballot.

Later in the day, the Democratic National Committee got involved, directing a telemarketing firm to contact as many Democratic voters as possible to inform them about the problem: "Voters have said they believe they accidentally punched the wrong hole . . . do not punch any other number . . ."

Later, Republican poll watchers would claim they did not witness any confusion at all. Of course they didn't. Voting for George Bush was simple because his name was first on the ballot and his punch hole was also first. There were no reported discrepancies by people who wanted to vote for George Bush.

The turnout in South Florida was incredible, possibly because Joe Lieberman, an Orthodox Jew, was on the ticket. For so many people this was such a proud day, a Jewish man running for vice president of the United States. It was a day many of my constituents had never expected to live to see. For many of my Jewish constituents Joe Lieberman's candidacy represented a profound realization that the always present glass ceiling for Jewish people had finally been shattered. The American dream had become so inclusive that now people of the Jewish faith could fully participate. This was their moment. So the elderly came out to vote by the thousands. It was a beautiful thing to watch; older people helping even older people get to the polls. I remember watching with great joy as two elderly ladies with oxygen tanks struggled proudly to cast their votes.

To go through all that and accidentally cast your ballot for the wrong person? And not just for any wrong person, but for a person my constituents considered evil? Many of these people had survived the Holocaust and perceived Pat Buchanan as unsympathetic to Jewish people—even anti-Semitic. People were traumatized. They were hysterical.

I told my staff that this was an awful situation. But even then we couldn't believe that these votes would make the difference in the election.

On Election Night, my staff and I watched the returns in our office because our computers allowed us to check the national numbers as well as results from Palm Beach and Broward Counties. When we saw that Pat Buchanan had gotten several thousand votes in my district, we realized that terrible damage had been done. Early in the evening the networks were calling Florida for Gore, and if that held up, these votes wouldn't matter. In fact, if either Gore or Bush had won Florida by more than a few thousand votes, all this confusion would have been irrelevant. Nothing more than a footnote. In the middle of the night, the networks reversed their early decision and awarded Florida—and the election—to George W. Bush. I finally went to sleep at four A.M., terribly depressed, believing George Bush had been named the winner.

Like everybody else, I was stunned when I turned on the TV very early the next morning. The networks had reversed themselves again and decided that Florida was too close to call. Gore had called Bush and rescinded the concession he'd made earlier that evening. Although Gore had easily won the national popular vote, the electoral vote count was so close that Florida's twenty-five electoral votes would determine the next president of the United States. It seemed as if the nearly impossible had happened—those few thousand votes could make all the difference in the world. Literally. I woke Eric at seven A.M. "Are you looking at your TV?" I asked. It took him a few seconds to understand the scope of the problem. "Well, I guess I'm lucky to be alive," he responded, referring to his misguided earlier bet.

The difference between me and most other Americans was that it was my responsibility to try to do something about it. Obviously I didn't know exactly what—nothing like this had ever happened in American history—but as the elected official representing the district in which the fiasco had occurred, it was my job to make sure the interests of my constituents were protected. And that is another aspect of a representative's job: to fight for the rights of your constituents. I asked Josh Rogin to get me on television as quickly as possible so we could tell the nation about what went wrong in Palm Beach County. That morning I was interviewed on MSNBC and CNN to tell America what the hell a butterfly ballot was and how it caused such great confusion among voters.

We then went directly to Theresa LePore's office in West Palm Beach. It was already a madhouse. Republican congressman Mark Foley apparently had gotten there about an hour before me and warned her, "Theresa, this is going to get crazy. You've got to get your act together." The media were starting to descend on Palm Beach County, and the lawyers would be right behind them, but at that point it wasn't yet clear to the media precisely what had gone wrong. The unofficial tally had George Bush ahead by less than 500 votes in the state—it had been as low as 292 votes—but we knew for certain that the confusion about the ballot had cost Gore at least three thousand votes, many more than necessary to make him president. Even Buchanan's campaign manager, his sister, Bay Buchanan, admitted, "There's clearly been a problem. This vote is much larger than one would expect for us."

Mark Foley dismissed the complaints, saying, "In the end there will be forty-six thousand people claiming they voted for Pat Buchanan by mistake . . . [T]he allegations . . . are nonsensical."

The initial problem was that nobody understood clearly what had happened—or what the legal remedies might be. As we quickly discovered, it wasn't simply people punching out the wrong hole. There were also 19,120 overvotes in Palm Beach County. An overvote means that the voter had punched out two holes, either out of confusion about the ballot or in an attempt to correct an initial mistake. Those 19,120 votes accounted for 4.1 percent of all the ballots cast in heavily Democratic Palm Beach County—and all of them had to be discarded.

There were also thousands of undervotes, in which the voters had failed to clearly mark their ballots by punching out the tiny cardboard rectangle.

In addition, an apparently large number of registered African-American voters had been taken off the voter rolls for no apparent reason. Later it was determined that the Republicans had hired a firm to remove the names of convicted felons from voter rolls—but rather than eliminating only the felon, they removed all voters with the same name. If a potential voter's name did not appear on the precinct rolls, clerks were supposed to call the supervisor's office to determine the voter's status—but because phone lines were jammed by complaints, they couldn't get through and many legally registered voters were sent home without being allowed to vote.

As the day progressed it was becoming evident that the election had been a catastrophe—and that tens of thousands of votes in mostly Democratic districts had not been counted. By Wednesday afternoon the demonstrations had begun. During the impeachment of President Clinton I'd learned the importance of public support. It was a chaotic scene, crowds gathered in front of the election office—Gore supporters to protest the vote, Bush supporters to claim that he had won the election honestly and prevent a recount.

Many of the same news and talk shows on which I'd been a guest during the Clinton impeachment proceedings began calling again. That first night I appeared on *Larry King Live* with Republican Mark Foley, who actually said, "I met with hundreds and hundreds of voters. No one came to me leaving the polls saying, 'I'm confused, I'm confused.'" Foley then went on to claim that Democrats made up the issue of ballot confusion only after they saw that Gore had lost. Initially, this was a major Republican talking point.

My conversation with Foley got a bit heated. We were already raising our voices, and this was only the first day. Things were happening so fast. It was during a commercial break that I first learned from a local reporter about the overvotes. As I told Larry King, "In fact, it may be as high as four percent of the ballots." On CNN's *Spin Room* I produced a copy of the memo Theresa LePore had issued, referring to it as "the smoking memo" because it was proof that the supervisor knew about the ballot problem before the polls had closed, proof that Democrats had not made up the issue after the fact. The Republicans dropped that particular talking point.

When Greta Van Susteren invited me to appear on her CNN show, I brought data with me proving that a terrible injustice had occurred and that the Republican claims were statistically impossible. But Greta wasn't interested in statistics, she just wanted good television. I was so naive at first that I really didn't believe that the media would allow the wrong person to become president. They had the story of the century right in front of them, but they just weren't interested in doing the investigative journalism that was necessary. I was astonished; they weren't going to investigate what actually happened in Palm Beach County.

The problem that we had cited with the design of the butterfly ballot had clearly caused several thousand people to mistakenly cast their votes for Pat Buchanan—more than enough votes for Gore to emerge as the winner in Florida. In addition, there were those incredible 19,120 double-punched ballots—almost all the double punches occurring in the presidential portion of the ballot. Throughout the rest of Florida the rate of double-punched ballots was less than half of 1 percent—or at most in Palm Beach County, 1,800 votes. There is no reasonable statistical basis for explaining the 19,120 double votes. One had to assume that people were confused by the ballot. Election law allows people counting the vote to consider the voter's intent. It seemed obvious that a significant number of voters, particularly Jewish voters, had not intended to vote for Buchanan. My mistake was that I believed the media would understand that, that the editorial boards of America's major newspapers would be morally driven to come out in favor of, not Gore, but honoring the votes of Americans.

That they stood by silently while the election turned on mistakes made by elderly voters was a disgrace. The media simply reported that Bush had begun assembling his cabinet and had started acting as the president-elect before a single investigation had taken place. The media outcry over these actions should have been deafening. Instead it was almost nonexistent.

The seven phone lines in my office continued ringing throughout the day. While the majority of callers were in tears and told us that they believed they had voted for Buchanan, many others were calling to tell me to shut up. Basically I was running from meeting to meeting. I met with lawyers, I met with Jesse Jackson, I went to several interviews and finally to a rally. I didn't stop. I spent a considerable amount of time discussing what our strategy should be with local officials like Commissioner Burt Aaronson. Citing a 1998 Miami election when the mayor of Miami had been removed from office because of absentee ballot fraud and his opponent placed in office, some people suggested that the results just be thrown out and that we push for a revote. Throw out the results and vote again? I didn't think there was a chance that would happen. You can't unring the bell. The dynamics of the election had changed so completely that a new vote would in no way be a repeat of the first vote.

There were several people who advocated for a statistical reassignment of votes. That, too, had been done before. In some local elections, a panel of judges had examined the results and statistically reassigned votes. I disagreed. I couldn't imagine that either side would agree to allow judges to assign votes based on a mathematical formula. We couldn't determine the presidency of the United States by using statistical probabilities. There were a lot of other suggestions. We were willing to consider anything reasonable. Anything legal. We investigated making the case that the ballot was illegal—which it was—and therefore the election didn't count. Florida law required that a punch hole be to the right of the candidate's name. On this two-page ballot, several holes were to the left of the name. Also, the law required that Al Gore's name be listed second, and technically Pat Buchanan's name was second. That's what caused the problem in the first place.

In retrospect, the only fair thing to do would have been to hold Florida's electoral votes in abeyance until all the votes cast in Florida were investigated by a panel of federal judges. This could have been expedited. The newspapers eventually did this and proved that Gore had won the state, which would have made him the president-elect by a margin of 24 electoral votes—but by the time they did this it was too late. George Bush had already been installed in the White House.

By Thursday, mobs of media and countless lawyers and protestors had gathered in West Palm Beach. The attention of the entire world was focused on my district. The situation was surreal. It just didn't seem possible that the presidency of the United States was going to be decided by a few hundred votes. And every day, it seemed, another problem with the election was raised. The courts couldn't even decide which ballots to count and how to count them: There were butterfly ballots and overvotes. There were absentee ballots from soldiers overseas postmarked a day late. Both sides were adapting strategies on the run. But as far as I was concerned, one thing was certain: Al Gore and Joe Lieberman had received the most votes in Florida and had won the election. No intelligent person who had access to all the facts could reach any other conclusion. To this day, Rush Limbaugh likes to talk about me and my role in the Florida recount on his radio program. Essentially, he claims I made up the whole controversy. But Limbaugh has never bothered to explain to his listeners how Pat Buchanan received almost 20 percent of his statewide vote total from a county that voted overwhelmingly for Gore—although Palm Beach County comprises roughly 6 percent of the statewide vote. In fact, of the seventeen Florida counties in which Buchanan received greater than 0.6 percent of the vote, only one, Palm Beach County, voted for Gore-Lieberman. Any response, Rush? Those people in Palm Beach County went to the polls intending to cast their vote for Al Gore.

The first lawsuits were filed a day after the election. Palm Beach County resident Andre Fladell, represented by local attorney Howard

Weiss, filed a suit demanding a new election. It was the beginning of a legal blizzard. In the next few weeks, many lawyers were going to earn a great deal of money as this case made legal history. It was almost impossible for me—for anyone, really—to keep up with all the legal maneuverings, there were so many lawsuits being filed. Eventually the Gore campaign decided that nothing could be done about the 3,407 Buchanan votes that had been wrongly cast. Attacking the butterfly ballot was a lost cause. The Gore people believed the only way they could win this election was by recounting the votes that had been properly cast but either miscounted or not counted. That meant they gave up on the more than nineteen thousand overvotes and focused on the undervotes, ballots that did not register a vote.

Because the Florida election had been decided by less than a quarter of 1 percent of the vote, Florida law required the votes to be recounted. A machine recount put Bush ahead by only 327 votes, but we requested a manual recount—as provided by law. We wanted that recount to start immediately, but Theresa LePore insisted on waiting until Florida's secretary of state, Katherine Harris, ordered it. That gave the Republicans time to get into court to try to prevent a manual recount.

The Republicans did everything they could to prevent the recount, and when it started, they tried to shut it down. The Palm Beach County recount focused on the undervotes. These were ballots on which voters apparently did not cast a vote in the presidential election. It required a large suspension of disbelief to believe that several thousand people had taken the trouble to stand in line to vote and then decided not to vote in the presidential election. In fact, once again the problem was with the ballot. For the vote to count, the voter had to punch a tiny piece of cardboard completely out of the ballot. If that piece of cardboard was hanging on to the ballot, as often happened, the optical reader wouldn't count it and it registered as no vote for the president. These little pieces of cardboard were called chads, and the tiny rectangles that had not been completely pushed through were known as hanging chads or pregnant chads. Under Florida law, election officials must consider the intent of the voter. Each one of those undervotes had to be examined by hand, one by one, to see if it was possible to determine the voter's intent. So in the greatest nation in the world, the most technologically advanced country in the history of mankind, everybody waited while three people held up every single ballot to a light and tried to figure out the voter's intent.

The Republican strategy was simple: Get George W. Bush into the White House at all costs. Do whatever was necessary and worry about how to rehabilitate later. Don't worry what you look like, don't worry about the consequences to the nation. The Democratic position was more confused and less disciplined. What a surprise! In fact, there was no unified strategy. I was right in the middle of it and at times I found myself wondering who was in charge. It was disorganized. At times the campaign was getting its information from us, and some of the time we really didn't know what was going on. To the outside world, I was on the inside, presumably speaking to the campaign leadership and working in concert with them. The real secret was that there was no inside. We're Democrats. Rather than the campaign leadership sitting down and deciding on a strategy and those of us in the middle of the debate executing it, they reacted to events as they took place. For example, it was apparent that the majority of the uncounted absentee ballots from soldiers serving overseas would favor Bush. It was probably several hundred votes. Under the letter of the law, these ballots should not have been counted. As usual the Republicans conveniently wrapped themselves in the American flag, screaming that we could not deprive our men and women overseas of the fundamental right to have their votes counted—while at the same time doing everything possible to stop the votes of elderly people in Palm Beach County from being counted—many of them being veterans themselves. The military aspect of the debate ended when Joe Lieberman appeared on *Meet the Press* and practically insisted that those ballots be counted.

On Friday I spoke at several rallies, telling a crowd of more than a thousand people in Delray Beach, "We're here today to protect the most important right and responsibility of an American citizen—to vote and have your vote counted. A ballot is not a puzzle, a ballot is not a maze . . ."

The Republicans countered with a rally of somewhere between twenty-four and forty people outside my Boca Raton office. Picketers chanted, "Overturn Wexler," and one of them told reporters, "Wexler does not reflect my views. For him to be on CNN every night as if he speaks for the entire country enflames me." Another Republican claimed I was inciting a riot by "bringing Jesse Jackson down here." I didn't bring Jackson anywhere, but I was not at all unhappy that he was there. The most important thing we could do in this situation was to keep the pressure on, try to sway public opinion, and eventually force some sort of equitable solution.

I spent a day with Jesse Jackson, mostly visiting African-American churches. Some Democratic leaders were afraid that Jackson would sensationalize the situation, allowing the Republicans to attack him and divert attention from the real issue. I believed that Jackson was doing exactly what he should be doing, continuing to raise awareness and keeping people actively involved in the protest.

I had barely slept since the election. When the first legal decisions seemed to be moving in our direction, the Republicans began physically trying to stop the recount. The GOP bussed down operatives from Washington, D.C., and Virginia and staged a riot to try to intimidate the Miami–Dade County Board of Elections into suspending the recount. These Republican efforts were disgusting, they were un-American—and sadly, they were effective. The situation got really nasty on Friday, as Eric Johnson, Josh Rogin, my aide Daniella Howard, and I went to the County Government Center for a CNN interview. Dozens of Republican and Democratic picketers were standing in large groups, performing for the cameras. As I walked toward CNN's trailer, someone from another TV station stuck a microphone in front of me and asked me a question. When I began answering the question, Republican protestors behind me raised their signs. It was the usual: Sore Losers, No Recount, the Bush slogans. One of these signs was made of heavy wood and was being swung close to my head. The situation was becoming violent. Someone standing nearby shouted, "Stick it in front of his face." As that heavy sign started coming down over me, Eric grabbed it to protect me from being clobbered by it and threw it to the ground.

That's when the sheriff moved in. The situation was so volatile that they immediately clamped down on the slightest provocation. The officer grabbed Eric and hustled him away. In the confusion, I had no idea what had happened to him. The crowd closed in and people began pushing and shoving. Josh grabbed me and we pushed our way through the crowd into a small telecommunications van. After we'd waited there several minutes, the police escorted us through the Republican crowd back to the parking lot where the interview was scheduled to be conducted. With a police guard standing behind me, I did the interview. Josh and Daniella eventually found Eric and explained to the officers what had happened. Reluctantly, they released him.

I don't know when the first death threats were called into my office. They were similar to the vulgar calls I'd gotten during the impeachment, except that there were many more of them. The stakes were much higher this time and everybody knew it. Soon after the calls and letters started arriving, I ended up getting my security detail back.

All other congressional business stopped. The electoral system of the United States had collapsed. The country had voted for its next president, and nobody had any idea who had actually won. The situation was so pathetic that Fidel Castro referred to America as "a banana republic." One thing was becoming quite clear: This election was not going to be decided by the voters. The courts were going to determine the next president. While I was convinced that my constituents had been disenfranchised by the illegal ballot, finding a practical remedy was going to be difficult. But as their representative, I persisted in arguing that no matter what remedy was chosen, for the result to be legitimate, each Florida vote had to be counted. At a rally in Boca Raton I told hundreds of elderly voters, "The will of the American people must be honored and determined by an impartial third party . . . Gore has the most popular votes, and Bush has more votes in the Electoral College. The media does a great disservice if it's concerned about wrapping this up quickly. This is about the right to vote and the right to have your vote counted."

What was also becoming clear was that my constituents were furious and they expected their representative to stand up for them. I had represented many of these people for a decade and I had never seen them so angry. While they had been truly upset by Republican attempts to impeach Bill Clinton, they had been able to keep their feelings under control. Not this time. This time many of them truly believed the Republicans were trying to steal the presidency. And they were absolutely right. I remember a ninety-year-old man from Delray Beach telling me that this was probably going to be his last presidential election—and he didn't want his last vote to have been for Pat Buchanan. Seventy-eight-year-old Boca resident Ben Packer told a reporter, "We want to tell the rest of the nation what our feelings are."

That was also my job.

The biggest hurdle we faced was that Republicans held all the key political positions in the state. Jeb Bush was governor and Katherine Harris—George Bush's Florida campaign chairman—was secretary of state and in charge of certifying the election. And as it turned out, the key was that Republicans also had a majority on the United States Supreme Court.

As far as I was concerned, the most important Democrat on the Palm Beach County Canvassing Board was Theresa LePore. That board consisted of Democrats LePore and Commissioner Carol Roberts and one Republican. I certainly wasn't angry with Theresa LePore. Her motives were absolutely correct; she'd tried to do the right thing by creating a ballot that was voter friendly. So I assumed that when decisions had to be made, she would be objective and try to minimize the ramifications of her honest mistake. That turned out not to be true. I was astonished when she voted against starting the recount. That didn't seem possible; a recount actually was the only possible way Ms. LePore could save her reputation. Why would she want to stop it? But she did.

What was worse, much worse, was that when the courts ordered her to start the recount, she shut down the office for the Thanksgiving holiday period. Meanwhile, Katherine Harris had announced that she would not extend the deadline for accepting the election results—and because the office had been closed, Palm Beach County didn't meet that deadline.

Prior to the election I had enjoyed a reasonable working relationship with Florida governor Jeb Bush. Each time he'd run for governor I had energetically supported his Democratic opponent. But when it became clear on his second attempt in 1998 that he was going to win, I had a cordial meeting with him. Both of us understood the importance to Florida of a good working relationship between the governor and members of Congress, even if there were partisan differences. For a time before the 2000 election our relationship was genuine and constructive. In fact, I made a point of complimenting him—saying often that he was engaged, smart, and principled.

When the postelection maneuvering began, I was among several people who urged Governor Bush to recuse himself from his position on the three-person election candidacy commission, to stay out of it, because obviously he was partial to his brother. And while he did announce publicly that he was not going to participate, privately he was quite active for his brother.

For six weeks we rode a political roller coaster. Almost three weeks after the election, Katherine Harris certified the results with George Bush ahead by 537 votes—but she refused to include the results from Palm Beach County, which were completed two hours after the Florida Supreme Court deadline expired. That meant that about fourteen thousand undervotes were not counted. On December 8, more than a month after the election, the Florida Supreme Court ordered a manual recount in all counties with a large number of undervotes. Finally, we were going to get a fair counting of the ballots. That's all I had been asking for—let my people's votes count—and that is precisely what the Republicans had desperately been trying to stop.

By this time most of the legal maneuvering had shifted away from Palm Beach County but I was still involved, making appearances on television, talking to state legislators I knew, keeping in touch with Joe Lieberman to find out what the campaign intended to do.

I was never optimistic. Republicans held the majority in both houses of Congress and it seemed plausible that this whole mess was going to get dumped there. But eventually the Bush campaign took its argument to federal court. This didn't surprise me, as there were major federal and constitutional issues involved. I did believe that the federal courts—especially the Supreme Court—would show more deference to the Florida courts. But citing the equal protection clause of the Fourteenth Amendment, claiming that voters' rights would be hurt if different standards were used to count ballots in different counties, the Supreme Court of the United States ordered the recount to be stopped. Justice John Paul Stevens's dissent lamented that the decision would only "lend credence to the most cynical appraisal of the work of judges throughout the land," and Harvard law professor Alan Dershowitz said eloquently that "the decision in the Florida election case may be ranked as the single most corrupt decision in Supreme Court history, because it is the only one that I know of where the majority justices decided as they did because of the personal identity and political affiliation of the litigants. This was cheating, and a violation of the judicial oath."

Amen.

The Republican-dominated Court added that their decision was not to be used as a precedent. It's almost as if the majority of the Supreme Court knew that its decision was misguided and that it undermined the credibility of the Court. Actually, the Supreme Court decision was worse than misguided—it resulted in the blatant theft of the presidency.

Every politician learns how to lose as well as win—and as a Democrat I had a lot of practice losing. Through most of my career I'd tried to salvage what was possible, stand up for my constituents, and use the influence I had as a member of Congress in areas where partisanship played less of a role, such as foreign relations and constituent services, where I could do some good. But this Supreme Court ruling infuriated me. I was just outraged by it. Like many of my constituents, I feel it is a wound that will never completely heal. I was determined that I would do everything possible to make certain nothing like Election 2000 ever happened again. I devoted myself to repairing our broken election system and rebuilding the confidence of the American people in our election process. In a column I wrote in a local newspaper I said, "Make no mistake, what we all witnessed in Florida was nothing less than a silencing of the people's will . . . By refusing to allow a full count of unread ballots, the Supreme Court did not run out the clock on Democrats, they ran out the clock on democracy . . .

"To my constituents I pledge to work to make certain that what happened in Florida will never happen again. I plan to take an active role in reforming the voting system in Florida and throughout the country."

15

The Paper Chase:
Making Your Vote Count

It's not the voting that's democracy, it's the counting.

—Tom Stoppard

Can one congressman make a difference on a national issue? I'd assumed so, but now I intended to find out. The reality is that sometimes issues find legislators. This one had found me. Nothing is more fundamental to a functioning democracy than voting rights, and the American system had broken down. Since my constituents had been the ones immediately affected, I felt compelled to learn all I could about voting machines, ballot design, and the science and methodology of elections. As a member of Congress, I had the bully pulpit—access to publicity—and both legal and legislative paths to follow.

My staff and I began by meeting in my office with several experts regarding the new electronic ATM-style voting machines that were being developed. And every one of them, literally every one of them, told us that the new electronic voting machines are not secure. Even the most sophisticated voting machines had glaring shortcomings. I've yet to meet a computer expert who will attest that these machines can't be tampered with or manipulated or won't malfunction. Computers are fallible. They can be hacked, they break, they crash, and design flaws happen. Knowing that, it is self-evident that American democracy cannot be solely dependent upon electronic machines to provide an accurate count of the vote. These machines are incapable of conducting any type of meaningful recount. Imagine that the world's most powerful democracy was just one computer glitch, one design flaw, or one hack away from total electoral chaos. This was the nightmare scenario I envisioned, which had to be prevented from happening. That's why I began a crusade for voter-verified paper ballots in Florida and then throughout the nation: ballots that can be recounted in close elections, ballots that can be audited, ballots that can be checked. This wasn't a partisan issue, and it wasn't rocket science. Most voters, people from all political perspectives, understood that it was just common sense.

I was astonished to discover that many elected officials didn't see it the same way I did. Some even argued that electronic voting machines are infallible. The last time we heard something like that, of course, was when the *Titanic* set sail.

This isn't a new problem. Originally America voted by paper ballot. When there are two means of verifying a vote, a machine tabulation and a supporting paper trail, there is a greater likelihood of an accurate vote tally with paper ballots. Also, the backup system gives voters more confidence in the integrity of the system and that their votes will be counted accurately. Since we first began dropping a paper ballot into a box, people have searched for a simple and secure technological way of making sure every vote is counted. More than a century ago, in 1892, when lever-operated voting machines began replacing paper ballots, people first began demanding a paper receipt. It was incredible to me that more than a hundred years later we were fighting the same battle.

If we'd had a voter-verified paper trail to follow in 2000, the world would be a much different place. After the 2000 election, Florida recognized that changes had to be made, and the state legislature passed the Florida Election Reform Act, which prohibited the use of punch-card machines—no more hanging chads. The "intent of the voter" was replaced by "a clear indication on the ballot" of the voter's choice. A year later, Congress passed the Help America Vote Act, which funded the purchase of electronic voting machines and instituted basic national voting procedures. As a result, a majority of Florida counties bought optical scan voting machines, which do provide backup voter-verified paper ballots—but fifteen other counties, including Palm Beach, Broward, and Miami-Dade, decided on touch-screen machines that do not provide a paper trail unless an expensive printer is attached. But no printers were certified for use in Florida by the state, which is why the machines never should have been allowed. In fact, the bipartisan commission set up by the state recommended a uniform election system, with all Florida counties using optical scan machines. But under pressure from Sandra Mortham, an ally of Governor Jeb Bush and a former Republican Florida secretary of state—who was paid handsomely by electronic voting machine companies to lobby on their behalf—the legislature allowed touch-screen voting machines to be used. In other words, nothing had changed. These fancy new machines did not produce a verifiable record of each person's vote. There was no way of verifying that the machines had correctly recorded each vote. And they completely eliminated the possibility of a recount.

I wrote letters to Governor Bush and to Glenda Hood, Florida's new secretary of state, complaining about the lack of a paper trail and asking them to purchase the printers. For some reason I have yet to understand, these people did not want a verifiable voting system. Bush was the biggest impediment, and he fought me ferociously until the day he left office.

Theresa LePore insisted that a paper trail was completely unnecessary, that the new technologies were easy to use, reliable, and efficient. Personally, I have wondered if she just wanted to make sure she would never be involved in another recount. Think of it this way: If touch-screen machines had been used in the 2000 election, there would have been no way of conducting a recount. Would anybody make a cash deposit at an ATM if the machine gave them no record of their deposit?

In Congress, New Jersey Democrat Rush Holt felt just as strongly as

I did about the need for a certifiable system and took the lead in filing federal legislation. I didn't know him well initially, but through this issue we developed a strong working relationship. When he originally filed his bill, the Republicans held the majority, so there was little chance it would pass.

Meanwhile, in several different elections, the new electronic machines proved to be a disaster. In a 2002 election for a seat on Boca Raton's city council, former mayor Emil Danciu was stunned when he finished third. His supporters claimed that when they touched his name on the screen, the machine tallied a vote for his opponent. It was later learned that after the election the cartridges from fifteen voting machines in his home precinct had been taken home by a worker. When they were finally examined, several of them proved to be blank. When the former mayor, represented by his daughter, Charlotte, sued the manufacturer, he learned that under Florida law the codes were considered to be trade secrets and the state was not permitted access to them.

The election for mayor of the small Florida town of Wellington was decided by only 4 votes—but 78 votes did not register on the machines at all. The election of a new mayor was the only race on the ballot. One of two things happened in Wellington—either seventy-eight citizens took the trouble to go to the polls for a local election but decided not to vote, or we had a big problem with the electronic voting machines.

In the Florida Democratic primary for governor that year, one precinct with more than a thousand registered voters reported no votes, and many other votes were not counted because the machines were shut down improperly. But Jeb Bush and Theresa LePore continued to defend the system. She continued to adamantly oppose a paper trail.

Those people who continued to believe in the integrity of electronic voting machines must have had their faith shattered in 2003 when the CEO of Diebold, the company making many of those machines, wrote to potential Bush contributors that he was "committed to helping Ohio deliver its electoral votes for the president next year."

Finally, the results of a Florida state house election were put into doubt after 134 people supposedly drove to the polls where there was only one race on the ballot but decided not to vote. The margin of victory was only twelve votes. Clearly, something was still very wrong. I realized I had no choice. I filed a lawsuit against Theresa LePore and Secretary of State Glenda Hood, contending that the new electronic voting machines were not in compliance with Florida law because they generated no paper trail and therefore could not be used in a manual recount. That was the first lawsuit I had ever filed in my life.

Glenda Hood responded that "it is a great disservice to create the feeling that there's a problem when there is not," because Florida had purchased and was using the best available technology.

I felt so strongly about the urgency of creating a paper trail that I decided to support a candidate for election against Theresa LePore. The 2000 election had changed her life. She told a reporter in 2005 that when she goes to a restaurant now, she always sits with her back to the wall. Each day she took a different route to work, and had stopped going to the grocery store. She was called every possible terrible name and received hate mail and death threats. She couldn't even shake hands with people without worrying that they might attack her. I never believed that she had created the butterfly ballot for anything but the proper reasons—but when she halted the recount and consistently refused to support a paper trail, I knew she had to be defeated. By this time she had left the Democratic Party and was running for her third term with no party affiliation—and the office itself had been made officially nonpartisan.

Members of Congress often get involved in local elections as well as national elections. We've been elected in a district populated by almost seven hundred thousand people, and our support for a candidate will sometimes make a difference. But it is rare that a congressman becomes deeply involved in an election for supervisor of elections. Usually the party nominates someone, and all the elected officials of that party support that candidate. This situation was very different. I actively tried to recruit several people to run against her, including former congressman Harry Johnston, a man of impeccable integrity, but either they didn't believe Ms. LePore could be beaten or they weren't interested in the job and turned me down. Finally a man named Arthur Anderson, a former school board member, announced that he was running, and I decided to support him. Arthur was carrying some political baggage: There were allegations that he had tax liens levied against him, that he hadn't made court-ordered child support payments, and that he had run afoul of some campaign finance laws. He was not the ideal candidate. But he made getting Palm Beach County a paper trail his number one issue, and as long as Theresa LePore stayed in power, there would never be a paper trail, which was unacceptable.

So I helped raise money for Anderson's campaign. I campaigned with him in every major condo, I attended rallies with him, I even brought down Joe Lieberman and Howard Dean to campaign for him. And nothing seemed to make a difference. The media came down hard on Arthur Anderson and almost unanimously supported LePore. Eventually she just stopped campaigning. It looked as if the election would result in a LePore landslide. However, since I was also up for reelection, we decided I would run television ads for my campaign in which I explained why I had gotten so deeply involved in the paper trail issue and why I was so pleased to be working with Arthur Anderson in the fight against Jeb Bush and Theresa LePore. LePore reacted by attacking me in the newspapers. Just as people were about to cast their vote, she turned the election from LePore versus Anderson to LePore versus Wexler. It was a huge upset. Anderson won—with no recount necessary.

Unfortunately, my court case did not proceed as well. We had filed the case in both state and federal court because Jeff Liggio, my lawyer, who had taken the case pro bono, wanted to try all possible legal venues. A Palm Beach County judge dismissed the state case because I did not have standing to sue. My election had not been affected by the voting machines and I couldn't show that my own vote had been affected. When we appealed that ruling, the court rejected our argument again, writing that voters are not guaranteed "a perfect voting system." Perfect? How about a just legal system, since Florida law required a manual recount that machines couldn't do!

U.S. District Court Judge James Cohn threw out the federal case, primarily because it was already being considered by the state courts, writing that the federal courts should not become "deeply involved with election legislation and election procedures, which the Constitution and the Supreme Court have delegated to the states." He did not mention the involvement of the Supreme Court in the 2000 election. A federal appeals court finally agreed with us, not on the issue of a paper trail, but simply that it was reasonable to sue in both state and federal courts.

It seemed as if I was in court all the time. I actually testified in the federal case, which was another first for me. Eventually we appealed all the way to the United States Supreme Court—ironically arguing as a precedent *Bush v. Gore*. We argued that Florida was disenfranchising its voters because some Florida counties use electronic machines that do not provide paper ballots, which would make a recount impossible, while the machines used in other counties do provide a paper trail. Our argument was that all voters had to be treated equally. But the Supreme Court refused to hear the case, effectively ending the legal path.

Just when it appeared that I had run out of options, political lightning struck. In 2006, Democrat Jim Davis and Republican Charlie Crist, "Chain Gang" Charlie, competed to replace two-term-limited governor Jeb Bush. Two excellent candidates. Jim Davis was a thoughtful and respected member of Congress and I supported him in both the primary and the general election. But Charlie Crist and I were old friends. We had worked closely together as state senators, and when Charlie was elected attorney general we conducted bipartisan town hall meetings together.

During the campaign, Charlie would occasionally call me to discuss the issues. Charlie has an unusual quality for a politician—he actually listens to people. I told Charlie flat out that guaranteeing a paper trail would be a bold and unexpected position for a Republican candidate for governor to take. I spoke with Jim Davis about it, too. I knew from my own polling that it was an issue South Florida voters cared about deeply; they were still angry about the 2000 election and, by a great majority, believed the problems had not been solved. Almost from the beginning, Crist was favorably inclined, but he had to learn more about it and find his own footing. Of course, I never expected he would actually support a paper trail, let alone champion it.

Ironically, Crist had been peripherally involved in the issue. As state attorney general, his lawyers represented the governor and the secretary of state in their battle against me. We'd discussed that, and I was never under any illusion that Charlie was going to take a position other than one supportive of Governor Bush.

Guaranteeing a paper trail became an issue in the gubernatorial election campaign. During a debate on his MSNBC show, *Hardball*, Chris Matthews asked both candidates where they stood on the issue and both men responded that they supported guaranteeing a paper trail. People expected that from the Democrat but were very surprised when the Republican took a position completely opposite to that of Jeb Bush. During the debate, Charlie had said a few things that were confusing about how a paper trail would operate, so afterward I talked to him about it.

In politics you learn there are few people you can ultimately trust. After the election and Charlie's victory, our discussions about a paper trail became very specific. On several occasions I told him his popularity would go sky-high in Democratic areas if he would do it. Even though Governor Crist is a Republican and we certainly have our differences of opinion, Charlie is someone I trust. We had a long history together, and we'd developed that trust when neither one of us needed the other and we weren't competitors. So it was real.

As an added impetus, in the November 2006 election to replace Katherine Harris as Sarasota's representative, the Republican won by 368 votes—but supposedly more than eighteen thousand people went to the polls, voted in other races, and amazingly recorded no vote in the congressional race. This was yet another example of something going dramatically wrong in a county using touch-screen voting machines, and no paper trail existed to figure out what had happened. Once again, disgusted Florida voters were left with an uncertain result. What a fitting legacy for Governor Jeb Bush as he left office!

One of new governor Charlie Crist's first actions was to appoint as secretary of state the election supervisor who had been the chief expert witness against me in my federal lawsuit. That was somewhat surprising—until Charlie called me and told me he was more committed than ever to creating a paper trail. I believed he meant it, although I wondered whether the forces of politics would allow him to do it. But he kept telling me he was seriously committed to it. When I told members of my staff about it they rolled their eyes and told me I was delusional. "No," I told them, "Charlie's for real. Charlie is committed to doing this."

Governor Crist and I continued to talk about it, and then one day he called to tell me, "I'm putting money in my budget to pay for a paper trail in every precinct in Florida." His administration developed its own proposal, with our input. It really was their work product, but the results were the same. In May 2007, as I stood a few steps to his side, Governor Crist came from Tallahassee to the office of the Palm Beach County supervisor of elections, Arthur Anderson, and signed legislation that required all voting in Florida be conducted on optical scan machines that used paper ballots—but also had a provision allowing the disabled to vote using a touch screen. In some ways, that provided at least a semblance of closure for the 2000 elections. Before the signing ceremony, Charlie gave me credit for persuading him to do it. The realization that we finally had a paper trail in Florida made me smile from ear to ear. It had been a very long battle, in which many people and organizations had fought alongside me. Imagine this: A Republican and a Democrat worked together to accomplish something important for the people, and Florida now has a guaranteed paper ballot voting system and has become the model for the nation. How very far we were from Washington, D.C.

16

Congress as Lapdog:
The GOP's Oversight of Oversight

We have forty million reasons for failure but not a single excuse.

—Rudyard Kipling

For six years the Republicans in Congress turned their backs on one of the most vital responsibilities of Congress: conducting oversight. President Woodrow Wilson said about the Congress, "Quite as important as lawmaking is its vigilant oversight of the administration." Every elementary-school child learns that a basic principle of effective government is a system of checks and balances that prevents any of the three branches from seizing power over the other two branches. The power of oversight is one of the checks. We're the guys who are supposed to make certain the government is functioning correctly, that the laws are being followed, that money is being spent for the purpose it was allocated for, and that the various executive agencies are all acting within their powers.

Please, stop laughing.

I know congressional oversight is supposed to work that way because

I've read it in the manuals. Obviously, it doesn't. Perhaps the one thing that disappointed me most about serving in the minority was the total lack of oversight we exercised over the Bush administration. During that time, wrote *The New York Times* in its scathing editorial of December 31, 2007:

> President Bush squandered America's position of moral and political leadership, swept aside international institutions and treaties, sullied America's global image, and trampled on the constitutional pillars that have supported our democracy through the most terrifying and challenging times. These policies have fed the world's anger and alienation and have not made any of us safer.
>
> We have seen the president, sworn to defend the Constitution, turn his powers on his own citizens, authorizing the intelligence agencies to spy on Americans, wiretapping phones, and interrupting international e-mail messages without a warrant.
>
> We have read accounts of how the government's top lawyers huddled in secret after the attacks in New York and Washington and plotted ways to circumvent the Geneva Conventions—and both American and international law—to hold anyone the president chose indefinitely without charges or judicial review . . .

Congress is supposed to be the fierce watchdog of the public's interest. The Republican Congress was more of a sleeping puppy. For six years they did nothing more than rubber-stamp the administration's policies. When the Democrats tried to hold a hearing or call witnesses, we were voted down. Who knows what we might have been able to accomplish if the House had simply done its job. Even if the Republicans had agreed with the administration on every issue, which obviously they did, it still should have been vital to exercise our oversight powers to help make better policy. I think it would be fair to say that was not done on a regular basis.

Actually, never.

Hardly any subpoenas were issued to the Bush White House by the Republican majority. In fact the Republican chairman of what was once known as the House Oversight and Government Reform Committee, Tom Davis of Virginia, removed the word *Oversight* from its name. One of Henry Waxman's first actions as the new chairman after the 2006 elections was to restore it. There's no question that the Republicans knew how to do oversight, because they had so much experience doing it during the Clinton administration. They never stopped. I'm certain the oversight powers had been used for political purposes many times before I got to Congress, but I don't believe they had ever before been used so irrationally, so vindictively, and in such a partisan fashion that the final result was the unjust attempted impeachment of the president. That was the ultimate oversight.

Ironically, following the 2006 election, Republicans in the House began complaining that Democrats were abusing their oversight powers by issuing a thousand subpoenas to the Bush administration. "Bush-bashing" they called it—while neglecting to mention that they had issued almost none. In fact, between 1997 and 2002 the House Government Reform Committee handed out 1,052 subpoenas and spent thirty-five million dollars to investigate the Clinton administration—and over the next three years issued only three subpoenas to members of the Bush administration, two of them to Energy Department officials during an inquiry about nuclear waste disposal at Yucca Mountain and one to the Defense Department, requesting documents relating to the response to Hurricane Katrina.

But of all the shameful things done—or more accurately, not done—by the Republican leadership in the House, nothing was more disgraceful than the abdication of any oversight of the Iraq War. Thousands of Americans were dying, thousands more were being maimed, and we were spending billions of taxpayer dollars, yet the Foreign Affairs Committee held not a single hearing about the war for two years. We had hearings about information that Yahoo! provided to the Chinese government, but not one hearing about Iraq. We spent half a trillion dollars in Iraq and never talked about it.

While in the minority, the only way Democrats could force the subject of Iraq to be brought up was to use a resolution of inquiry, a parliamentary tactic requesting specific documents from the administration, which requires the relevant committee to debate an issue and bring it up for a vote or bring it to the full House for a debate and vote. Democrats have used it many times with a perfect lack of success. We always got voted down—but at least we forced the Republicans in the House to acknowledge that a war was being fought and we were approving billions of dollars to fund that war without conducting any oversight. I almost had a resolution of inquiry passed in 2006. When it was disclosed that the National Security Agency was conducting a domestic surveillance program, specifically by collecting telephone data, I filed a resolution of inquiry in the Judiciary Committee demanding "all documents in the possession of the President and the Attorney General, including all legal opinions, relating to requests made without a warrant by the National Security Agency or other Federal departments and agencies to telephone service providers, including wireless telephone service providers, for access to telephone communications records of persons in the United States." For the first time in American history—at least as far as we know—the federal government was getting the records of trillions of completely legal phone calls made . . . possibly by you.

Truthfully, like the numerous other resolutions we'd filed, I expected the Republicans to vote it down. But they made a parliamentary error. This was so-called privileged legislation, meaning that if the committee failed to act on it within fourteen days I would be allowed to bring it to the floor of the House. I introduced it just before the Memorial Day recess, and Congress adjourned for two weeks. By the time we were back in session, the required fourteen days had passed. I now had the option of bringing it directly to the floor, where the Republicans would be forced to vote *against* investigating the government for illegally wiretapping the telephones of completely innocent American citizens. That wasn't a good issue for them.

This was particularly embarrassing for the Republican Judiciary Committee chairman at that time, James Sensenbrenner. It would mean putting the Republicans on the spot in a very public way. But he was also having his own problems with the Department of Justice. Months earlier he'd requested some innocuous documents and been completely ignored. So he offered me a deal: If I agreed not to bring the resolution to the floor, he would agree to hold hearings in committee and report it out of committee.

We'd spent years getting nothing. If I brought it to the floor it would be voted down. This offer was better than nothing. At least it would give us the opportunity to debate the wiretapping program. We could bring national attention to this invasion of privacy. So I accepted his offer. We debated my resolution in the committee, and with Sensenbrenner's support it passed unanimously and was sent directly to the Department of Justice.

Where it was ignored. And there was nothing Democrats could do about it. That's how bad things were in committees for the Democratic minority. Only when the Republicans were forced into an oversight role did the House show the slightest interest in investigating the actions of the executive branch. The quaint notion that we were a coequal branch of government, which had been so ingrained in the system by the Founding Fathers, was completely ignored. We had become subservient to the executive branch.

That began to change after the 2006 elections. One of the first things Nancy Pelosi did was hire two hundred new staffers to begin investigations into the Bush administration, ranging from which top officials revealed the name of covert CIA operative Valerie Plame and destroyed an active CIA front company in an effort to discredit her husband, to the conduct of the administration in the Iraq War.

The Bush administration has tried to fight these investigations, claiming repeatedly that Congress has no constitutional authority to investigate wartime strategy, that the only powers granted to Congress are the authority to declare war and then fund that war. Just give them the money. When Democrats insisted that the House had the right to investigate how that money was being spent, the administration cried that Democrats were trying to deprive troops in the field of food and armor. This was the worst kind of cynicism—the Republicans, with the support of the right-wing radio propagandists, were trying to persuade the public that by asking questions, the Democrats were undermining the troops in the field.

Well, the right of the House to question the conduct of the executive branch in war goes all the way back to 1791, to the Second Congress, when General Arthur St. Clair led an underequipped and undertrained army into battle against the Native Americans settled along the Wabash

River in Ohio. In that disaster, 657 troops were killed and 271 were wounded. A resolution was introduced in the House, then meeting in Philadelphia, asking President Washington to initiate an investigation of this military debacle. The majority felt that forcing the president to launch this investigation was disrespectful and perhaps beyond the powers of Congress, and defeated the resolution 35 to 21. But several months later, perhaps due to public pressure, which grew as news of this defeat spread throughout the young country, the House created a committee to investigate the expenditure of funds for St. Clair's mission, and it authorized this committee to collect the pertinent records and documents and conduct the necessary interviews to figure out what had gone wrong.

President Washington resisted. Sound familiar?

Nothing like this had ever been done before and no one was certain how to proceed. The president's cabinet agreed that in order to determine if the money the House had provided had been properly spent, Congress had the right to conduct this investigation. The investigation revealed a widespread mismanagement of military stores and supplies. Specifically, the muskets issued to the soldiers were found to be defective and the ammunition they were using was of especially poor quality.

General St. Clair and his soldiers were cleared, and the quartermaster general was found to be responsible for these failures.

This was the very first House investigation into the actions of the executive branch and it established the right of House committees to compel executive branch officials to testify. And for two hundred years that's the way the House conducted its business—until the Republican decision to acquiesce to the Bush administration changed the balance of power between the three branches of government.

Every effort the Democrats made to conduct any oversight was resisted by the Republicans. Some of the actions they allowed the Bush administration to get away with were clearly unconstitutional. In 2005, for example, NBC News obtained a 400-page Defense Department document listing secret domestic surveillance operations conducted by the government without first obtaining a warrant; in other words, cases in which the government was spying on American citizens without any judicial review. The administration defended itself by claiming that every organization it had investigated was linked to al-Qaeda and that these operations were necessary for national security.

One of the dangerous groups on the list was located in my district. This "credible threat" to America was called The Truth Project, and it consisted of eight mostly elderly people who met at a Quaker Meeting House and whose entire purpose was to hand out counterrecruitment pamphlets in local high schools. Among the members were a seventy-nine-year-old grandmother and a Korean War veteran named Richard Hersh, a former teacher, who had a nerve disease that caused him to use a wheelchair. Probably the most subversive action ever taken by Hersh was stationed on a corner in Delray Beach holding up a HONK FOR PEACE sign. These were hardly the kinds of people the Bush administration could consider a threat to America, and certainly proved that Bush and Cheney were not telling the truth when they claimed that these warrantless wiretaps and surveillance activities were aimed only at conversations between Americans and terrorists. This was exactly the kind of abuse of power that had been carried out by the Nixon administration during the Vietnam War. If there ever was a situation that required oversight, this was it. When Chairman Sensenbrenner refused to hold a committee hearing, or give the Democrats a room in which to hold our own hearing, the ranking Democrat on the committee, John Conyers, called a meeting. A meeting has no official status, just people getting together to talk—even if it has all the trappings of an official hearing. Among several people we invited to testify was Richard Hersh. On a Friday morning in early January 2006, we met in a small room in the basement of the Rayburn building.

Also testifying was former Reagan administration associate deputy attorney general Bruce Fein, who pointed out angrily, "The Founding Fathers understood that men were not angels and that 'Trust me' was not a good enough protection for our civil liberties. And accordingly, they created a tripartite system of government whereby the legislative, executive, and judicial branches would be restraints upon one another."

When Hersh testified I asked him, "Have any of your members ever traveled to Pakistan?" They had not. "Have any of your members ever traveled to Afghanistan?" Nope. In fact, he explained, he wasn't certain that any members of this group actually had a passport.

Then he explained how the United States government had spied on his group. In addition to an agent infiltrating their meetings, he said, "Agents rummaged through trash, snooped into e-mail, hacked Web sites, and listened in on phone conversations. Indeed, address books and activist meeting lists have disappeared."

Your tax dollars at work. Going through the garbage of people who dared to disagree with the decisions of the Bush administration. When it was my turn to make a statement, I said, "I think most Americans, when they hear descriptions of surveillance and wiretaps say, 'Well, that can't happen to me. I'm just going to work. I'm just driving my kids to school. I'm just a retiree. I just go to church or synagogue. I just go and exercise my religious rights the way I wish' . . . And there shouldn't be a single American that today remains confident that it couldn't happen to them, because that is how it happened in Palm Beach County."

This meeting got some media coverage, but not at all equal to the dangers to our constitutional rights it exposed. And most frustrating to me was the fact that the Republicans once again had completely abrogated their oversight responsibilities. They were complicit with the administration in refusing to even hold a hearing after learning about these widespread abuses of Americans' civil liberties, and they then tried to prevent the American people from learning the truth.

Before the 2006 elections the Republicans lived in fear that we would take control of the House—because with that control came subpoena power. The right-wing radio zealots were screeching warnings to their true believers that the Democrats would use that power to launch witch hunts whose sole purpose was to destroy the president. Nothing much was said about investigating the ineptitude as well as the malfeasance of the administration.

One of the primary objectives of oversight is not to uncover intentional wrongdoing, but rather to figure out why things went wrong and find ways to fix them. The job isn't only to point out the glaring failures of the government to deal with the devastation caused by Hurricane Katrina, for example, but rather to understand why FEMA was unprepared to deal with a major emergency and make those changes necessary to ensure that it will be capable of dealing with the next catastrophic event.

Since Nancy Pelosi proudly accepted the gavel from Denny Hastert, we have used our oversight powers to try to look beneath the cloak of secrecy that the Republicans had pulled over the actions of the Bush administration, to reveal to the American public how their trust and dollars have been misused. In our first one hundred days in office we conducted more than six hundred oversight hearings, including more than seventy-five hearings about Iraq, ranging from why our troops did not have sufficient armor to why our strategy has failed so completely. We held more hearings about the war in three weeks than the Republicans had held in three years.

In a relatively short time, these oversight hearings revealed the attempt by the Bush administration to politicize the entire executive branch, from the surgeon general to the attorney general's office, to an extent that had never before been done. For example, we learned that the surgeon general was told which medical conditions were politically correct—and that in every speech he gave he was to mention George Bush's name three times on every page. We learned that Attorney General Gonzales populated his office with young and inexperienced graduates of a very small religious college and fired eight competent U.S. attorneys solely for political reasons. In fact, during a Judiciary Committee hearing when I asked the attorney general who had decided those eight U.S. attorneys should be fired, he looked at me and admitted he didn't know. The attorney general runs the Justice Department, yet he claimed he did not know who had made such significant decisions. That did not sound believable to me. I challenged him. "So a group of people put Mr. [David] Iglesias [New Mexico] on the list [to be fired]? . . . You've also said you didn't put him on the list. So somebody other than you, other than the president, other than the vice president, other than every deputy attorney general that has come to this committee, put him on the list. But with all due respect Mr. Attorney General, you won't tell the American people who put Mr. Iglesias on the list to be fired. It's a national secret, isn't it! . . . You know who put him on the list, but you won't tell us."

Eventually the pressure put on the Bush administration became too strong and Gonzales was removed from his job—and by making his ineptitude public, these oversight hearings contributed to that necessary change.

The list of the failures of the Bush administration sometimes seems endless. The head of FEMA, Michael "Heck of a job" Brown, was a political appointee whose major qualification for that sensitive job was his loyalty to the administration—and the result of the inability of the government to respond to the Katrina disaster was chaos, misery, and death. When *The Washington Post* revealed that wounded Iraq War veterans were not receiving the proper housing or treatment at Walter Reed Army Medical Center, oversight hearings under the new Democratic majority led to the hospital's leadership being replaced and the conditions improved. On issues ranging from the enforcement of civil rights legislation to investigating industry-too-friendly energy and environmental policies, from the illegal torture of war prisoners to the funding of religious-oriented abstinence programs, the House has finally resumed its duty to oversee the executive branch.

17

He Betrayed His Country, Not His Wife: Why Cheney (and Probably Bush) Should Be Impeached

---

Bush and Cheney are clearly guilty of numerous impeachable offenses. They have repeatedly violated the Constitution. They have transgressed national and international law. They have lied to the American people time after time. Their conduct and their barbaric policies have reduced our beloved country to a historic low in the eyes of people around the world. These are truly "high crimes and misdemeanors," to use the constitutional standard.

—George McGovern,
Washington Post editorial, January 6, 2008

One thing you almost have to respect about the Republicans: They have no shame about using their power to bludgeon opponents into submission. Using their right-wing radio and TV attack henchmen to broadcast their positions, they have been extraordinarily effective in creating a united bloc. I see it in my office. After Limbaugh and his sycophants attacked me for daring to question General Petraeus, my office was deluged with phone calls from all over the country. Some of the callers were polite, but most were spewing rage.

The Republicans have perfected the art of rallying their base around a cause—usually appealing to patriotism, religion, or bias. Sometimes their ability to manipulate their base is nearly Orwellian. A perfect example is President Bush's commutation of the prison sentence of Vice President Cheney's former chief of staff, I. "Scooter" Libby. As part of the administration's disinformation campaign to hide its prewar propaganda effort, Libby had revealed the identity of a covert CIA agent to the press. Just imagine that: Bush and Cheney built their entire case for war around the threat that Saddam Hussein possessed weapons of mass destruction, and in order to cast doubt on evidence indicating that Iraq did not have those weapons, they revealed the identity of a CIA agent—Valerie Plame Wilson—whose husband was assigned to gather information about those weapons. These so-called patriots revealed the identity of a covert CIA agent solely for political purposes, destroying the network she managed and potentially putting lives in danger. The magnitude of such reckless behavior is breathtaking. In their race to war they stopped at nothing. Nothing mattered—the truth, decency, integrity—none of it mattered when it came to manipulating Americans into believing that we were justified in launching an attack on Iraq. If a Democratic president had committed these acts he would have been impeached and strung up on the Washington Monument; but the administration's conservative base not only defended these actions, it justified them. It celebrated them. This "base" even had the audacity to support administration attacks on the CIA agent whose career had been destroyed. Eventually, Special Counsel Patrick J. Fitzgerald began to uncover these crimes and the subsequent cover-up. While the right wing sought to discredit Fitzgerald and his investigation, he doggedly pursued the truth. And as usual in the Bush administration, the truth was well hidden.

Libby was the sacrifice the administration tossed to the court to protect the vice president and Bush political adviser Karl Rove. He was the firewall that prevented the investigation from delving deeper into the White House. By lying to the special prosecutor, Libby made it virtually impossible for Fitzgerald to uncover the truth. President Bush initially declared boldly that he would fire any member of his administration who had leaked Plame's identity to the media. Months later, when it became clear that top-level members of his administration were responsible—specifically, the vice president's key political adviser—and that they had lied about their involvement, the president amended that promise, saying he would fire anyone convicted of a crime associated with leaking that information. Libby was convicted of lying to federal investigators trying to unravel this White House conspiracy. Lying under oath. It was far worse than the charges on which the Republicans had based their attempt to impeach President Clinton, since Libby's lies dealt with national security, not personal infidelity.

I remember so well that throughout those impeachment proceedings, Republicans insisted that their actions had nothing to do with the fact that Clinton had sexual relations with Monica Lewinsky, but rather that he had lied under oath about it. They spoke with grandeur about the importance of the truth to maintaining the integrity of our judicial system.

Except, of course, when a Republican is lying. These same Republicans now insisted that Libby had done nothing wrong; that this was just a political witch hunt. Libby was found guilty of four felonies, including two counts of perjury, one count of lying to FBI agents, and another of obstructing a federal investigation. A federal judge sentenced him to two and a half years in prison and a $250,000 fine. Conservatives were enraged. In July 2007, two weeks after Libby had been convicted, I was in Paris meeting new French president Nicolas Sarkozy's foreign minister. I remember getting a message from my office informing me that President Bush had commuted Libby's sentence. The president had reduced the sentence to the fine and two years' probation; Libby would not go to prison. In announcing this decision, Bush said the punishment remained "harsh," primarily because Libby's reputation "is forever damaged," but that he believed the jail sentence was excessive.

Excessive? The man destroyed the career of a top CIA officer, put lives in danger, and certainly compromised the security of the United States, and his punishment was that his reputation was damaged? Polls eventually found that 70 percent of Americans disagreed with this action. I assumed they agreed with me—the president was protecting himself and the vice president. The president was using his constitutional power to grant pardons and commute sentences to cover up possible crimes committed by the people closest to him and the vice president.

Bush's motives were evident: He was rewarding Libby for protecting the administration. While no one will ever know for certain, it seems plausible that Libby knew that he would be protected if he took the fall for the administration. If Bush truly believed the thirty months in prison were excessive, he could have reduced them to many fewer months. The president has the power to reduce a sentence to whatever term he deems appropriate. But in fact, based on federal sentencing guidelines, which Bush purportedly supports, it was a standard sentence. Because of President Bush's actions, Libby's penalty for committing four felonies was no jail time—and the confidence that numerous true right-wing believers would offer him profitable employment in the future. And in exchange, Cheney was protected.

This was just another in a long series of examples of right-wing hypocrisy: When Bill Clinton left office in 2001, among those people he pardoned was fugitive financier Mark Rich, who had evaded a huge tax bill and whose former wife had been a large contributor to the Clinton Library fund. Among those people who had written to Clinton requesting the Rich pardon were Israeli prime minister Ehud Barak and Spanish king Juan Carlos I. And among the lawyers representing Rich in the request for a pardon was—irony is sometimes quite beautiful, isn't it—Scooter Libby. Republicans contended angrily that the Rich pardon was "bought" by those contributions and held several hearings in the House and Senate, including one in the Judiciary Committee titled "The Controversial Pardon of International Fugitive Mark Rich." For political reasons, Republicans held a full-court press on this controversy and scored serious political points.

In contrast, the Democratic majority responded to the Libby commutation by doing . . . nothing. Nothing. Several members of the House and Senate claimed calmly to be outraged, but took no action. The silence from the Democrats was deafening. Once again, I was frustrated. We were in the majority, finally, and we were doing nothing to respond to an unpopular president who was acting with complete impunity. Well, I wanted to put the Republicans on that same record, I wanted to force them to respond to the commutation of Libby's sentence. Did they support the commutation of the sentence of a man who had risked compromising our national security for political reasons and then lied about it to a federal investigator, or were they against it?

Perhaps if I hadn't been so profoundly affected by the Clinton impeachment I wouldn't have felt so strongly about this. But having watched Republicans misuse the political and legal systems for a decade, I had finally reached the point where I needed to do something.

The question was, How should Congress respond to Bush's decision? While still in France I talked with several members of my staff and we began to consider the options. Among the options available was a resolution censuring the president. While a censure doesn't have legal ramifications, it is a powerful and public means of confronting a president. Only three times in history has Congress debated censuring a president, and only once has a president actually been censured—in 1834, when the Whig Party censured Democratic president Andrew Jackson for refusing to turn over documents relating to his decision to defund the Bank of the United States. So it is a rare and serious action.

I worked on the resolution with my legislative director, Ellen McLaren. When I got back to Washington I filed it just like any other bill, dropping it into the hopper in front of the chamber. As I explained at the time, "This presidential intervention is an unconscionable abuse of authority by George W. Bush, and Congress must step forward and express the disgust that Americans rightfully feel toward this contemptible decision . . . This deceitful chain of events began with the administration's falsifying of intelligence on Iraqi nuclear capabilities. It is clear that the perjury of Mr. Libby in this case effectively protected President Bush, Vice President Cheney, and other administration officials from further scrutiny . . ."

The resolution stated, "President Bush has finally and unalterably breached any remaining shred of trust he had left with the American people and rewarded political loyalty while flouting the rule of law . . ."

When Congress reconvened, I approached several members of the House to gather support. Sixteen other members sponsored my censure resolution. But our party leadership was not enthusiastic. I spoke with them on the floor, as other legislation was being considered. "We need to do something," I said. "We just can't let the president get away with it again."

One leader assured me, "We're going to do something. We just haven't decided what yet."

Fine. I didn't care what we did or who did it—so long as we did something. Unfortunately, we never did. One means of killing a bill or a resolution is to just let it sit there. Taking no action kills it without forcing anyone to vote on it. That was one way the Republican majority prevented almost all Democratic legislation from being considered during their twelve years in power. And that's what the Democratic leadership did in this situation.

It is also what the Democratic leadership did when Representative Dennis Kucinich (D-OH) introduced a bill to impeach Vice President Cheney in April 2007. However, Kucinich refused to be subdued, and the following November he resubmitted that bill as a privileged resolution, a parliamentary maneuver that forced the bill to the House floor. Having already taken impeachment "off the table," majority leader Steny Hoyer introduced a motion to table it, to ignore it. But the Republican leadership, sensing another opportunity to embarrass Democrats, orchestrated their members to vote against Steny's motion. Apparently both the Republican and Democratic leadership believed that debating the impeachment resolution on the House floor would reflect badly on the Democrats. So the Republicans wanted to force the Democrats to debate the issue. It was the Murtha strategy all over again. If the Democrats voted to table it, the Republicans would argue that Democrats agreed that Cheney had done nothing impeachable. The Republican maneuver "succeeded" when most of their members and a group of Democrats committed to holding Cheney accountable— including me—voted against tabling. I for one would have welcomed a debate about the blatant abuses of Dick Cheney on the floor of the House and in front of the nation.

Steny Hoyer then called a vote requesting that the bill be sent to the Judiciary Committee for consideration. This time almost all Democrats—including me—voted with our leadership to refer the bill to committee, but the only way I could justify that vote was if we were truly serious about debating it in committee.

It was clear that the public agreed with Kucinich that Vice President Cheney had abused his office. In fact, an American Research Group poll taken a week after Kucinich filed his bill showed that 70 percent of voters believed Cheney had abused his power and 43 percent felt he should immediately be removed from office. Among Democratic voters, those numbers undoubtedly were substantially higher.

What was clear to me was that many Democrats and Independents were becoming as disillusioned as I was with our refusal to hold the Bush administration accountable.

Now we had a choice. We could either let the resolution die quietly in the Judiciary Committee or we could actually schedule hearings. We could call witnesses. Former White House press secretary Scott McClellan had admitted that Vice President Cheney and his staff provided false information to him about the outing of covert CIA agent Valerie Plame Wilson. Hearings would allow us to question him about what he described as being used to "unknowingly [pass] along false information." Former White House counsel Harriet Miers and White House chief of staff Josh Bolten had defied Congress by ignoring subpoenas to testify. Impeachment hearings break through these outlandish claims of privilege and enable us to determine the full extent of the malfeasance of the Bush administration.

Before the November vote in the House to table the resolution, I approached Judiciary Committee chairman John Conyers while we were both on the House floor. I have the utmost respect for John, who earned his liberal credentials long before I was elected to Congress. "They've ripped the scab off the wound," I said. "I think we should go ahead and bring this up."

Believe me, the Republicans were not going to push Conyers around. Like me, he had voted against tabling it. I don't want to put words in his mouth. He didn't promise me he would schedule hearings.

Truthfully, I believe that if it were his decision alone he would have done that, but he is a savvy, experienced legislator. He operates in the reality of leadership.

Initially, I didn't fully comprehend the extent of the anger felt by mainstream Democrats, but when I was back home in my district I became convinced that the appetite for impeachment was widespread even among Independents and disgruntled Republicans. As has happened before in my district, people stopped me in the supermarket aisle, at the deli, or when I was speaking at a school and asked quite forcefully, "So, Wexler, why aren't we holding these people accountable?"

It became clear to me that Congress was behind the country on this issue, way behind. I listened to my constituents and had discussions with some national leaders on the issue, among them author John Nichols, who'd written *The Genius of Impeachment,* and Dave Lindorff, the author of *The Case for Impeachment.* I spoke with the founders of respected online groups such as Bob Fertik of Democrats.com and David Swanson of AfterDowningStreet.org, who also made convincing cases to me. Ultimately I had no choice. To uphold the Constitution, I had to call for impeachment hearings.

While I understand as much as anyone in Congress the complexity, emotional cost, and traumatic consequences of impeachment hearings, I also know that this situation is almost the precise opposite of the Clinton impeachment. Unlike Bill Clinton, George Bush and Dick Cheney have betrayed the country, not their wives. Holding hearings would give us the opportunity to prove that the administration had intentionally distorted intelligence to lead us into an unnecessary war, ordered the illegal wiretapping of American citizens, and obstructed justice to prevent the special prosecutor from learning all the facts about the outing of a covert CIA agent. These hearings would permit us finally to look behind the curtain of the most secretive administration in American history. I wrote to my constituents explaining why I had voted against the motion to table the impeachment resolution and my fervent desire to begin hearings, "It is time for Congress to expose the multitude of misdeeds of the administration."

Various bloggers and Web sites ran my letter or portions of it. Before I knew it, the netroots came alive and liberal talk radio starting buzzing. The response to a simple e-mail to my constituents was extraordinary. My office received hundreds of letters and thousands of phone calls.

I then decided to write an editorial calling for hearings and outlining my reasons. When I was on the floor of the House, I learned that other members were hearing the same dissatisfaction in their districts. Illinois representative Luis Gutierrez and Wisconsin representative Tammy Baldwin, both Democrats, felt the same powerful anger in their districts and both quickly agreed to sign on to the editorial. Together we submitted it to several major newspapers, intending it to be published on the editorial page—but we were turned down by all of them. The fact that three members of Congress all sitting on the House Judiciary Committee were calling for hearings to investigate credible allegations of crimes committed by the vice president of the United States apparently wasn't important enough. In fact, when we stated publicly that those papers refused to publish the article, they were deluged by complaints from readers. The editorial-page editors of two prominent national newspapers called Josh Rogin to complain that they hadn't rejected the editorial, but had "passed on running it" or "didn't have enough space that week."

It was clear the national media wasn't interested, so I decided to take the message directly to the people. I published the editorial on top progressive blogs such as *Daily Kos* and *The Huffington Post*. I also decided to galvanize the significant grassroots support for impeachment hearings in a quantifiable way that the media and Congress could not ignore. With the aid of a talented media specialist in my district, Brian Franklin, we established a Web site, WexlerWantsHearings.com, and invited people to sign our online petition. Initially we hoped we could get as many as 50,000 signatures, but in just the first week we got almost 120,000—without a single mention of the existence of this Web site in the mainstream media. Eventually, several hundred thousand people joined our call for impeachment hearings. Fittingly, our Constitution's hometown paper, *The Philadelphia Inquirer,* finally ran our editorial. I then made an impassioned plea to my colleagues on the floor of the House to begin the hearings immediatel.

I didn't call for impeachment hearings for partisan motives or political payback. I simply wanted Americans to see and hear the unvarnished evidence. The outcome of such hearings was certainly not preordained. I wasn't suggesting impeachment proceedings whose objective was to politically harangue the administration. As I envisioned these hearings, they would be a sober and objective presentation of the facts without hyperbole or political gamesmanship. The evidence alone would determine the outcome. But the issues—grave abuses of power—were just too serious to ignore.

Certainly there were legitimate arguments made against these proceedings. Many people reasoned that we'd been through this gut-wrenching process with President Clinton and it had ripped apart the nation. I responded by suggesting that the worst possible legacy of the Clinton impeachment would be to discourage future Congresses from examining valid allegations of constitutional violations against members of the executive branch. Should that happen, the tragedy of Clinton's impeachment would be compounded. I was convinced that Congress needed to send a strong message, not just to Bush and Cheney but to all our future presidents and vice presidents, that impeachment is always on the table—no matter whether they have been in office one day or one week or only have months remaining in their term. Holding fair hearings would establish that Congress takes its constitutional authority seriously and would stand in clear contrast to the kangaroo court engineered by Republicans against Clinton.

Moreover, the Constitution is not a smorgasbord. We do not have the luxury of picking and choosing which constitutional protections and prescriptions are to be enforced. No, that is the most compelling attribute of our Constitution. It is timeless. It is subject to amendment, but it is a universal law. The freedoms embodied in the Bill of Rights are not to be selectively enforced, and neither is the duty of Congress to protect the nation from an executive who abuses his or her constitutional authority.

If we fail to hold hearings, many of the abuses of the Bush administration will remain secret forever. I strongly believe, and the hundreds of thousands of Americans who signed up on my Web site agree, that George Bush and Dick Cheney, working together, have done more than any other president and vice president to dismantle the delicate system of checks and balances that have governed this country for more than 225 years.

After demonstrating a stark willingness to steal the presidency of the United States, President Bush and Vice President Cheney have not hesitated to eviscerate the Constitution when it stood in the way of their political aims. Unfortunately, the theft in Florida was only the opening salvo in Bush and Cheney's total disregard for the civil liberties of Americans and the constitutional framework that we cherish.

If seven years of living under the thumb of the Bush administration has taught me anything, it is that Congress desperately needs to reestablish itself as a legitimate, coequal branch of government. Through the excessive use of executive privilege, President Bush has skirted and ignored the law as passed by the House and Senate, has significantly weakened Congress as an institution, and has created an unprecedented imperial presidency. The GOP, which led Congress for twelve years under the iron-fisted stewardship of Newt Gingrich, Tom "The Hammer" DeLay, and Denny Hastert, enabled George W. Bush's neutering of Congress by refusing to engage in oversight of the executive branch during Bush's first six years in office.

There is no more urgent and noble calling for the new Democratic majority than to stand up against and confront this executive overreach by Bush and Cheney. Democrats must be true to our priorities of universal heath care, public education, and expanding economic gains for middle- and lower-income Americans. But we have an even loftier mission—to restore the promise and guarantees of the United States Constitution. We must reassert the rightful role of Congress in ensuring that the civil liberties of Americans are sacred. No more secret wiretaps and a hollow right to privacy. It must be more than a mere slogan: Democrats must really stand for the little guy—the average American—against the entrenched interests that dominate Washington and the GOP fear-mongering that has been the hallmark of the Bush and Rove model.

The truth is that we have never been subjected to more abusive behavior by an administration than by the one currently occupying the White House. The Bush administration makes Nixon's team look like Girl Scouts. As former senator George McGovern wrote in a *Washington Post* editorial, "I have not been heavily involved in singing the praises of the Nixon administration. But the case for impeaching Bush and Cheney is far stronger than was the case against Nixon and Vice President Spiro T. Agnew after the 1972 election. The nation would be much more secure and productive under a Nixon presidency than with Bush. Indeed, has any administration in our national history been so damaging as the Bush-Cheney era?"

DURING THE GOP reign over Congress, the Republican Party governed almost universally to satisfy their core constituency, the right-wing true believers. Their agenda didn't match the needs of the country, but it did match the ideology of their political base. Rather than focusing on those issues that mattered to the everyday lives of Americans, the GOP built their political agenda around divisive social issues. The so-called wedge issues. Rather than working on improving our school system, they waged a battle against gay marriage. Instead of working toward universal health-care coverage, they passed legislation prohibiting Americans from playing poker online. Instead of tackling global warming, they rallied pro-life activists around the tragic case of Terri Schiavo. Instead of conducting judicious oversight hearings on the Iraq War debacle, they fought valiantly to protect Christmas.

In political terms, the Republicans moved the middle to the right—and thus moved the mainstream closer to their conservative position. When Democrats regained the majority, we tried to govern from the middle, believing we could be passionate moderates or triumphant triangulators. This strategy, however, has achieved precious few results with an incorrigible Bush-Cheney White House blocking substantial progress. And it makes you wonder: If Republicans govern from the right and Democrats govern from the middle, when does the left get to govern? As a progressive, I fear my party has become more docile in the majority than we were in the minority.

We're trying to expand our relatively slim majority by being cautious. Instead, we should be galvanizing Americans behind a progressive agenda. The facts favor our side. Rather than blurring the differences between Democrats and Republicans, we should highlight them and fight for our principles. A Democratic Party that voters believe is vigorously representing the interests of consumers and health-care patients will be viewed as a party with conviction and be rewarded at the ballot box. A Democratic Party that has the gumption to insist that personal privacy still matters, that America is strongest when we honor the principles set out in the Geneva Conventions and when we lead, rather than resist, scientific advances, will be a party that earns the trust and confidence of a clear majority of Americans.

After eight long years of Bush and Cheney, if we give the American people a clear choice, they will pick us overwhelmingly. But if we show them caution, hesitation, and meekness, they will remain frustrated, even despondent over the state of our government. I believe that if more liberals start "breathing fire," we Democrats will finally build a lasting majority.

ACKNOWLEDGMENTS

Thirty years ago as an idealistic high-school senior, I boldly declared to a classmate, whose exuberant smile I found quite captivating, that my dream was to go to Washington. What I didn't realize at seventeen was that my classmate would become my wife and that Laurie would unwittingly teach me the skills and expose me to the knowledge that would enable me to fulfill that dream. Everything I believe in, everything I cherish and hold dear, I do so because of the strong foundation provided by our blessed life with our three children, Rachel, Zachary, and Hannah. I am quite grateful for the passion and spirit that the five of us enjoy together as a family, and it is this good fortune that allows me the confidence to write this book.

I also want to express the profound respect I have for my parents, Sandra and Ben Wexler, and my mother and father-in-law, Roslyn and Larry Cohen, and acknowledge the never-ending love and devotion that they individually and collectively so generously give to me, Laurie, and our children.

I want to acknowledge my heartfelt appreciation and gratitude to my chief of staff and friend, Eric Johnson. Eric believed in this book before I did and went far beyond the call of duty to guide it to fruition. He has devoted too much of his personal time and energy, as well as his considerable talents, to this book and even more to our political partnership. I value immensely Eric's judgment and loyalty.

I also am especially thankful to my deputy chief of staff, Josh Rogin, who traded in his legal career to return to my office. He labored long hours on weekends and evenings to organize our thoughts and memories about several extraordinary political events. Josh's intelligent wit, honesty, and even temperament are always invaluable.

I am the beneficiary of a dedicated and faithful staff in Florida and Washington. I am incredibly fortunate that a nucleus of wonderful men and women have chosen to work together in my office and on my campaigns for more than a decade, some almost two.

I feel as if I have known and cared about my two longest-serving coworkers, Wendi Lipsich and Eva Dominguez, my entire life. As my district director, Wendi tirelessly toils in Florida on my behalf and represents me better than I could represent myself. I greatly admire her earnest devotion to our constituents, and the love that so many feel for Wendi is well deserved. I have worked with Eva since I was elected to the Florida Senate in 1990. Over the years, Eva has assisted thousands of people with their health-care and immigration problems. She has touched so many lives in such a profound way. I still expect that someday Eva will become the president of Paraguay, her native-born country.

My passion for foreign policy is shared with my staff director of the Europe Subcommittee, Jonathan Katz. Over the past twelve years, Jonathan has developed a true expertise in international relations, and his insights and knowledge have ably guided me throughout my tenure in Congress and in this book. We have traveled and learned together in faraway places, and I am thankful for his extraordinary dedication.

Ellen McLaren is the unsung hero in my Washington office. As my legislative director, Ellen plays an essential policy role and keeps me on the straight and narrow. Her thoughts and suggestions about this book made it a much better read.

I am grateful to all those who have worked for me and with me, past and present, including Suzanne Stoll, Todd Adams, Pat Agatheas, Jared

Allen, Hina and Imran Awan, Debra Armentrout, Courtney Bafer, Brian Baker, Sally Belson, Jill Benson, Lori Berman, Lynne Brenes, Theresa Brier, Kevin Cutro, James de Jesus, Ted den Dooven, Darcy Farnan, David Feinman, Jennifer Tabach Gerst, Dana Kelly, Rhona Kirsner, Jacob Kurtzer, Joshua Lipman, Mariana Maguire, Lale Mamaux, Ivy Meeropol, Joan Moore, Ashley Mushnick, Virginia Neale, Jesper Pederson, Tom Plante, Beverly Razon, Beverly Robinson, Shelley Rood, Betsy Rothstein, Anthony Samson, Susan Silver, Nicole Silverstein, Shelley Simpson, Halie Soifer, Amy Spigel, Meril Stumberger, Lisa White, and Gene Wilk.

I would like to thank my friends and supporters, who are too numerous to list, and who have put their faith in me and supported my efforts year after year. I am so grateful for your continued support and help.

I also want to thank all the members of Congress and staff who contributed their stories and memories to this book. And to those who read the book before publication and made suggestions to improve it, including Tiffany Muller, David Beattie, Scott Simpson, Brian Franklin, and Daniella Howard, an invaluable member of my Florida staff.

I want to express my appreciation to my publisher, Tom Dunne, and all the great people at St. Martin's Press, especially my editor, Joel Ariaratnam, who had excellent suggestions for improving this book.

Finally, this book is the brainchild of an especially talented and thoughtful author, David Fisher. During our collaboration, David patiently extracted my thoughts and ideas and organized them into a remarkably readable manuscript. He interviewed countless people to create a more thorough and interesting book. David endured my less-than-accommodating schedule and even worked with me in a hospital waiting room while my mother had knee surgery. I am eternally grateful to David for his extraordinary efforts and am especially proud of our work product.

—*Robert Wexler*

I would also like to thank Eric Johnson, Josh Rogin, and those other members of Congressman Wexler's office who so graciously gave so much of their time and expertise to our effort. And, of course, I am tremendously grateful to my beautiful wife, Laura, my partner in all my efforts, as well as my sons, Jesse and Beau, for accepting my absences without complaint.

—David Fisher

INDEX